SOTHEBY'S

THE

COUNTRY HOUSE GUIDE

HISTORIC HOUSES ASSOCIATION

D0809125

SOTHEBY'S
THE
COUNTRY HOUSE GUIDE

HISTORIC HOUSES ASSOCIATION

GEORGE PLUMPTRE

A WARD LOCK BOOK

First published in the UK 1996
by Ward Lock
Wellington House
125 Strand
LONDON
WC2R 0BB

A Cassell Imprint

Distributed in the United States
by Sterling Publishing Co., Inc.
387 Park Avenue South, New York, NY 10016 – 8810

Distributed in Australia
by Capricorn Link (Australia) Pty Ltd
2/13 Carrington Road, Castle Hill NSW 2154

A British Library Cataloguing in Publication Data block for this book may be obtained from the
British Library

ISBN 0 7063 7519 X
Design by Christine and Paul Wood
Maps by Eugene Fleury
Printed and bound in Spain

PREVIOUS PAGE: Stowe, Buckingham.

CONTENTS

PREFACE

I am delighted to introduce this book, written by George Plumptre. The Historic Houses Association has long felt the need for a guidebook covering virtually all of its Member houses that are open regularly to the public, a need that has now been met thanks to the generous sponsorship of Sotheby's.

The entries for all the individual houses have been written in close collaboration with the owners concerned. They include the practical information the visitor needs – where to go and when to go there – with a summary of the particular interest of each of the properties and, in many cases, anecdotal material about the history of the buildings, or the families involved with them over the years. We believe that this will make the book more interesting than many similar publications.

We hope that all of its readers will find it useful in planning their visits to historic houses and that it will add to their understanding and pleasure when they get there.

William Proby
President, HHA.

INTRODUCTION

This new edition of THE COUNTRY HOUSE GUIDE is an exciting advance from the original guide published in 1994. The book has colour illustrations, maps and an index.

While hearteningly few of the houses included in the first edition have dropped out, there are a number of new entries. These include houses which have begun opening to the public since 1994, such as Mount Stuart on the Isle of Bute, as well as National Trust houses occupied by families who are HHA members, such as West Wycombe Park in Buckinghamshire and Coughton Court in Warwickshire, and a selection of houses not in private ownership but members of the HHA, such as Fairfax House, York, and Tredegar House and Margam Park, both in South Wales.

As this book is not an annual gazetteer, the details about times of opening are not date-specific because these obviously change from year to year. However, the periods during which most houses are open remain constant, and the relevant information given is as accurate as possible.

It is worth noting that the majority of houses are open for pre-booked parties and by appointment for periods outside the advertised opening period and such details can be obtained by telephoning the house. Equally, the grounds and gardens of a large number of houses may be open for longer periods – and often for more hours on an open day – than is shown in the details of their entry and, again, such information can be obtained by telephoning.

The entry prices shown are for 1996, except in cases where the entry specifies that they are 1995 prices. In all entries the first figure shown is the price for an adult, the second the price for children. Concessions mean that there is a combination of possible reductions for Senior Citizens, groups, family or season tickets. Such details can be obtained by telephoning. All the details given were correct at the time of going to press.

The new additions to the book have not changed the major characteristic: that the houses are, with only one or two exceptions, occupied family homes. Their architectural and artistic qualities are hugely enhanced by the warmth of family inhabitance which in most cases has been continuous for generations, in some for hundreds of years.

The evolution of the country house from uncomfortable, often squalid, medieval castles and towers was a vigorous, complex process. The web of links between land and estates, architecture, art and gardening, social advancement and vanity, developed with inextricable links through successive generations. In the evolutionary process, old houses were replaced as architectural fashions changed, and their surroundings were similarly gardened or landscaped. At the same time many succumbed to disaster: fire, bankruptcy or the lack of an heir.

Today the situation is rather different. The emergence of new country houses, dependent as in the past upon a landed estate for much of their economic support, has slowed almost to a halt. This has sharpened the focus on owners of historic houses who preserve and maintain, against increasing economic odds, such a considerable part of our national heritage. The old saying that the country house is Britain's supreme contribution to civilization may be something of an old chestnut, but it loses none of its relevance for this.

Public support of houses by visitors can often make the difference between their survival as viable, lived-in entities and being broken up in a sale. It is this support that THE COUNTRY HOUSE GUIDE hopes to stimulate. Sotheby's are proud to be able to play a part in encouraging visitors, for any contribution to future health and survival, and to the appreciation of owners' unstinting hard work, will be of lasting value.

George Plumptre

SOUTHERN ENGLAND

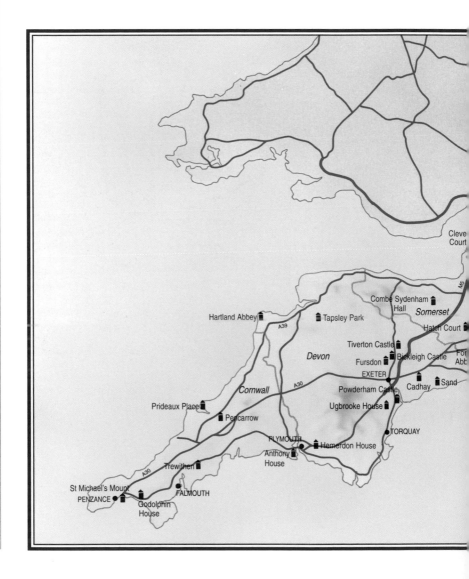

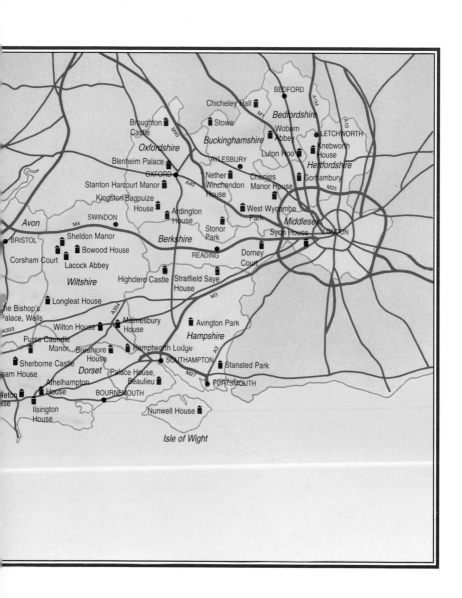

Luton Hoo, *Luton*

The Luton Hoo Foundation
Tel: 01582 22955

Off A6129 (M1 exit 10), south of Luton

Open: Apr to mid-Oct, Fri, Sat and Sun, p.m
(telephone for further details and for group bookings)
£5.50, children £2.50

Edwardians were exacting in their demands for quality and comfort, but not necessarily purist over architecture or decorative styles. When the South African diamond magnate, Sir Julius Wernher, bought Luton Hoo in 1904, he commissioned C.F. Mewes, the architect of the Ritz Hotel, to completely remodel the house, but retain the austere

Greek Ionic portico that was the only surviving feature of earlier work by Sir Robert Smirke. The result may have been architecturally curious but it was undeniably splendid, in the lush Francophile Beaux-Arts style enjoyed by plutocrats of the period.

Luton Hoo already had a long distinguished history of occupation for seven hundred years, with an eighteenth-century zenith when the 3rd Earl of Bute (Prime Minister and tutor to the future George III) bought the estate. He commissioned Robert Adam to rebuild the seventeenth-century house and create a new suite of interiors. Adam's work, and the new contents, were universally admired. Bute's great-grandson, the 2nd Marquess, commissioned Smirke to remodel the entrance front. The major addition was the monumental portico that, when the house was destroyed by fire in 1843, was all that survived. Sold shortly afterwards by the Butes, the house was subsequently rebuilt by the Victorian industrialist who had bought it, and who subsequently sold the property to Wernher. All that remained from the Bute heyday was – and is – 'Capability' Brown's expansive park where he created some of the most skilfully serpentine lakes for which he was so renowned.

For Wernher, Luton Hoo was to be a place of luxury and display. The interior decoration achieved its peak in the circular main staircase which ascends round the white marble group 'L'Amore degli Angeli' by Borgonzoli, but most rewarding are the collections built up by Sir Julius and continued by his son, Sir Harold (who divided the house into private residence and public museum). Sir Julius's forte was European works of art; Sir Harold brought in most of the outstanding eighteenth-century English furniture, his mother the equally distinguished English porcelain of the same period and his wife, Lady Zia, daughter of Grand Duke Michael of Russia, the Fabergé collection for which Luton Hoo is perhaps best known.

WOBURN ABBEY, *Woburn*

The Marquess of Tavistock and Trustees of the Bedford Estates
Tel: 01525 290666

In Woburn on A4012 (M1 exits 12 and 13), 13 km (8 miles) north of Dunstable

Open: Jan to end Mar, Sat and Sun, 11–4; Apr to end Oct, daily, 11–5 (last admission)
£6.50, children (12–16) £3, concessions
Tea room

A pioneer of commercial opening to the public, which began in 1955 in response to the death duties facing the present 13th Duke of Bedford, Woburn's high profile occasionally hides the distinguished history of its family and the wonderful works of art with which it is filled. Crammed might be more accurate, for in 1950 raging dry rot demanded that two sides of the quadrangle, whose plan had survived from the old Cistercian monastery, should be demolished, and the available room space was halved.

The Russells have been collecting and commissioning for generations, since John, 1st Earl of Bedford brought them to prominence during Henry VIII's reign. They were later aided by judicious marriages to heiresses, notably Rachel, daughter of the Earl of Southampton. Although her husband was executed after implication in the Rye House Plot of 1683, her fortune, including the Bloomsbury estate in London, passed to their son who became the 2nd Duke.

The 4th Duke was the statesman among a politically distinguished family and he commissioned Henry Flitcroft to build the Palladian west wing which today presents its confident façade to the park, and to design the wing's interiors. After 1786 the grandson of the 4th Duke commissioned his friend, the Prince of Wales's architect, Henry Holland, to rebuild the south and east wings (the latter was part of the 1950 demolition). Holland also designed the Chinese Dairy that is shown as a Chinese Temple in Humphry Repton's *Red Book* for the park that he laid out for the 6th Duke. Holland's riding school and tennis court were demolished; his conservatory was transformed by the 6th Duke and Jeffry Wyatville into a sculpture gallery.

Woburn contains one of England's premier private collections. The state dining-room is devoted to Van Dyck, another to Reynolds and the smaller dining-room to twenty-two Canalettos, all commissioned by the 4th Duke. Other highlights are works by Velasquez, Claude and Cuyp. Flitcroft's long gallery contains George Gower's celebrated Armada portrait of Elizabeth I; the room's Corinthian columns are repeated in Holland's library whose superb volumes on natural history and horticulture reflect successive Russells' pioneering interest in gardening and farming. The English and French furniture and works of art provide an intriguing insight into the connoisseurship and changing taste of different generations.

DORNEY COURT, *Windsor*

Mr and Mrs Peregrine Palmer
Tel: 01628 604638

In Dorney on B3024, 3 km (2 miles) west of Eton and Windsor

Open: Easter weekend; May, Sun and Bank Holidays; June to end Sept, Mon, Tues and Sun; 2–5.30 (last admission 5)
£4, children £2, concessions
Home-made teas

The twentieth century has often conspired against England's country houses, not least those close to London. Dorney Court is a short distance from sprawling Slough and tourist-ridden Windsor and within earshot of the M4 and Heathrow flight-paths. It is a mark of its unassailable establishment that all this can be forgotten as one approaches through fields and ancient woods to a memorable first view: a symphony of patterned rose brick, leaded windows, barge-boarded gables and towering chimneys, all rising above clipped yew hedges.

It is as authentically medieval as it looks and, as such, a rarity. In 1924 *Country Life* called it 'one of the finest Tudor manor houses in England'. But the house was substantially built before Henry Tudor ascended the throne and it is the craftsmanship of transition from basic medieval to more decorative Tudor that is most fascinating, both inside and out. From the eighteenth century the main front was disguised by the imposition of a Palladian façade, but Peregrine Palmer's grandfather painstakingly removed this and exposed the original structure.

In 1537 the wealthy grocer Sir William Gerrard (or Garrard) who was Lord Mayor of London bought the Dorney Court estate and established four hundred and fifty years of unbroken continuity. His daughter married Sir James Palmer from Kent and they inherited Dorney. From 1620 the succession has been unbroken from father to son. Seventeenth-century Palmers were distinguished royalists; Sir James was knighted by his friend Charles I and his son was Charles II's cupbearer. More personal service was provided by Sir Roger Palmer whose wife Barbara was the king's mistress and eventually

Duchess of Cleveland. A skilful ambassador for the King, Sir Roger was made Earl of Castlemaine, an ennoblement as much in recognition of his wife's contribution as his diplomatic prowess.

This period is wonderfully evoked in the great hall where, above the linenfold panelling, Tudor, Stuart and eighteenth-century portraits line the walls. Over the fireplace are Sir Roger and Barbara by Lely and the other portraits include works by Johnson and Kneller. A shrewd-looking Sir James, an outstanding miniaturist, his likeness complete with earring, looks down from the gallery at one end where there is also a rare group of seven eminent Turks presented to Lord Castlemaine when he was in the Levant. Across the hall the irregular octagonal parlour has a low timbered ceiling and a striking carved chimney-piece. The Chinese lacquered bureau is one of the most interesting pieces of furniture in the house.

Above the parlour the great chamber is now the principal bedroom. This and the other oak-panelled bedrooms continue the same mood as the main rooms downstairs. The exception is the dining-room, decorated in William and Mary style with a patterned plaster ceiling and painted and gilded panels. On the stairs hangs one of the heroes of the British Raj, Field Marshal Sir Donald Stewart, the first man into Delhi after the Mutiny and eventually commander-in-chief in India.

The brick-towered church is adjacent, as one might expect of a medieval manor and contains an amazing Gerrard tomb dated 1620. The gardens around the house add greatly to the overall picture and recall Dorney's most distinguished horticultural incumbent, John Rose, the Palmers' gardener who grew the first pineapple in England and was immortalized in the painting by Danckerts, presenting the fruit to Charles II who made him gardener at St James's Palace.

HIGHCLERE CASTLE, *Newbury*

The Earl of Carnarvon
Tel: 01635 253210

On A343 6.5 km (4 miles) south of Newbury

Open: May to end Sept, Tues to Sun, also Bank Holiday Mon in May and Aug, 11–5 (last admission 4)
£5, children £2.50, concessions
Restaurant

Highclere is a vast and impressive nineteenth-century nobleman's house designed by Charles Barry, standing on the crest of a superb 'Capability' Brown park. The finest neo-Elizabethan house in England, it is a worthy precursor to Barry's Houses of Parliament.

The elaborate interior is a mixture of Baronial, Gothic, Italianate and rococo revival of considerable opulence and character. A good collection of European furniture and mostly English paintings reflect a long family history at Highclere dating from the seventeenth century. The most unusual contents — and most celebrated — are the remaining part of the Egyptian collection of the 5th Earl, of Tutankhamun fame. These were dramatically rediscovered in 1987 by his grandson, the present earl, and are shown in an imaginative pictorial reconstruction of the 5th Earl's patronage of Howard Carter's excavations.

STRATFIELD SAYE HOUSE, *Reading*

The Duke of Wellington
Tel: 01256 882882

1.6 km (1 mile) off A33, 18 km (11 miles) south of Reading
Open: May to end Sept, daily except Fri, 11.30–4
Prices available on request
Restaurant

The nation proferred £600,000 to the victor of Waterloo to purchase a suitable country house and estate. The 1st Duke of Wellington settled on Stratfield Saye because of its surroundings and the warm friendliness of the house. A plan by Benjamin Wyatt for a 'Waterloo Palace' shows what might have been, an early-nineteenth-century version of Marlborough's Blenheim. Instead the duke remained at Stratfield Saye, adorning the house with trophies from his campaigns, and stamping each room with his personality. The long façade with embracing wings is immediately welcoming and remains faithful to its original date of 1630, when commissioned by Sir William Pitt, James I's Comptroller. The most important interiors are eighteenth-century in origin and executed for the Pitts (who had become the Lords Rivers). The impressive library ceiling and decoration is attributed to William Kent, while the house's showpiece, the gallery, was added along the east front by George Pitt around 1745.

But in all the rooms the Duke of Wellington's additions account for Stratfield Saye's memorable atmosphere. He himself planned the water-closets and central heating system which were pioneering luxuries during the early-nineteenth century. The library bookcases were filled with his leather-bound volumes of history and many others that came from Napoleon's library.

Indeed the presence of the Duke's great rival and his family are ever-present, from the tricolour banners in the hall, to the busts along the gallery and the important collection of Dutch and Flemish paintings in the drawing-room. They were part of the baggage captured from Joseph Bonaparte after his defeat by Wellington at Vitoria in

1813, which the French general had himself acquired from the Spanish royal collection. On discovering their identity, Wellington immediately offered them back to Ferdinand VII of Spain, to which the king graciously replied, 'His Majesty, touched by your delicacy, does not wish to deprive you of that which has come into your possession by means as just as they are honourable.' The greater part of the collection is at Apsley House and was presented with the house to the nation by the 7th Duke in 1947.

The Duke so enjoyed the effect of the gallery, lined with prints, that he created a print room of his own next door and decorated other rooms in a similar manner. Following its redecoration by John Fowler, the gallery is Stratfield Saye's most impressive room, an unforgettable combination of classical features such as the Ionic columns at both ends and chimney-pieces, the later prints, the series of busts added by the Duke, and the wonderful black and gold wall decoration and Boule furniture. The music room is dedicated to the memory of Wellington's charger at Waterloo, Copenhagen (who is buried in the grounds). Among all the trophies and memories of the Duke's military glories, and the impressive family portraits, Stratfield Saye never loses the sense of, first and foremost, being his home. Nothing confirms this more than the charming picture of the Duke in the last year of his life with his grandchildren, by Robert Thorburn, that hangs in the small drawing-room; a scene that exemplifies early-Victorian family virtues.

CHENIES MANOR HOUSE, *Chenies*

Lt Col and Mrs Macleod Matthews
Tel: 01494 762888

In Chenies off A404 (M25 exit 18)

Open: Apr to end Oct, Bank Holiday Mon, Wed and Thur, 2–5
£4, children £2 (gardens only half-price)
Home-made teas

The village of Chenies has well resisted the urban and motorway encroachment around it; the tranquil manor house tells of past grandeur and adoption by the present owners to become a characterful family home. John Russell, who became 1st Earl of Bedford and founded the distinguished dynasty, acquired the manor by marriage and expanded it to suit his position of importance within Henry VIII's court and to entertain his monarch. Elizabeth I signed papers regulating the imprisonment of Mary, Queen of Scots while staying at Chenies, and both monarchs held privy councils in the house.

Building on the pre-existing fifteenth-century manor, Russell's house extended to two courtyards, the inner of which enclosed the present buildings and others that were reduced c.1750 to a garden wall. What remains today is the fifteenth-century hall-house and tower that he altered in 1526, and the 'new wing' that he added to provide extra lodgings. The deep-toned brick has an immediately Tudor feel, as do the crow-stepped gables, but the best feature are the superb chimneys whose builders were later taken by Henry VIII to work at Hampton Court; the similarity is clearly evident. A visit by the King to Chenies was one of the occasions of the adultery by his feckless wife, Katherine Howard, which led to her execution.

During the Civil War a garrison of parliamentary soldiers was kept at Chenies in the upper armoury which is a fine early example of a long gallery, stretching over the lodgings of the new wing. The Russells did not occupy Chenies after 1627 and following deterioration during the occupancy of successive tenants, alterations in the eighteenth century reduced the house to its present size. Surviving old details in parts of the lodgings wing, and sixteenth-century furniture and tapestries perpetuate the Tudor atmosphere while the main dining-room and drawing-room have a later, more airy feel.

During their time at Chenies the Macleod Matthews have developed a widely admired garden, whose flower borders and formal sunken garden are perfectly in keeping with the Tudor period of the house. An interesting recent addition is the Chenies hedge maze.

CHICHELEY HALL, *Newport Pagnell*

Trustees of the Hon Nicholas Beatty
Tel: 01234 391252

On A422 (M1 exit 14), 3 km (2 miles) east of Newport Pagnell

Open: Easter Sun and Mon; May Bank Holidays; Aug, Sun and Bank Holiday; 2.30–6. Open to parties all year by arrangement
£3.50, children £2
Tea Room

Photographs do not do justice to Chicheley Hall and it is only when visiting that the Baroque vigour and vertical ingenuity of the house's exterior are fully appreciated, facing the lime avenue that provides an ideal approach. The brickwork is of a glorious deep hue and the succession of main façades present carefully planned architectural variety. The house was long attributed to Thomas Archer, its bravado suited his individual style of Baroque.

In fact it was designed between 1719 and 1723 (two decades later than originally thought) by Francis Smith of Warwick for Sir John Chester. The move from exterior façades to interior rooms marks an intriguing progression from Baroque to Palladian illustrating what was happening in fashionable circles at the time. Sir John Chester was one of the first patrons of William Kent; he and other friends funded Kent's first visit to Italy, during which the young Kent painted the ceiling of Chicheley's hall, a room designed by another emerging Palladian, Henry Flitcroft. It is the most expansive room in the house and, with the supremely elegant staircase beyond, makes for a memorable introduction.

The architectural note continues in the panelled drawing-room and through the house the ensemble of rooms are intimate but faultlessly proportioned. Hudson's portrait of Sir John clearly indicates that he was a man of taste, but does not reveal his obvious sense of humour; his upstairs library appears to be another elegant but conventional panelled room until it is discovered that the panels swing open to reveal hidden bookshelves.

Much of the furniture and other contents of Chicheley confirm that Sir John was a discerning collector; good examples are the set of four gilt mirrors in the drawing-room. His family continued to own Chicheley, leaving his work remarkably untouched, until 1952 when the house was bought by the 2nd Earl Beatty, son of the distinguished admiral, who introduced a rich new vein of interest. The house now contains many memories of the admiral's naval career, especially in the top-floor Beatty museum and in his sitting-room. Elsewhere there are stirring paintings by W.L. Wyllie of Jutland and Beatty's flagship, the *Lion*, being towed past the Forth Bridge. The admiral's personality is impressed by portraits by Sargent and de Lazlo.

Chicheley's gardens retain a rare feature of early eighteenth-century formality in the three-sided canal designed by George London of the fashionable London and Wise partnership.

NETHER WINCHENDON HOUSE, *Aylesbury*

Trustees of Will Trust of J.G.C. Spencer Bernard
Tel: 01844 290101

Off A418, 10 km (6 miles) south-west of Aylesbury
Open: May, daily; Aug Bank Holiday Sun and Mon; 2.30–5.30
£2.50, children £1.50

Set in peaceful water meadows around the River Thame, Nether Winchendon's first impression is both curious and intriguing. An avenue of Dawn Redwood trees – a first example of the rarities elsewhere in the garden – leads towards an imposing battlemented screen of Gothic arches; beyond is a courtyard enclosed on two sides by the house. The initial impression that the house is eighteenth-century Gothic, albeit of a charmingly unorthodox style, is correct. It was the work of Sir Scrope Bernard, a clever eighteenth-century politician who took on the house from his brother Sir Francis, Governor of New Jersey and then of Massachusetts at the outbreak of the American War of Independence.

Hints of an older house in the entrance front become strong suspicion at the east end and are confirmed along the south-facing garden front. Scrope's Gothic accounts for the castellated towers, theatrical gable and arched windows, but above are swirling Tudor chimneys pointing to the older building which Bernard extended and remodelled. From the twelfth century Nether Winchendon belonged to Notley Abbey. During the latter decades before Henry VIII's Dissolution of the Monasteries it was let to Sir John Daunce, a prominent civil servant during Henry VIII's reign, who was an executor of the will of Henry VIII and whose son married Elizabeth, daughter of Sir Thomas More.

Daunce's original lease document was sealed 'the 7th day of September in the 19th year of the reign of our Soverieign Lord King Henry the Eighth', and he left a strong stamp on the house. He added a parlour (now the drawing-room), on the east end, where the carving of the frieze and ceiling is sophisticated Renaissance work and includes Sir John's portrait in profile. His monarch is the subject of the rare tapestry in the dining-room (formerly the great hall), depicting Henry VIII being confirmed as Defender of the Faith.

In 1559 the house was bought by William Goodwin who was probably responsible for the chimneys and the Elizabethan west wing. Goodwin had bought the house to set up his daughter who was marrying a Tyringham, and thereafter Tyringhams were in occupation for some two centuries. They added the cupola to the heterogeneous skyline. During the eighteenth century the house passed to Bernard cousins whose descendants have remained in occupation. Most of the portraits are of the Bernards who are responsible for other interesting contents. The dining-room contains Romney's portrait of the philanthropist Thomas Bernard, elder brother of Sir Scrope whose wife Harriet commissioned the unusual early Worcester, Barr, Flight and Barr porcelain. Harriet's portrait, probably by Hoppner, hangs in the drawing-room.

STOWE, *Buckingham*

House only: Stowe School
Tel: 01280 813650

6.5 km (4 miles) north-west of Buckingham

Open: 23 Mar to 14 Apr; also 7 July to 8 Sept; daily 2–5 (Sun, 12–5)
£2, children £1

The pleasure grounds and their buildings at Stowe have been much in the public eye since being given to the National Trust in 1989; so much so that the house has assumed a secondary position. At the same time visitors might suspect that the series of sales from the collections of the Dukes of Buckingham, and the occupation of the mansion by Stowe School together mean that there is little to see. They would be wrong to make this assumption. This palace is full of echoes and evidence of its past grandeur. The architecture survives as do the interiors, notably the series of state rooms, heralded by Vanbrugh's North Hall and Borra's Pantheonic South Hall.

An excellent guide book fleshes out the history and gives a good impression of what the rooms would have looked like when fully furnished. The remaining chimney-pieces, full-length portraits by Beechey, a pair of Atheniennes, dated *c.*1780 and attributed to Valdre, sculpture by Veyrier, Banks and Trentanove, together hint at the splendours that have gone.

The grounds, which constitute the most important eighteenth-century landscape in Britain, are administered by the National Trust who are carrying out an ambitious programme of restoration to the various temples and other buildings by eighteenth-century architects including Vanbrugh, Kent and Gibbs.

WEST WYCOMBE PARK, *Nr High Wycombe*

The National Trust / Sir Francis Dashwood, Bt
Tel: 01494 524411

At west end of West Wycombe, off A40

Open: June, July and Aug, Sun to Thur, 2–6 (last admission 5.15)
£4, children £2, concessions

The Dashwoods acquired West Wycombe in 1698 as part of a family settlement. Alderman Thomas Lewis married Elizabeth, daughter of his friend Alderman Francis Dashwood and as part of a subsequent agreement, Lewis transferred his West Wycombe estate to his two Dashwood brothers-in-law, Sir Samuel and Sir Francis. It was an uncharacteristically dull and dusty legal start, for a family who within a generation would positively sparkle, and build and adorn one of the liveliest, most engaging contributions to English Palladian architecture.

Having bought out his brother, Sir Francis built the original house in 1708. He died in 1724 when the stage was set for his son, Sir Francis, 2nd Bt, who was sixteen at the time. The young heir spent the next few years on a series of Grand Tours, when pranks and roistering went hand-in-hand with more serious connoisseurship: seeking out works of art and commissioning buying agents, and carrying out antiquarian studies of ancient Roman landmarks. In 1733 he was one of the co-founder members of the Dilettanti Society, about which Horace Walpole wrote a decade later: 'The nominal qualification is having been in Italy; and the real one, having been drunk: the two chiefs are Lord Middlesex and Sir Francis Dashwood, who were seldom sober the whole time they were in Italy.'

Throughout his life Sir Francis balanced the serious with the frivolous and outrageous: the notorious Hell-Fire Club which met at Medmenham (and occasionally in the caves) on his estate; the Dilettanti Society; Fellowship of both the Royal Society and the Society of Antiquaries; an active political career (including being, from 1762 to 1763 Chancellor of the Exchequer – admittedly of debatable success); and partner with his American friend, Benjamin Franklin, in a revised edition of *The Book of Common Prayer*.

West Wycombe was, however, his most lasting and greatest achievement and its creation continued throughout his life from 1735 to his death in 1781. Roughly midway through, in 1763, he inherited the Le Despencer barony from his mother. At different times he employed and was advised by a variety of architects and craftsmen: Isaac Ware, John Donowell, possibly Giovanni Servandoni and definitely one of his pupils Morise Lewes Jolivet, Nicholas Revett, Giuseppe Borgnis, William Hannan and, quite possibly, a variety of others but much of the house's interior work cannot be fully appointed.

The one constant was Sir Francis's own involvement, approving or rejecting schemes and often initiating new schemes. He was one of the few patrons at the time to commission an important design from Robert Adam and then reject it for the proposal from another architect (Nicholas Revett).

The house's north front was completed by 1753, facing over the park with the church and mausoleum perched on a hill to the left and with the lake in the foreground, which, from 1774, was adorned with Revett's magical Music Temple on the island. The relationship between house and landscape was paramount in Sir Francis's plans and, indeed, the west front in particular, designed by Revett and copying the Temple of Bacchus at Teos, was as important as a garden temple as a portico for the house.

The east front has another portico, Ionic and designed by Donowell, but it is the south front, with its double colonnade, which is West Wycombe's most remarkable architectural feature. Tuscan below, Corinthian above, it defies the accepted arrangement of the Classical orders but such unconventionality does nothing to detract from the extraordinary lightness of the arrangement.

Sir Francis paid as much attention to the houses's interiors: the hall and saloon filling the centre between north and south fronts, the drawing-rooms and tapestry room, and the music room that fills the whole east end of the house. There are many highlights and rarities: the staircase of mahogany inlaid with satinwood and ebony; the Brussels tapestries woven to designs by Teniers, in the eponymous room; Sir Henry Cheere's marble chimney-pieces and doorcases; and Borgnis's painted ceiling for the music room, the house's most impressive interior.

The furniture, paintings and works of art complete the ensemble: furniture by Chippendale and, more unusual, the Frenchman Pierre Langlois; busts by Scheemakers, Roubiliac and Rysbrack; portraits, topographical views and original architectural studies for the house and park temples; and the outstanding array of Italian Old Masters that Sir Francis either collected or ordered during his visits to Italy. There is much else to enjoy, both in the house and outside in the park. There has been an admirable lack of change by Sir Francis's successors, the present owner's grandfather and father each carrying out limited alterations to the interiors. The present Sir Francis has carried out extensive restoration to both house and the buildings that adorn West Wycombe's landscape and now the place retains the atmosphere of a masque that its builder created. This has not changed since 1943 when Sir John Dashwood gave the house and grounds to the National Trust, and the present Sir Francis lives in the house and remains the owner of the contents and surrounding estate.

GORHAMBURY, *St Albans*

The Earl of Verulam
Tel: 01727 854051

Off A4147, 3 km (2 miles) west of St Albans

Open: May to Sept, Thur, 2–5
£4, children £2.50, concessions

Proximity to London was an important priority for Tudor courtiers and among the quantity of seats in Essex and Hertfordshire, Gorhambury occupied a distinguished place as the home of Sir Nicholas Bacon, Lord Keeper of the Great Seal (whom Elizabeth I visited and chided: 'My lord, what a little house you have gotten!'), and subsequently his more famous son, Sir Francis. During the seventeenth century Gorhambury passed to the Grimstons, who became baronets, viscounts and, at the beginning of the nineteenth century, earls.

The ruins of the Bacon home make a picturesque folly in the park, but the present house is radically different, an impressive Palladian villa with broad steps leading up to a monumental portico, the whole building austerely white since refacing with Portland stone during the 1950s. The entrance hall is as imposing as the outside, and here the visitor is introduced to Gorhambury's historically important collection of portraits. Bacons and Grimstons, relations and marital connections, hang alongside monarchs and other leading figures, particularly from the sixteenth and seventeenth centuries. Sir Francis is represented as Lord Chancellor by Van Somer, and his nephew Sir Nathaniel, probably the best amateur painter of the seventeenth century, shows his skill with two large still lifes and a rakish self-portrait complete with earring. The Grimstons begin with a portrait of Edward Grimston dated 1446.

If the eighteenth century is not so densely illustrated, it provides the house's visual highlight in the drawing-room, Reynolds' conversation piece of the four children of the 2nd Viscount Grimston (one of whom rebuilt the house), a worthy complement to the group by Van Dyck in the dining-room of the Earl of Northumberland with his wife and daughter. The library is arranged in Sir Francis Bacon's 'divisions of knowledge' and the two splendid marble chimney-pieces, designed by Piranesi and bought in Rome, are rare trophies of the rebuilder Grimston's grand tour.

KNEBWORTH HOUSE, *Knebworth*

The Lord Cobbold
Tel: 01438 812661

On B197, 5 km (3 miles) south of Stevenage

**Open: end Mar to mid-Apr and end May to early Sept, daily; mid-Apr to mid-May, weekends and Bank Holidays; Sept weekends; 12–5.
Telephone for specific dates
Prices available on request**

There is more than a hint of imperial fantasy about the glimpse of Knebworth from the passing road that says much about the house's long, eventful and occasionally eccentric history. A medley of towers, turrets, heraldic beasts and battlements dance between trees. They beckon enticingly and confirm on closer inspection that Knebworth is a Victorian revival of Henry VII's period. Not just a revival, however, for Sir Robert Lytton fought at Bosworth with Henry VII, became a royal confidant, bought Knebworth in 1492 and altered the old manor into a square around a courtyard. Through either direct descent or by marriage the family have lived there ever

since. The house remained little changed until the early-nineteenth century when it was Gothicized by the redoubtable Elizabeth Bulwer-Lytton.

Her son, Edward Bulwer-Lytton, wrote distinguished but now unfashionable historical novels extolling the period when his home was originally built. He set about remodelling it in suitable style, as viewed through Victorian eyes, with the help of the architect, H.E. Kendall, and the interior decorator, John Crace, and today's exteriors are the result. Bulwer-Lytton's later political career brought him a peerage which was elevated to an earldom in the next generation, for his son who served as Viceroy of India. An evocative exhibition records Lytton's involvement in India at the height of the British Raj. The 2nd Earl continued the imperial connection of service in India and these three generations brought to Knebworth a rich and distinctive mixture of Victorian and Edwardian arts, politics and society. Tragically two successive Viscount Knebworths, sons of the 2nd Earl, died – the eldest in a flying accident in 1933, the younger at El Alamein in 1942. Knebworth passed to their sister, Lady Hermione, who married the 1st Lord Cobbold, parents of the present owner.

Bulwer-Lytton was responsible for almost all the house's exterior appearance, but inside the hands of successive generations survive to present a picture of absorbing variety. There is important early-classical seventeenth-century panelling in the banqueting hall. Crace's work is particularly evident in the fantastical state drawing-room, while the entrance hall and Bulwer-Lytton's library were among alterations by Edwin Lutyens who married Emily, daughter of the 1st Earl. Family portraits span the centuries from Sir Robert the original builder to the 1st Lord Cobbold in his Garter robes. There are a number of Bulwer-Lytton: in his study by E.M. Ward, in Byronesque pose by Van Holst, and by his friend Daniel Maclise, whose important historical picture 'Edward IV visiting Caxton's Printing Press', hangs in the state drawing-room.

Distinguished friends and acquaintances also appear; Sir Philip Sydney painted by Jan de Critz; Disraeli hangs in the drawing-room; there are quantities of letters from Dickens to his friend Bulwer-Lytton; Churchill's 1930s' painting of the banqueting hall survives, as does a slightly earlier humorous sketch by Rex Whistler for remodelling the exterior. And in case any visitors think that the early-eighteenth-century members of the family are hard done by, they should visit the adjacent parish church where the last three Lyttons of direct descent from Sir Robert are commemorated in lofty Baroque monuments of immortal splendour.

SYON HOUSE, *Brentford*

The Duke of Northumberland
Tel: 0181-560 0881/3

On north bank of River Thames, between Brentford and Isleworth

**Open: Apr to end Sept, Wed to Sun and Bank Holidays; Oct, Sun; 11–5
(last admission 4.30)
Prices available on request**

The square castellated exterior of Syon which remains largely as built by Lord Protector Somerset during the reign of Edward VI gives little hint of the superb suite of interiors created over three hundred years later by Robert Adam for the 1st Duke of Northumberland. Today Syon survives to perpetuate the spirit of the riverside villas that once lined the River Thames westward from London, to which a steady traffic of gaudy barges travelled up and down stream. The Brentford gate built by Adam announces the Percy seat in emphatic style with the ducal lion on top of the tall arched gateway. Inside the house, only Harewood and Kedleston similarly illustrate his unmatched skill at creating a succession of individual but harmonious grand classical interiors.

In 1750 the properties of the 'proud' Duke of Somerset — which included all the Percy estates — were divided and Syon, with Alnwick Castle and Northumberland House in London, were inherited by the Duke's only child, Lady Elizabeth Seymour. She married Sir Hugh Smithson who acknowledged his wife's legacy by assuming the name of Percy. By special remainder he was able to inherit the earldom of Northumberland on the death of the Duke of Somerset and then in 1766 he was elevated to a dukedom.

Four years earlier he commissioned Adam to work on all three houses: Syon, Alnwick and Northumberland, beginning at Syon. Adam's work was a masterly combination of the atmosphere of a classical villa and elements that hinted at Syon's past and incorporated the social requirements of his patron. The great hall which greets the visitor is one of his most successful and impressive essays in Roman classical; the ante-room beyond is decorated in richer style and leads to the dining-room. The drawing-room was for ladies, but mainly an introduction to the gallery beyond which Adam made out of the old long gallery.

Throughout the rooms the standards of decoration and fittings are unfailingly high. Joseph Rose executed plasterwork and the splendid gilded figures and panels of trophies in the ante-room; Francesco Zuccarelli painted the exquisite lunette portraits which line the long gallery between Adam's groups of Corinthian pilasters. Adam himself designed much of the furniture, designed the Roman statues in the hall, ordered the figures and busts in the dining-room, and designed the black and white marble floor in the hall whose pattern lines are mirrored in the ceiling. The composition of detail which was his superlative quality when planning interiors is fully revealed. In the drawing-room the collection of royal Stuart portraits match the decorative quality and if this is not so prominent in the other rooms open to the public, not designed by Adam, the paintings and works of art amply compensate.

ARDINGTON HOUSE, *Wantage*

Mrs Desmond Baring
Tel: 01235 833244

In Ardington off A417, 3 km (2 miles) east of Wantage

Open: May to Sept, Mon including Bank Holidays; 2.30–4.30
£2.50
Home-made teas by arrangement

John Betjeman was a regular visitor to Ardington and considered the dining-room 'the nicest in Oxfordshire'. Certainly its warm panelling and cheerful plaster decoration encourage conviviality, but it does not begin to rival the staircase hall which is Ardington's glorious forte. The hall's quality was no doubt partly responsible for the rueful comment by a descendant of the house's builder, Edward Clarke, that the house had been 'the proximate cause of the ruin of the family'.

Clarke may have over-reached himself but he did so in style. Gervase Jackson-Stops attributed Ardington to one of the Strong family of master-masons who worked, among other places, at Blenheim and Greenwich. Ardington was built between 1719 and 1720 and is both ambitious and assured; the main south- and north-facing façades were precisely symmetrical and identical, and the detail of the three different shades of brickwork speak of superior craftsmanship.

If the main façades are identical, the hall provides their link, stretching from one side of the house to the other. The 'imperial' staircase rises in two flights to a half-landing and returns via a central 'flying' flight to the first floor. The twisted oak balusters continue the vein of craftsmanship. For the staircase enthusiast it is heady stuff, hardly less impressive to the ordinary visitor.

Despite Edward Clarke's extravagance the family stayed on at Ardington until 1831 when it was sold to Robert Vernon whose collection of pictures now hang in the Tate and National Galleries. After a period as a subsidiary house of the Lockinge estate it was rented in 1939 by Mr and Mrs Baring. They bought the house in 1960 and since then have carried out discerning restoration such as removing the stone rendering applied by Vernon which detracted from the brickwork. Barings now look down on the elegantly furnished rooms, including Batoni's portrait of John Baring whose son Francis established the bank, while Lance's painting of Ardington in 1845 provides a happy link with the past – showing the house to be unchanged since then.

BLENHEIM PALACE, *Woodstock*

The Duke of Marlborough
Tel: 01993 811325

In Woodstock on A34

Open: mid-Mar to end Oct, daily, 10.30–5.30 (last admission 4.45)
Prices available on request

Blenheim is England's most monumental palace, and one can only understand its scale by knowing of the unique set of circumstances that produced it. Marlborough's victories enabled England to become a force to be reckoned with in Europe, and needed to be celebrated accordingly. At the time his wilful wife, Sarah, was at the height of her influence over Queen Anne whose favourite she had long been. When the decision was made to present to the victorious Duke a royal estate where the nation would build him a suitable seat, Vanbrugh was chosen as architect, rather than his senior, Wren. The project was presented to Vanbrugh by the 1st Duke as the man most likely to build in suitable style.

Vanbrugh had just completed his first house, Castle Howard, and proven his extraordinary Baroque flair. Now he had the opportunity to build on a heroic scale. A soldier himself, he had clear ideas about how such military successes should be immortalized in stone, which Blenheim does, triumphantly. He was supported by an impressive team: Hawksmoor, who had assisted him at Castle Howard, Grinling Gibbons, whose carved stone adorns the roofscape, James Thornhill and Louis Laguerre, to paint interiors.

While the construction of Vanbrugh's exteriors is consummate Baroque architecture, Blenheim was always going to be 'first a monument and only second a house'. Originally it was surrounded by formal gardens on a similar scale but 'Capability' Brown's park, laid out later, is more suitable and the lake that he created by damming the River Glyme achieved lofty fusion between palace, Vanbrugh's bridge and landscape. Garden formality is retained on two sides, however, and the early-twentieth-century Water Terraces of the French designer, Achille Duchêne are ideally suitable.

Vanbrugh's heroic scale extended into the Great Hall. Once the visitor can come to terms with the proportions, he can immediately begin to appreciate the decorative variety and quality which continues majestically from room to room. Alterations have been made, in particular by the 9th Duke, but they do not detract from Vanbrugh's original effect. There are marble doorcases surmounted by the Marlborough arms as Prince of the Holy Roman Empire, tapestries illustrating Marlborough's campaigns and fine ceilings, gilded, painted and stucco, depicting him kneeling to Britannia, as well as portraits and marble busts of the great soldier, his Duchess and Queen Anne.

The Duchess outlived her husband by twenty-two years, dying in 1744 after a lifetime of quarrelling. Vanbrugh was eventually banned from Blenheim following their running battles over the building of the palace. Marlborough's titles and Blenheim were inherited by his eldest daughter, Henrietta, whose nephew, the 5th Earl of Sunderland, subsequently became the 3rd Duke. Successive generations of the family appear to have lived easily within the vast portals and they have made important additions. Much came to Blenheim from the Sunderland inheritance, although the famous Sunderland library was sold in the 1880s. The house has assumed an additional mantle as the birthplace of an even more revered Englishman than the 1st Duke, Sir Winston Churchill. Amid all the splendour it is difficult to imagine Blenheim as occupied by any one family, but two superb groups from different periods, Reynolds' of the 4th Duke and his family and Sargent's of the 9th Duke and his family, face each other across the Red Drawing-Room and convey the ducal inheritance from generation to generation.

BROUGHTON CASTLE, *Banbury*

The Lord Saye and Sele
Tel: 01295 262624

On B4035, 3 km (2 miles) south-west of Banbury

**Open: mid-May to mid-Sept, Wed and Sun; also July and Aug,
Thur and Bank Holiday; 2–5**
£3.50, children £2, concessions
Tea Room

Broughton's placid stone façades reflected on all sides by its broad moat are a memorial to the medieval and Tudor status of its owners but conceal conflict and violence. The 1st Lord Saye and Sele was dragged from the Tower of London by Jack Cade's rebellious mob and beheaded by them in 1451. His son died fighting for Edward IV at the battle of Barnet. A century and a half later the 8th Baron gathered at Broughton the men opposed to Charles I's determination to rule without parliament. Although Lord Saye and Sele supported opposition to the King, he deplored the later execution of his monarch. Thereafter family history was quieter, Broughton abandoned for long periods for a more fashionable home in Kent. The extravagance of the Regency 15th Baron dissipated the family fortunes and at the same time allowed their home to slumber on without damaging alteration.

The original moated house was built around 1300. A century later, when Broughton was owned by the great William of Wykeham, the licence to crenellate produced extensions and the gatehouse through which one still approaches, having crossed the bridge over the moat. The 2nd Lord Saye and Sele married Margaret Wykeham in 1451 and thus Broughton passed to the family who have lived there ever since. A hundred years later the medieval house was incorporated into the present far larger Tudor building, completed in 1554 by the 6th Baron, whose son was responsible for much of the interior work.

The surviving medieval house is best seen in the chapel, the vaulted undercroft (now the dining-room) and the groined passage with a similar vaulted ceiling. Certainly here the castle atmosphere is very strong but the more extensive Tudor rooms are invitingly domestic if expansive. As was usual, the great hall was made out of the old medieval hall, although its Gothic ceiling is one of the few eighteenth-century features in the house and may easily have been the work of Sanderson Miller, the gentleman-architect who was a near neighbour. At the same time the long gallery was also Gothicized – albeit in restrained manner – and today the predominance of Tudor and Stuart family portraits along its spacious length retains the feel of its original period.

The most important Tudor features inside Broughton are chimney-pieces and overmantels, in particular the stucco overmantel in the King's Chamber where James I once slept. The overmantel is unique in England and contemporary work of the most comparable style is at Fontainebleau in France. Equally interesting but later is the interior porch through which one enters the oak room with geometric panelling between Ionic columns. The porch dates from the Restoration of Charles II, celebrated with vigour by the 8th Lord Saye and Sele during the last two years of his life, to atone for his earlier parliamentary loyalty. No doubt the same sentiments inspired him to purchase the fine seascape by Peeters set in a panel over the fireplace, showing Charles II setting sail for England from Scheveningen.

KINGSTON BAGPUIZE HOUSE, *Abingdon*

Mrs Francis Grant
Tel: 01865 820259

Off A415 and A420, 8 km (5 miles) west of Abingdon

**Open: Apr to Sept, Bank Holiday weekends and selected weekends
and preceding Wed, 2.30–5.30 (last admission 5)
£3, children £2.50, concessions
Home-made teas**

Although its architect is not known, Kingston Bagpuize House is confidently dated 1670; while there is no firm reason to dispute this, it makes the house precociously advanced in style and the more intriguing for having been built for modest squires, the Latton family. Today from the passing road its tall symmetry and warm balance of brick, with stone quoining and window dressing is immediately impressive. It must have been more so when one approached along a formal avenue to gates and a paved forecourt; today the drive leads along the edge of the west park to the present front door on this side of the house.

Many of the architectural features are unusual for the period, but the overall effect presents a house far more imposing than its size would suggest. Inside the same feeling of transition from a Restoration house towards more spacious William and Mary and eighteenth-century style is equally strong. The rooms, many with fine panelling, are a symmetrical progression focusing on the saloon that was the entrance hall, beyond which is the interior's best feature, the cantilevered staircase.

The garden was largely created by Miss Marlie Raphael, who bought the house in 1939 and who was a notable plantswoman. There is a fine collection of unusual trees and shrubs, especially in the woodland garden and shrub border. A terraced walk is surviving evidence of the Tudor house that was replaced. At one end of the terrace a gazebo is built over a Tudor cockpit and beyond the terrace lies Miss Raphael's woodland garden. After Miss Raphael's death in 1976 the house was inherited by her niece, Lady Tweedsmuir (at the time Lady Grant), and in 1995 she handed on the property to her son, Francis Grant.

STANTON HARCOURT MANOR, *Stanton Harcourt*

Mr Crispin and the Hon Mrs Gascoigne
Tel: 01865 881928

Off B4449, 14.5 km (9 miles) west of Oxford

Open: Apr to end Sept, selected days, 2–6
£4, children £2
Teas (in aid of church) on Thur, Sun and Bank Holidays

Harcourts trace their lineage back a thousand years to Normandy and they have been at Stanton Harcourt since the end of the twelfth century. Such ancient families who later prospered – as did the Harcourts – often forsook their old medieval manorial homes, which may possibly have been enlarged during Tudor times, for a grand new seat elsewhere in their estates, only to return this century to more manageable and domestic circumstances.

Stanton Harcourt dates from 1380. Some of the original parts survive as rare medieval buildings and the house expanded through the next two centuries, at its peak enclosing an inner and outer courtyard. After 1688 the family departed. Simon Harcourt became the most distinguished lawyer of Queen Anne's reign, was Lord Chancellor and was made a Viscount. He was described by one contemporary as 'a second Cicero'. He built a new house at nearby Cokethorpe. It was his grandson, the 1st Earl, however, who established the family in even greater style at Nuneham, where the foundations for his new house were built with stone from the by then ruinous Stanton Harcourt. Palladian Nuneham became a renowned eighteenth-century seat, especially admired for its park and gardens developed by the 2nd Earl.

Nuneham remained the family seat until the mid-twentieth century but after wartime requisition the last Viscount Harcourt (Mrs Gascoigne's father) decided to return to Stanton Harcourt, restoring the parts that remain today and creating the romantic gardens around the old buildings and medieval moat, ponds and stews.

The main house is the 1540 gatehouse extended by Lord Harcourt, but historically the most important part is the detached great kitchen, a square building with an octagonal timbered roof shaped like a cone to collect the smoke which was released by opening wooden louvres. There is no other surviving kitchen like it in England. Also detached from the main house is Pope's Tower which was the chapel of the medieval manor, but derives its name from occupation by the distinguished poet in 1717 and 1718, when it was semi-ruined but habitable. Pope completed the translation of the fifth volume of Homer's *Iliad* during his stay and his message on a pane of glass survives, 'In the year 1718 I Alexander Pope finished here the fifth volume of Homer.'

Nuneham may have gone but the paintings and works of art that graced its rooms are now at Stanton Harcourt and views by Paul Sandby confirm the house's imposing situation. If the portraits of the Lord Chancellor and his ambassador grandson, as well as other distinguished Harcourts, hang in less spacious surroundings than originally envisaged for them, they happily combine with eighteenth-century furniture in particular to perpetuate the family's distinguished patronage.

STONOR PARK, *Henley-on-Thames*

The Lord and Lady Camoys
Tel: 01491 638587

On B480, 8 km (5 miles) north of Henley

Open: Apr, Sun and Bank Holidays only; May, June and Sept, Wed, Sun and Bank Holidays; July, Wed, Thur and Sun; Aug, Wed, Thur, Sat, Sun and Bank Holidays; 2–5.30
£4, children under-14 free
Tea room

Hidden halfway up one of the most stunning valleys in the Chilterns, Stonor has been the home of the Stonor family for more than eight centuries. As befits its age and distinguished length of unbroken occupation, it evolved like so many English country houses, from the medieval hall to the Elizabethan 'E'-shaped house. Its present mellow façades, surrounded by deer park with noble trees, perpetuate an atmosphere of antiquity.

During the eighteenth century decorations such as glazing-bars for the windows were added and interiors remodelled, some with a Gothic flavour. Stonor is the classic recusant house with its chapel, strong Catholic traditions and memories of Edmund Campion, who was hidden here and kept a clandestine printing press. During the twentieth century the addition of Francis Stonor's collection of Italian Baroque paintings, drawings and works of art greatly enriched the more traditional country house furniture and family portraits. The deeply embedded Catholicism notwithstanding, the collection has brought a very Roman and slightly exotic feeling to the house.

CLEVEDON COURT, *Clevedon*

The National Trust / Sir Charles Elton, Bt
Tel: 01275 872257

On B3130, 2.5 km (1½ miles) east of Clevedon

Open: April to end Sept, Wed, Thur, Sun and Bank Holiday Mon, 2.30–5.30
(last admission 5)
£3.40, children £1.60
Tea room

Approaching Clevedon Court, the visitor cannot fail to detect its ancient origins; tell-tale signs are the curious combination of unsymmetrical blocks, the variety of windows and often massive, undecorated stonework. During the 1320s Sir John de Clevedon built the house against the remnants of thirteenth-century defensive buildings from which the stone tower survives. After passing to the Wake family, in 1709 Clevedon was bought by Abraham Elton, a prosperous Bristol merchant, whose family have lived there ever since and who, during the eighteenth and nineteenth centuries, were instrumental in making Clevedon a fashionable resort. They passed the property to the National Trust in 1960. At this time the west wing, originally Tudor, but altered out of all recognition, was taken down, returning the house to its medieval size.

It retains an intense air of antiquity. The visitor enters into the medieval screens passage and an even more remarkable survivor from the fourteenth century is the square window of the first-floor chapel, whose patterns of ogee tracery allow the light to flood in. Elizabethan (and later) alterations have been incorporated both inside and out: windows, re-faced façades, chimneys, chimney-pieces and panelling. The portraits reveal generations of Eltons and an interesting connection with the novelist William Makepeace Thackeray, who often stayed at the house with the scholarly 6th Baronet, and who is reputed to have written sections of *Henry Esmond* here. Outside, to the north, terraced gardens provide a perfect setting for the house and at one end of the largest terrace is a fine eighteenth-century Gothic octagonal temple.

ANTONY HOUSE, *Torpoint, Nr Plymouth*

The National Trust / Sir Richard Carew Pole, Bt
Tel: 01752 812191

Off A374, 3 km (2 miles) north-west of Torpoint, 8 km (5 miles) west of
Plymouth via car ferry

Open: Apr to end Oct, Tues to Thur and Bank Holiday Mon,
also June, July and Aug, Sun; 1.30–5
(last admission 4.45)
£3.80, children £1.90, concessions

Of all National Trust houses, Antony preserves the feel of a family home as well as any. Elegant, early-eighteenth century, surrounded by a park influenced by Humphry Repton, and gardens created by nineteenth-and twentieth-century Carew Poles, it commands memorable views down to the Lynher estuary. The overall effect is both welcoming and rewarding.

The Carews had been one of Cornwall's leading families long before Sir William built Antony in 1720. The two-storey – or 'double-pile'– house with an attic and dormer windows is most remarkable for the silvery hue of its stone. In sunlight, when viewed from a distance, the effect is almost ethereal. In 1771 Antony was inherited by Reginald Pole who assumed the Carew name. He consulted Repton and and made alterations to the house, and in 1906 a Jacobean wing was added, but demolished during the late-1940s. But the changes have not detracted from the house's original appearance and this is most obvious in the entrance south courtyard, enclosed on two sides by brick pavilions and opposite the house by a wall and central gates.

The interiors are restrained in decoration, with a number of rooms panelled in oak, which allows the fine furniture and paintings to present themselves without competition. There are portraits by Ramsey, Reynolds, Romney and Hudson (showing Sir John Pole and his wife in fancy dress), and an important portrait of Charles I at his trial by Edward Bower. Most charming is the portrait by Thomas Beach of Sir John de la Pole's three children with cricket bats.

Repton's *Red Book* of designs for the park can also be seen in the house, and for many visitors Antony's garden and parkland setting is as enjoyable as the house itself. The woodland garden belongs to the Carew Pole Garden Trust and has evolved since Repton's day to become one of Cornwall's most majestic gardens, combining landscape with a host of ornamental and often rare flowering trees and shrubs.

GODOLPHIN HOUSE, *Breage*

Mrs S.E. Schofield
Tel: 01736 762409

Off A394, 8 km (5 miles) north-west of Helston

Open: May and June, Thur; July, Aug, and Sept, Tues, Thur and Bank Holidays; 2–5 (10–5, Thur in Aug)
£3, children £1

Even in days of lengthy travel Godolphin was too remote to be the main seat of great men, and tucked below wooded Godolphin Hill it perpetuates an atmosphere of rarely disturbed slumber. The Godolphins' prosperity was built on tin mining before, at the end of the seventeenth century, a family meteor appeared in the form of Sidney, 1st Earl of Godolphin who served Charles II, James II, and William III before becoming Queen Anne's Lord High Treasurer and the most important man in England. His son married the 1st Duke of Marlborough's daughter who became duchess in her own right, but their only son died childless and Godolphin passed to the Dukes of Leeds who added the name to their own but never occupied the house.

Much of the house was demolished at the beginning of the nineteenth century, the rest became a farm and was sold in 1921. The future looked bleak when, in 1937, Mrs Schofield's husband bought the property and carried out commendable restoration. Godolphin as originally built was most interesting for its use of local granite and other materials and Mr Schofield followed this example in every aspect of his work. The main front is both welcoming and unusual, very long and low, its seventeenth-century colonnade with pillars of local granite stretches between identical fifteenth-century towers. The Schofields also hunted down much of the most interesting original contents, pride of place going to Wootton's painting of the Godolphin Arab, one of three eighteenth-century stallions from which all British racehorses descend. Charles II is reputed to have slept in the king's room when, as Prince of Wales, he escaped to the Scilly Isles.

PENCARROW, *Bodmin*

The Molesworth-St Aubyn family
Tel: 0120 884 1369

Off A389 and B3266, 6.5 km (4 miles) north-west of Bodmin
Open: Easter to mid-Oct, daily except Fri and Sat, 1.30–5
(11–5, June to mid-Sept and Bank Holiday Mon)
£3.80, children £1.80, concessions
Light lunches and cream teas

Pencarrow's ochre-stuccoed Palladianism is a cheerful contrast to the granite houses and windswept landscape of Bodmin Moor. Only one side, facing a courtyard and roofed with grey Delabole slate, confirms that the mid-eighteenth-century house was built around an older one. If the house is mainly eighteenth-century, its surroundings are a fine example of Cornish Victorian plantsmanship. Visitors do not actually drive down the rare avenue of monkey-puzzle trees that leads from lodges on the Camelford road, but take a later turning and follow a mile-long drive that winds between banks of rhododendrons and camellias grouped around a comprehensive collection of conifers. The planting has been steadily renewed and extended by successive generations, not least the present occupant, Sir Arscott.

Financial stewardship of the Duchy of Cornwall during Elizabeth I's reign founded

the Molesworth fortunes which prospered through the seventeenth and eighteenth centuries. It was Sir John Molesworth, 4th Bt, who began remodelling the house and the work was finished by his son. Pencarrow was one of the few houses by the Yorkshire architect, Robert Allanson, who died aged only thirty-eight. The various rooms retain high quality Georgian interiors: elegant marble chimney-pieces, and doorcases surmounted by broken pediments. The outstanding decorative feature is the rococo stucco ceiling in the music room depicting the Four Seasons. Such details, and the arrangement of the hall where marbled pillars support a vaulted ceiling with a cantilevered stone staircase beyond, confirm that Allanson had all-round talent in the best eighteenth-century tradition.

Limited but significant alterations were made by Sir William Molesworth during the 1830s. He made the entrance hall into a library with bookcases below panels carrying a series of family portraits, and panelled the music room where the major addition was the early-Georgian carved wood alcove that he inserted to contain an Italian marble figure of the Borghese Venus. All his additions are still intact and their different periods give the house greater depth of interest.

The Molesworths – and, from 1839, Molesworth-St Aubyns – have been discerning commissioners and collectors as the portraits and other works of art at Pencarrow confirm. The eighteenth-century figures around the library are all enjoyable but outshone by the dashing Northcote of the 6th Baronet over the fireplace. The dining-room portraits are exclusively by Reynolds, except for one by his 'tutor' Hudson, and demonstrate how a privileged selection of Cornish houses benefitted from his being a 'local' artist. The most delightful eighteenth-century family picture, however, is the Arthur Devis conversation piece of the 'four Misses St Aubyn' in the ante-room. Raeburn's later full-length of the sporting 7th Baronet overlooks the staircase.

The pictures are by no means confined to portraits. There are seascapes by Charles Brooking, two important mid-eighteenth-century views of London Bridge and the Tower of London by Samuel Scott, landscapes by Richard Wilson, and Dutch pictures in the boudoir. The Pencarrow bowl, containing a Chinese artist's impression of the house, is the charming highlight of a good collection of Oriental porcelain and the furniture throughout – English, French and Italian – is of equal quality.

PRIDEAUX PLACE, *Padstow*

The Prideaux-Brune family
Tel: 01841 532411
On edge of Padstow, 11 km (7 miles) north-west of Wadebridge
Open: Easter Sun to mid-Oct, Sun to Thur, 1.30–5;
also Bank Holiday Mon, 11–5
£4, accompanied children (14 and under) £1, group rates
Tea Room

Prideaux's first impression is almost military; battlemented terrace walls with toy-fort-like little towers flanking steps up to the long front of the house whose age is not immediately obvious. Visitors are left guessing throughout most of their tour and none would predict the variety that appears. For Prideaux is an originally Tudor house altered during the eighteenth century, given Strawberry Hill Gothic additions during the early-nineteenth, and full of other unexpected treats. Its immaculate appearance is thanks to dedicated restoration carried out since 1988 by the present owners and still continuing.

Shrewd Tudor Prideauxs did well out of the Dissolution, gained the property which had belonged to the Priory of Bodmin and in 1592 Nicholas Prideaux had completed his 'new house', built on the Elizabethan 'E'-plan with gables and castellated bays. New, but not the first house, for during the restoration work a few years ago a slate panel of an original thirteenth-century building was revealed. Sir Nicholas's portrait hangs over the fireplace in the dining-room where part of the dark panelling is his work, but his most sensational interior was the great chamber with its richly worked ceiling depicting the story of Susannah and the Elders, concealed by an eighteenth-century ceiling until a few years ago when this was removed and the original restored.

The house was altered by Edmund Prideaux after his Grand Tour in 1739. He removed the gables from the entrance front and inserted the Georgian sash windows. His most dramatic additions, however, and the house's most surprising contents, were from the nearby house of Stow, Restoration home of the Grenville family, Earls of Bath, which was demolished only a generation after it was built. The panelled Grenville room contains carving by Grinling Gibbons that has been sumptuously regilded during recent restoration. There are also three inset paintings by Verrio and the Earl's vast wine cooler. Prideaux's shallow rising cantilevered staircase also came from Stow.

In 1799 the Rev Charles Prideaux married a Brune heiress and celebrated the match by adding the Gothic wing and rooms which complete the house's development. The Gothic exteriors face south and inside the cleric's tour-de-force was the library where Gothic furniture complements the lofty arched window with heraldic glass, and the ribbed ceiling.

Charles Prideaux-Brune also commissioned one of the most interesting groups among the house's fine paintings, all by the Cornish artist John Opie, who was born and brought up on the estate and was paid twenty guineas and a suit for five pictures. His pictures hang in the morning room with the most romantic of the family portraits – both in looks and story. It is Humphrey Prideaux painted on his Grand Tour, by Rosalba Carriera, who became so enamoured with her sitter that she slid a love letter into the portrait's frame; sadly it lay undiscovered for over two hundred years. The Grenville room contains an important collection of royalist Caroline portraits and generations of the family hang in the hall. Among a host of fine works of art one of the most intriguing is an astrological clock made in 1800 by a Padstow craftsman, which shows the position of the stars and other details, all in relation to Padstow.

Impressive evidence of the on-going work can be found at Prideaux inside and out. Alec Cobbe has redecorated the drawing-room with a series of panels containing Cornish scenes; the Gothic dairy is undergoing complete restoration and Edmund Prideaux's eighteenth-century garden, with an Ionic temple built with stone from Ralph Allen's quarries at Bath, is being extensively restored.

ST MICHAEL'S MOUNT, *Marazion*

The National Trust / The Lord St Levan
Tel: 01736 710507 / 710265

At Marazion, 0.8 km (½ mile) south of A394

Open: Apr to end Oct, Mon to Fri, 10.30–5.30 (last admission 4.45)
£3.50, concessions

Romance and history wash around St Michael's Mount with the waters of Mount's Bay from which the island rises up, surmounted by its cluster of granite buildings. Accessible either by the centuries-old causeway at low tide, or by boat at other times, it blends legend with ancient Christianity, and more recent battles, before peaceful occupation as a family home in a manner that cannot fail to fascinate visitors. In 1954 the Mount was given to the National Trust by the 3rd Lord St Levan, with the family continuing to lease parts of the house and its grounds.

The Mount's strategic position meant that it was built upon in prehistoric times and frequented by the earliest traders who passed around the Cornish coast. In 1135 a Benedictine priory was established as a dependancy of the much larger Mont St Michael off the coast of Normandy. There are traces of twelfth-century buildings that survive from the priory, but after the Dissolution of the Monasteries only the church, the refectory and the Lady Chapel survived.

Sold by the crown in 1599, the Mount was occupied by successive governors who maintained it as a fort. In 1646 the future king Charles II lodged on his escape to the Scilly Isles and later that year the Royalist Basset family, the governors at the time, surrendered to the Parliamentarians. The Mount was granted to Captain John St Aubyn and in 1659 he bought the island and began the occupation as a family home that has been continued by his descendants ever since.

St Aubyn's son was made a Baronet and the 3rd and 4th Baronets, during the 1730s and 1750s, carried out extensive work to improve the collection of buildings that constituted the house. The old Lady Chapel was transformed into the Gothic Blue Drawing-Rooms by the 4th Baronet. A cloud was cast over the family's legitimate descent by the popular 5th Baronet who had fifteen children – all illegitimate. On his death in 1839 (when between twenty and thirty thousand mourners followed his coffin to its burial-ground), the family estates on the mainland passed to relations, but the eldest son of the 5th Baronet inherited the Mount and was succeeded by his younger brother who was created a baronet in his own right. His son, Sir John, was made the 1st Lord St Levan in 1887 and employed his cousin, Piers St Aubyn, to design a new wing for the castle.

St Aubyn was well-known as a builder of churches (mainly in Cornwall but also including the Temple Church in London). He remodelled the old buildings, using the same granite stone so that his work makes for a balanced whole, and built a new wing some way down the slope. The main group of buildings cluster around the fourteenth-century church and the original priory refectory has become the Chevy Chase Room, whose timber ceiling was renewed during the nineteenth century. The room is named after the hunting scenes in the fascinating plaster frieze which extends around the whole room and carries the date 1641. In a loyal flourish (probably to make up for his earlier loyalty to the Parliamentarians), Colonel St Aubyn put up the royal coat of arms on the end wall to celebrate the restoration of Charles II in 1660.

Quite different in appearance and atmosphere are the delightful blue drawing-rooms with rococo Gothic plasterwork of superb delicacy and freshness and Chippendale Gothic chairs of similar quality. Portraits by the Cornishman, Hudson, of the creator of the rooms, the 4th Baronet, and his wife, hang there along with a delightful family group of them with their children by the little known artist, George Roth. As well as a distinguished Gainsborough of Lord de Dunstanville, the 5th Baronet was painted by another Cornish artist, John Opie, and there is a rare Opie landscape of the Mount in moonlight. The painting's combination of charm and mystery in many ways encapsulates the Mount's appeal.

TREWITHEN, *Grampound Road*

Mr and Mrs Michael Galsworthy
Tel: 01726 882763

On A390, between Probus and Grampound
Open: Apr to July, Mon (including Bank Holidays) and Tues, 2–4
£3, children £1.50
Tea room

Visitors approach Trewithen through undulating parkland containing venerable holm-oaks and arrive at the forecourt enclosed by the house's trim north façade and flanking cupola-topped stable blocks. It is a welcoming arrival, but the house's *tour de force* lies on the other, south-facing side. Tree-felling by government order during the First World War, in the beech wood protecting this side of the house, inspired George Johnstone to open up a broad 180-m (200-yd long) lawn stretching away from the house. Today, to look back to the pink-tinted stone façade, the view flanked by towering tree magnolias, banks of rhododendrons – many raised by Johnstone – and other woodland plants, is one the most memorable house and garden vistas in England.

The present Trewithen was built by Philip Hawkins shortly after he purchased the estate in 1715. His ancestor John had left the family's native Kent as a recusant Catholic during the troubled reign of Mary Tudor and sought peace in distant Cornwall. By the early eighteenth century the family were prosperously established in Cornwall and Philip employed the London architect Thomas Edwards who designed the neat Palladian house that survives hardly altered today. After his death in 1738 Philip's work was continued by his nephew, Thomas Hawkins, who had married a sophisticated London heiress, Anne Heywood. They employed Sir Robert Taylor who designed the saloon, now the dining-room, with fine rococo plasterwork and imposing colonnaded arcades with vaulted alcoves at both ends. Anne's indulgent father regularly produced presents for the new house; their correspondence mentions a set of six Chippendale dining-chairs still in the house.

The other main rooms are warmly panelled and retain furniture and pictures from Thomas and Anne Hawkins' time as well as additions by later generations. The last Hawkins was always called C.H.T.; his father, John, a distinguished horticulturalist and Fellow of the Royal Society, planted the holm-oak acorns from his Sussex estate, Bignor Park. C.H.T.'s sister married a Johnstone and the family descent continued to George Johnstone, grandfather of the present owner. Among the Hawkins' portraits there are others to tell of these family connections; Raffles – including Sir Stamford – ancestors of George Johnstone's wife whose connection also brought the Reynolds portraits of Zachariah Mudge and his wife (whose son Thomas became the famous clockmaker).

In 1991 Patsy and Janet Swanborough completed a delightful bird's-eye view of Trewithen showing the house in its garden setting, the combination which quite rightly draws most visitors. Despite being paralysed from his waist down following a hunting accident in 1932 George Johnstone continued to expand the garden. One of his rhododendrons was named after his wife, Alison. After his death she named an equally well-known variety of camellia 'Glenn's Orbit' in 1962 because it was sent up to the Royal Horticultural Society and received its Award of Merit on the day that the American astronaut completed his space orbit of earth. First, George Johnstone's daughter, Elizabeth, and subsequently his grandson, Michael Galsworthy, have maintained and built on his garden.

BICKLEIGH CASTLE, *Tiverton*

Mr and Mrs O.N. Boxall
Tel: 01884 855 363

On A396, 6.5 km (4 miles) south of Tiverton
Open: Easter week; May, Wed, Sun and Bank Holiday; June to early Oct,
daily except Sat; 2–5.30
£3.50, children £1.80
Tea room

Bickleigh Castle's thatched Norman chapel is probably the oldest complete building in the county, its main body dating from 1100. It survives from the period when the castle was orginally built, in a then strategic and now picturesque position on the wooded slopes of the River Exe. From 1410 it belonged to the Courtenays of Powderham who rebuilt the castle as a fortified manor, but of their home only the gatehouse survived from the Civil War when General Fairfax 'sleighted' the castle, demolishing the two main wings. By this time Bickleigh had passed by marriage to the Carew family; Thomas Carew eloped with Anne Courtenay but was forgiven after brave service at Flodden and other battles, and Bickleigh was Anne's dowry when they married.

After Fairfax's devastation Sir Henry Carew restored the gatehouse and built the thatched farmhouse which became the main dwelling. But after his death in 1681 with no heirs the place fell into disrepair until this century when successive owners have carried out restoration. The work has been carried on by the present owners who purchased the property in 1970. The arrangement of the buildings – chapel gatehouse, farmhouse, cottages and barns – makes a harmonious vernacular group and the old moat is the focus of the garden.

The gatehouse retains its vaulted entry with an armoury and guard room on the ground floor and a great hall stretching over both on the first floor. The armour has a suitable feel, as does the Tudor furniture in the guard room, all added by the present owners. The most prized survivor from the Civil War is a carved stone overmantel in the farmhouse's garden room. The dining-room contains samplers collected by Mrs Boxall and the watercolours, plaster reliefs and charcoal studies in the farmhouse were done by her mother and sisters. The thatched barn contains an enjoyable museum and exhibition of the *Mary Rose*, Henry VIII's ill-fated warship of which Sir George Carew was vice-admiral, and a later collection of Second World War spy and escape gadgets.

CADHAY, *Ottery St Mary*

Lady William-Powlett
Tel: 01404 812432

On B3176, 1.6 km (1 mile) north-west of Ottery St Mary
Open: Spring and Aug Bank Holiday Sun and Mon; also July and
Aug, Tues, Wed and Thur; 2–6 (last admission 5.30)
£3, children £1.50

Following the lime avenue that leads to Cadhay, one gets an impression of approaching an undiscovered house, a feeling that strengthens as the warm stone gables first appear. Undiscovered and long-established, John Haydon's 'fair new house', built between 1546 and 1550, in fact extended an existing house incorporating a medieval great hall dating from 1470 or earlier. Sometime after 1587, when he married Joan Poulett, John's great-nephew Robert filled in the empty south side to link the house around its central courtyard, and made the long gallery on the first floor of the new wing.

The timber roof of the great hall survives in one upstairs room but the courtyard plan is certainly later, confirmed by the sophisticated pattern of flint and sandstone on the internal walls of the courtyard. It is called the court of the Sovereigns because of its stone figures of Henry VIII, Edward VI, Mary Tudor and Elizabeth I, positioned at first-floor level over doorways. Dating from 1617 (carved beneath Elizabeth I with Robert Haydon's initials) and set in niches flanked by classical columns and other decoration, they would appear to be a local craftsman's Renaissance flourish.

After two centuries of occupation the Haydons sold Cadhay in 1736 and thereafter it belonged to a number of owners. In 1910 it was bought by W.C. Dampier Whetham (who became Sir William Dampier), who carried out extensive and careful restoration. The house's plan makes for an easy progression of rooms around the courtyard: the dining-room to one side of the entrance hall leads to an adjoining trio of sitting-room, living-hall and drawing-room along one side; on the first floor each corner of the house contains a main bedroom. Some of Cadhay's most interesting paintings are the fine portraits of Lady William-Powlett and her husband and daughter, by the Australian artist M. Cohen.

FURSDON, *Thorverton*

E.D. Fursdon
Tel: 01392 860860

Off A396, 14.5 Km (9 miles) north of Exeter
Open: Easter Mon to end Sept, Thur and Bank Holidays only, 2–4.30
£3
Home-made teas

For more than seven centuries generations of Fursdons have occupied this part of Devon by continuous male succession, but not always on the well-chosen site of the present house, perched overlooking its terraced garden which projects the view south over the undulating, wooded valley below. The house was built during the eighteenth century, retaining the shell of an older building, and around 1815 its present appearance was completed with the addition of the library wing, and the central colonnade which links the two slightly projecting wings and adds an agreeable note of decoration to the unpretentious entrance façade.

Although, like the exterior, Fursdon's interiors are principally eighteenth-century in appearance, evidence of the older house has appeared on a number of occasions. In the drawing-room on one side of the entrance hall the field panelling with a frieze and Corinthian columns is c.1732, but two archways in the oak screen at the far end of the room were recently discovered to be early-Tudor doorways, probably leading into the original house's great hall. The drawing-room has pale panelling and gives a sense that little has changed; which indeed it has not done in much of the house. A watercolour of the interior dated 1860 shows a sofa table in the library in the same position as today and the Lely portrait of Fursdon's most formidable chatelaine, Grace Fursdon, hangs over the same doorway. While she stirred strong likes and dislikes, her granddaughter, another Grace, drove a rejected lover to fire a pistol at her own portrait which hangs nearby; the shot-hole is still visible in the back of the canvas.

An adventurous recent addition is the fine Axminster carpet, specially woven and incorporating into its pattern the Fursdon crest of five feathers. The most delightful exhibit in the house, ideally displayed in rooms of intimate size, is the costume collection. Among eighteenth-century pieces are a rare mantua or court-dress, worn once in 1753 by Elizabeth Fursdon and a tiny pair of child's shoes dated 1772, that belonged to George Fursdon aged one.

HARTLAND ABBEY, *Bideford*

Sir Hugh Stucley, Bt
Tel: 01 2374 41264

At Hartland Point, 24 km (15 miles) west of Bideford, 8 km (5 miles) from A39
Open: Easter to Aug, Bank Holiday Sun and Mon; May to end Sept, Wed;
also July, Aug and Sept, Sun; 2–5.30
£3.50, children £1.50, concessions
Tea room

Hartland is reputed to have been the last abbey in England to fall during Henry VIII's Dissolution, no doubt because of its remote, secluded position in a narrow wooded valley that runs inland from the dramatic Atlantic coastline at Hartland Point.

The setting survives unspoilt and, as one approaches Hartland, the tower of St Nectan's Church stands loftily on the seaward hill beyond, a reminder of the original reason for the abbey's foundation in 1160. The walk to the sea from Hartland remains as breathtaking as it was when taken by medieval monks, and the shrub and walled gardens have just been opened to visitors, adding to the enjoyment outside the house.

Part of the old building is incorporated into the present house. The remodelling began in 1704, an unusually long time after the Dissolution, when an heiress of the Luttrell family, who had been in occupation for a century, married Paul Orchard. Their work is commemorated in a stone in the south wall inscribed 'P.O. & M 1705'. More extensive work was carried out during the 1770s by their son, also Paul, who removed the abbey's great hall and chapel and rebuilt them in Gothic style.

The outside is Orchard work, the inside substantially Stucley, carried out by Sir George Stucley (whose great-grandmother was an Orchard). Paul Orchard II's three new rooms – drawing-room, hall (made into the billiard room) and dining-room – were impressively redecorated. In the drawing-room linenfold panelling was copied from the House of Lords. Above the panelling an Exeter artist painted a series of panels showing Stucleys in heroic role at successive medieval events of English history. Sir George employed Sir G.G. Scott whose most dramatic addition was the Alhambra corridor which he carried out in 1862 after Sir George had visited and been inspired by the Moorish original in Granada.

Good family portraits include works by Reynolds, Hudson, Northcote and Beechey, all of whom were West Country artists by origin. Hudson (Reynolds's tutor) lived in Bideford and the house contains his fine full-length portrait of Catherine, Lady Bampfylde. She was an ancestor of the Hon Lady Stucley, daughter of Lord Poltimore. Their family heritage mixes happily with the Stucleys'. The impressive 1835 group of six coach-horses by Davis in the inner hall belonged to the Lord Poltimore of the day.

An exhibition of documents dating from the founding of the abbey includes the seals of most English kings and queens since the early thirteenth century. There is also the vindicating account by Sir Lewis Stucley of his escorting Sir Walter Raleigh to the Tower. The sporting parson, Jack Russell's hunting equipment hangs on one wall and a photograph of Emperor Haile Selassie opening Hartland fete in 1938 adds an exotic note.

HEMERDON HOUSE, *Plymouth*

J.H.G. Woollcombe
Tel: 01752 841410/337350

3 km (2 miles) from Plympton, 8 km (5 miles) east of Plymouth north of A38

Open: May to Sept, selected days and Bank Holidays, 2–5.30
£2.50

The austerity of Hemerdon's neatly rendered Georgian exterior is quickly dispelled as one enters the hall where family history combines with welcoming rooms and interesting works of art. To the plan of main rooms, hall, library, drawing-room and dining-room, which is contemporary with the house's construction, subsequent generations have added an overlay of character so that the library has a mellow Victorian air and, throughout, the house is a family home – as it always has been.

Woollcombes have given fine service on many occasions. In the hall is a perfectly crafted model of HMS *Victor* commanded by George Woollcombe between 1824 and 1827. Also in the hall the highlight of a collection of swords is the weapon belonging to Lieutenant William Woollcombe of the 71st (Highland) Light Infantry, which he used at Waterloo. The upstairs landing is dominated by the powerful Victorian portrait by J.C. Horsley of Thomas Woollcombe, a leading figure in the extension of the Great Western Railway to nearby Plymouth and beyond into Cornwall. An unexpected discovery is the primary version of Reynolds's portrait of the Earl of Bath. But without doubt Hemerdon's outstanding painting, purchased in 1828, is the large Northcote in the drawing-room, entitled 'The Worthies of Devon'. It shows a distinguished group, all originating from the county, comprising Sir Joshua Reynolds, John Gay, Lord Ashburton, George Monk, the Duke of Albemarle, Sir Francis Drake, Sir Walter Raleigh, the 1st Duke of Marlborough, Sir Richard Grenville, John Mudge and Dr Huxham.

The antiquarian enthusiasm of one member of the family is hinted at by Hamilton Smith's watercolour, 'The Landing of the Black Prince with Prisoners including the King of France', which also hangs in the drawing-room. More immediately at home are the charming Devon landscapes executed during the 1820s and 1830s by William Bath, which complement the four watercolours of Dartmoor by Hamilton Smith in the first-

51

floor passage. In a house where interior decorative features were used sparingly, the handsome double arch in the hall is especially effective, as are the large Regency bookcases in the library which also contains good Chinese porcelain.

POWDERHAM CASTLE, *Kenton*

The Lord and Lady Courtenay
Tel: 01626 890243

In Kenton, off A379, 3 km (8 miles) south of Exeter
Open: March to end Oct, daily except Sat, 10–5.30
£4.40, children £2.95, concessions
Tea room

Few families are more suited to live in a castle than the Devon Courtenays: Plantagenet knights, great crusaders, and described in *Burke's Peerage* as 'one of the most illustrious races among the nobility'. During the Middle Ages they married into both French and English royal families, and the English family descends from a Courtenay who accompanied Eleanor of Aquitaine to England for her marriage to Henry II. During the crusades they provided three emperors of Constantinople. The earldom of Devon was conferred in 1293, although between 1556 and 1831 it fell into abeyance and only a quirk of genealogy allowed it to be reclaimed.

Today the skyline of turrets and battlements evokes memories of Sir Philip Courtenay (knighted by the Black Prince after Poitiers), who built the original castle between 1390 and 1420. But appearances are deceptive; almost all exterior and interior are the work of later generations. Damage suffered during the Civil War when Parliamentary forces besieged Powderham forced the family to depart until 1740 when they returned after steady renovation by Sir William Courtenay. His son was created Viscount Courtenay and he ushered in the nineteenth century which witnessed Powderham's elevation to a house of wide-ranging artistic quality.

Portraits by the Devon-born artist Thomas Hudson hang in many houses in the county, but few rival his work at Powderham, especially the group of the 1st Viscount with his wife and children. Hudson's group was emulated for the next generation by Matthew Peters who painted the 2nd Viscount with his wife and twelve children — eleven girls and one boy. Two more girls were subsequently born.

The lone son, who inherited as 3rd Viscount and later revived the Devon earldom, became the family's most flamboyant character. As a young man he was embroiled in a scandal with William Beckford; later in life debts and an enduring bad reputation forced him to leave England first for America and then Paris, where he died in 1835.

There is constant variety in the interiors: the grand staircase hall, made in 1750 on the site of the medieval great hall and rising through two storeys with memorable rococo plasterwork; the sombre dining-hall added in 1837 and subsequently decorated with linenfold panelling which supports panels of arms tracing the long family history; or the 3rd Viscount's music room designed by James Wyatt. It still has its organ at one end, the 3rd Viscount himself painted the circular wall panels and his portrait – one of a number by Richard Cosway, better known as a miniaturist – hangs over the fireplace. The pink drawing-room added during the 1760s exemplifies the eighteenth-century grace successfully married to Powderham's ancient, warring origins. Its bow windows look out across the deer park to the River Exe.

SAND, *Sidbury*

Lt Col P.V. Huyshe
Tel: 01395 597230

Off A375, 1.6 km (1 mile) north-east of Sidbury
Open: Easter, May and Aug, Bank Holiday Sun and Mon;
also July, last week-end; 2–5.30 (last tour 4.45)
£3, children/students 60p
Tea room

Sand is an ideal example of a largely Tudor house so expertly restored during the early-twentieth century that this later work is difficult for the casual observer to detect. It is the more enjoyable in that the Huyshe family rebuilt Sand during the 1590s shortly after they acquired the property in 1560 and have retained ownership ever since. Between 1908 and 1909 Rowland Huyshe, assisted by the architect E.H. Harbottle, carried out the restoration, which included rebuilding a wing demolished early in the nineteenth century, thereby restoring the house's harmony.

Rowland's work is part of the stone entrance front that greets visitors but the effect is pure Tudor; the cross-gabled wings embrace the central portion with mullioned and transomed windows for the hall and the two-storey gabled porch set to one side. Small gables over the upper windows stick up from the parapet in front of the roof. Tudor details continue inside: the newel stair, doorways and chimney-pieces but most decorative is the stained glass in the hall, which includes a panel of a crowned pomegranate, the badge of Catherine of Aragon.

Close to the present house is the old hall house that was superseded, which retains its fine timber roof. In the garden is a rare 1600 thatched summerhouse with Tuscan columns, which carries the arms of Rowland and Anne Huyshe, who built the house, and a part-Greek, part-Latin inscription of admirable piety: 'The fountain of true fragrance is to be in fellowship with God.'

Tapeley Park, *Bideford*

Hector Christie
Tel: 01271 860528

Off A39, 1.6 km (1 mile) south of Instow

Open: Easter to end Sept, daily except Mon (open Bank Hols), 10–6
£2.50, children £1.50
Tea room

The house stands proudly above the Torridge estuary looking across to Bideford. The drive leads dramatically up from the water's edge. Passing a blasted obelisk, you ascend to an elevated plateau with spectacular views out to sea. The plain eighteenth-century house of the Cleveland family was imaginatively reclad by John Belcher at the turn of the century. Inside his work is even more apparent. He remodelled the interior for Lady Rosamund Christie, whose husband inherited the house through his mother. It is her collection that gives the interior its distinctive character. She had a passion for grand eighteenth-century furniture and late nineteenth-century works of art. Here are to be discovered marvellous pieces of French and Italian eighteenth-century furniture nestling beside particularly fine inlaid cabinets from the Morris workshop at Merton. Late nineteenth-century paintings by Leighton and Richmond hang near good eighteenth-century family portraits. Bronzes by Leighton and marbles by Gibson and Benzoni give the interiors an aesthetic period flavour enhanced by the sumptuous collection of *pâte-sur-pâte* Minton china arranged in the hall.

Outside the Italian gardens are early-twentieth century. In front of the main house, beyond the gaggle of geese, are regular displays of jousting. As the delightfully idiosyncratic guide book hints, this is a house well worth crossing North Devon to see.

TIVERTON CASTLE, *Tiverton*

Mr and Mrs A.K. Gordon
Tel: 01884 253200

In Tiverton

Open: Easter Sun to end June and Sept, Thur and Sun; July and Aug, Sun to Thur, also Bank Holiday Mon; 2.30–5.30
£3, children £2/free
Tea room

In one corner of the main courtyard of Tiverton Castle an unmistakably Norman tower stands as testament to the place's ancient history stretching back to the reign of Henry I. On his orders Richard de Redvers built a castle to command the strategic crossing-point of the River Exe and Redvers remained until 1293 when Tiverton and its lands passed to their kinsmen, the Courtenays. Much of the castle was built by Hugh de Courtenay around the turn of the fourteenth century. During the Wars of the Roses its fortune followed the ups and downs of its owners until Sir Edward Courtenay was reinstated in the family honours by Henry VII. His son William married Katherine,

daughter of Edward IV and, in her own description, 'daughter, sister and aunt of kings'. The connection was too close to her nephew, Henry VIII, and their son, who had been made Marquess of Exeter, was beheaded in 1539. Katherine had died in 1527; her funeral was probably the most sumptuous event in the town's history.

Alterations were made during Elizabeth I's reign by the Giffard family who were still in occupation during the Civil War when the castle was damaged by Fairfax and his Parliamentary army. Ruined sections, the old tower and fourteenth-century Courtenay gatehouse survived but the main house today was built during the late-seventeenth century by a wealthy Tiverton merchant.

The present owner inherited from his uncle, Ivar Campbell, who had bought the castle in 1960, restored many of the buildings and decorated and furnished the interiors. The collection of paintings, furniture and clocks remain and the work on the castle has been continued by the Gordons. Suitably there is a collection of Civil War armour; few other places offer holiday accommodation in surroundings with such an ancient history.

UGBROOKE HOUSE, *Chudleigh*

The Lord Clifford of Chudleigh
Tel: 01626 852179

In Chudleigh

**Open: mid-July to early Sept, Tues, Wed, Thur and Sun, grounds 1–5.30,
house tours 2 and 3.45**
£4, children £2, concessions
Tea room

Ugbrooke is a four-square castellated eighteenth-century house, mostly designed by Robert Adam but altered later. It has been the seat of the Lord Clifford of Chudleigh since the first of their title, Charles II's great minister, Clifford of the Cabal.

Set in beautiful rolling Devon countryside, the house's exterior is impressively simple, a contrast to the pretty suite of Adam rooms and a rich marble Catholic chapel. The 1st Lord Clifford's Dutch paintings (of which he was a pioneering collector) are on view along with his portrait, one of Sir Peter Lely's masterpieces, and a great many other portraits of the family and their various relations. Francis Towne was a drawing master here and there are unusually interesting watercolours and pastels.

'Capability' Brown gave Ugbrooke a suitable parkland setting, with lakes and majestic trees. Around the castle, terraced gardens make the most of views out to Dartmoor.

ATHELHAMPTON HOUSE, *Puddletown*

Patrick Cooke
Tel: 01305 848363

On A35, 1.6 km (1 mile) east of Puddletown
Open: Easter to end Oct, daily except Sat, 11–5
£4.50, children £1.50

It was one of the great country house escapes of recent years that Athelhampton was not destroyed by a potentially disastrous fire in 1992. It says much for the determination of the owners that the house was restored in time to re-open to the public in 1994. The fire was the latest in a series of challenges that have faced the ancient manor and make its survival the more to be enjoyed. The outstanding medieval and early-Tudor architecture of the two wings enclosing the forecourt was described by Robin Fedden as 'one of the most picturesque sights of Dorset'.

The central battlemented part of the entrance façade was built by Sir William Martyn, Lord Mayor of London. His oriel bay with three-tier windows is superbly delicate. The other wing is early-Tudor where Ham stone window mullions shine out from the grey walls and the high gables topped by heraldic beasts are theatrically Renaissance in style. The most important room of Martyn's wing is the hall with its unique timbered roof.

Nineteenth-century decay was followed by restoration, first after 1848 but later and more substantially from 1891, by Alfred Cart de Lafontaine. His work was typical of the high standard displayed by Edwardian enthusiasts of medieval and Tudor styles. He introduced linenfold panelling to many of the rooms including the hall and King's room. Perhaps Lafontaine's most telling addition was to commission F. Inigo Jones to lay out the gardens whose water features, clipped yew, and stone architecture perfectly complement the house.

Lafontaine's work lasted half a century but when Robert Cooke bought Athelhampton in 1957, decay had once again set in. He and successive generations of his family have once again rejuvenated the old manor. Robert Cooke was succeeded by his son Robin, a Member of Parliament, after whose death the work at Athelhampton has been continued by his son, Patrick. In the process new touches were added; Robin Cooke's expert knowledge of the Palace of Westminster accounted for wallpaper whose pattern reproduced the one designed by Pugin for the House of Lords. The most notable additions to the house have been the furniture while the gardens have been both restored and extended.

ILSINGTON HOUSE, *Puddletown*

Mr and Mrs P. Duff
Tel: 01305 848454

In Puddletown on A35, 6.5 km (4 miles) north-east of Dorchester
Open: May to end Sept, Wed, Thur, Sun and Bank Holidays, 2–6
£3
Lunch and tea by prior arrangement

Ilsington House was built by the splendidly named Theophilus, 7th Earl of Huntingdon in 1690. Its symmetrical façade in pure William and Mary style hides an intriguing past and evidence of rejuvenation since being bought by Mr and Mrs Duff in 1977. The house passed to the Walpole family when the Prime Minister's son (who succeeded his father as Earl of Orford) married Huntingdon's granddaughter, Margaret, and the Orfords retained ownership until 1862.

The house was let between 1780 and 1830 to General Garth, an equerry to George III, as the King paid annual visits to Weymouth. Garth added marble chimney-pieces and the plasterwork in the upstairs long library, but his period of occupation also produced a long-suppressed scandal. George III's daughter, Sophia, gave birth to a son at Gloucester Lodge, Weymouth, in complete secrecy. General Garth formally adopted the boy and brought him up at Ilsington as his son. Sophia died unmarried but the boy grew up to be troublesome and attempted to blackmail the royal family.

The story adds an enjoyable element to the house and gardens which the Duffs have extensively restored. The important entrance hall that Huntingdon modelled exactly on the one at Kensington Palace is a major success, with the original oak panelling being restored, while the house's most impressive room is the upstairs long library, whose balcony overlooks the garden. As well as their restoration, the Duffs have brought to Ilsington a collection of paintings, sculpture and ceramics of considerable distinction; as well as many modern works the 'ruralist' and Pre-Raphaelite schools are well represented.

PURSE CAUNDLE MANOR, *Sherborne*

Mr and Mrs Michael de Pelet
Tel: 01963 250400

In Purse Caundle, off A30, 6.5 km (4 miles) east of Sherborne
Open: Easter Mon; also May to Sept, Thur, Sun and Bank Holidays, 2–5
£2.50, children free
Teas by appointment

Dorset is richly endowed with gabled village manor houses, but few rival Purse Caundle which has all the essentially manorial elements: medieval origins; an initial impression of architectural modesty disguising one or two expansive flourishes; variety in interior scale and atmosphere; and retained connections with the village surrounding it. The latter could hardly be more emphasized, Purse Caundle village hall is a ground floor room. The manor also gives one of its best features, a delicate oriel window dating from 1480 with Gothic carving on its stone exterior, to the gable end overlooking the passing village lane.

On most sides the arrangement of gables seems irregular and only from the garden is an impression of symmetry given by the long Tudor wing with a deliberate E-shape of three gables. The irregularity confirms that the house evolved from the initial mid-fifteenth century building put up by the Long family through a series of Tudor additions by their cousins, the Hanhams. Admirable but expensive Royalist support during the Civil War impoverished the Hanhams, the manor was originally sold to a cousin and then, in 1648, away from the family to John Hoskins. Mr and Mrs de Pelet bought the manor in 1984, becoming the sixth owners since 1900, some of whom had carried out important and often urgent restoration; in 1959 a large section of the roof collapsed and had to be rebuilt.

The house's centrepiece is the fifteenth-century great hall, its timber roof original except for Tudor tiebeams. It is unusually light for such a room, thanks to a tall five-bay mullioned window inserted by Lady Victoria Herbert during the 1920s. Above a panelled screen at one end is a balustraded minstrels' gallery, at the other end the contrastingly intimate parlour has seventeenth-century panelling decorated with Corinthian pilasters. Upstairs the rooms boast a total of seven barrel ceilings, all inserted by the Hanhams during the late-sixteenth century, the most splendid of which is in the great chamber

which has the oriel window at one end. Lady Victoria decorated the great chamber with its William Morris wallpaper, but otherwise the manor is greatly enhanced by the de Pelet's decoration, pictures and furniture and, not least, the atmosphere of an established family home.

PARNHAM HOUSE, *Beaminster*

Mr and Mrs John Makepeace
Tel: 01308 862204

On A3066, 2.5 km (1½ miles) south of Beaminster
Open: Apr to end Oct, Wed, Sun and Bank Holidays 10–5
£4, children £2 (under 10 free)
Restaurant

As with many country houses, Parnham's history is one of centuries-long ownership by one family, followed by a rapid succession of owners through the twentieth century. Happily in 1976 stability was brought by John Makepeace who established his distinguished furniture workshop at the house, its craftsmanship well suited to the architectural setting.

From all sides, whether across the entrance forecourt or from the gardens, where balustrading and yew topiary extend the house's gabled and battlemented architecture, Parnham presents an immensely satisfying combination of mellow Ham stone, arched mullioned windows and turreted gables.

The house was extended from a medieval building in two stages during the sixteenth century and retains a strongly Tudor appearance and character, not least because the subsequent period of major alteration was the early-nineteenth century when John Nash remodelled the garden façades, added the theatrical element of pinnacles and battlements to the original gables and designed a Gothic dining-room inside. In 1896 the house was sold for the first time in its history. Early in the twentieth century Dr Han Sauer, advised by Captain Lindsay who helped the Duke of Rutland restore Haddon Hall in Derbyshire, consciously evoked the house's medieval and Tudor origins, bringing in fine panelling and Renaissance plasterwork, and making the architectural additions to the garden that blend so well with the house.

During the Second World War Parnham House was requisitioned by the Army and used as one of the strategic planning bases for the invasion of Europe. While the contemporary furniture and college have given Parnham its reputation, the combination of house and garden alone is of considerable merit.

SHERBORNE CASTLE, *Sherborne*

Simon Wingfield Digby
Tel: 01935 813182

Off A30, south of Sherborne

Open: Easter Sat to end Sept, Thur, Sat, Sun and Bank Holidays,1.30–5
£4, children £2, concessions
Tea room

Sherborne Castle faces its ruined Norman predecessor across the lake of its expansive park, laid out by 'Capability' Brown, which belies the proximity of the eponymous town. Sir Walter Raleigh acquired Sherborne at the height of his popularity with Elizabeth I and transformed a hunting lodge into an impressive Elizabethan house. After his disgrace it was granted by James I to John Digby who became the 1st Earl of Bristol. That title died out but the Digbys have remained. The name became Digby Wingfield and subsequently Wingfield Digby after the marriage, in 1796, of the Lady Charlotte Digby and William Wingfield.

Inside and out, Sherborne bears witness to successive generations. Raleigh's Elizabethan house was extended by Lord Bristol with four wings ending in towers and the interiors combine remaining features of their work such as decorative ceilings and doorways, with later Georgian and – more particularly – Victorian alterations. The decorative riches are more than matched by the array of paintings, furniture and works of art. The Strawberry Hill Gothic survives intact while the Victorian alterations echo the earlier Elizabethan and Jacobean styles. Digby portraits through more than two centuries include many distinguished works by Cornelius Johnson, Van Dyck, Lely,  Reynolds, Gainsborough, Batoni, Landseer and Sir Francis Grant. The range of English furniture is equally impressive; the French furniture is one of Sherborne's many rewarding surprises, as are the outstanding collections of Kakiemon Japanese porcelain, Japanese lacquer and English, Chinese and Continental porcelain.

Although the old terraced gardens that Raleigh would have known were swept away by Brown, the visitor can still enjoy 'Raleigh's Seat' where he sat smoking his pipe until a servant – to whom the habit was unknown – threw a bucket of water over his master whom he feared was on fire.

WOLVETON HOUSE, *Dorchester*

Capt N.T.L. Thimbleby
Tel: 01305 263500

On A37, 1.6 km (1 mile) north-west of Dorchester
Open: May to end Sept, Tues, Thur and Bank Holiday Mon, 2–6
Prices available on request

Approaching Wolveton to be confronted by the formidable gatehouse, the visitor could be forgiven uncertainty about what to expect. Wolveton's long and often melancholy history takes some time to unravel and in the process a distinguished past followed by decline and partial salvation emerge. Thomas Trenchard's house built at the turn of the sixteenth century – of which the gatehouse is the major surviving part – became a grand twin-courtyard Tudor house at the hands of his grandson, George. Towards the end of the eighteenth century, however, the family had effectively deserted Wolverton for another home and thereafter the great majority was neglected, partly ruined and contents and fittings removed. Decline was arrested in the 1860s; nonetheless after the Second World War the house as it had survived, the gatehouse and one side of the main Elizabethan courtyard, were divided into three dwellings. Only in the time of Captain Thimbleby has restoration made the best of the many outstanding features that survive.

Such a background suggests a house of uneven appearance introduced by the gatehouse; the flanking circular towers are different in size and the arch through which the drive passes is not central. Through here in 1506 came Wolveton's most illustrious visitors, Archduke Philip of Austria and his Spanish wife, Joanna, daughter of Ferdinand and Isabella. En route from the Netherlands to claim the throne of Castile, a storm inconveniently forced them into Weymouth harbour and they accepted Sir Thomas Trenchard's hospitality before travelling to Windsor to visit Joanna's sister, Catherine of Aragon, who was waiting to marry the future Henry VIII. The gatehouse's defensive purpose is recalled in the guardroom on one side; on the other is the chapel replacing the free-standing chapel that formed one side of George Trenchard's main courtyard. Here carved panels of *c.*1510 depicting the signs of the Zodiac and the occupations of the month give a taste of other fine carving to be found in the house.

The south front that overlooks the garden is principally Elizabethan but the stair turret at one end is part of Sir Thomas's house. The north front has been considerably altered at different times and the porch is Victorian. Inside, the great hall has lost all its original decoration and the outstanding Elizabethan rooms are the dining-room and parlour, both with plaster ceilings. The former has a plaster overmantel while the parlour has a notable carved oak overmantel and doorcase which extends to the ceiling.

A stone groin-vaulted passage contains carving of unusual quality and the monumental stone staircase with a pierced balustrade of open arches is both impressive and rare. The classical stone doorcase at the top of the stairs confirms the refinement of detail as well as a distinctly Renaissance style and leads into the great chamber which retains its fine carved fireplace the height of the room. It is an enjoyable idea that among the carved figures the Red Indians may have been described by Raleigh who often visited Wolveton. One of Captain Thimbleby's most important improvements has been to remove internal divisions in this room. The garden retains a Tudor bowling green and the Norman church, to which Sir Thomas added the west tower, is worth a visit.

AVINGTON PARK, *Winchester*

Mr and Mrs J.B. Hickson
Tel: 01962 779260

Off B3047, 6.5 km (4 miles) north-east of Winchester
Open: May to Sept, Sun and Bank Holidays, 2.30–5.30
£2.75

Avington's handsome entrance façade, its monumental white Doric portico recessed between rich brick wings and flamboyantly surmounted by lead statues of Minerva, Juno and Ceres, as well as its lavishly decorated state rooms, survive as evidence of the house's rollicking Restoration and indulgent eighteenth-century past. They are maintained by the enthusiasm of the Hicksons who have owned the house for some forty years, and are happily preserved despite the house being divided into eight units.

George Brydges was Charles II's groom of the bedchamber and rebuilt his home at Avington to accommodate the King on his frequent visits to Winchester; the cathedral prebendar refused to allow the King's mistress to stay in the hallowed close and Charles later referred to him as 'the ugly little man who would not give poor Nelly [Gwynne] lodgings'. Brydges' rebuilding was greatly assisted by the fortunes of his wife, Anna-Maria, who had previously been the Countess of Shrewsbury. Disguised as a page, she attended the duel between her husband, Shrewsbury, and her lover, the Duke of Buckingham, and had the satisfaction of seeing her husband killed.

Avington's entrance front is attributed to the architect, John James. He worked as clerk of the works at Greenwich under the royal surveyor, Sir Christopher Wren, and the portico is comparable to Wren's Royal Hospital. James was a Hampshire man, his own home, Warbrook House in the north of the county, has two similar porticos.

Brydges died in the lake at Avington trying to save his pet dog. He was succeeded by his son who in turn was succeeded by his cousin, James Brydges, Marquess of Caernarvon, who became the 3rd Duke of Chandos and a man of legendary wealth and extravagance. His wife built the wonderful church at Avington, completed in 1771, which retains its Georgian box-pews and other furnishings. Her husband's improvements were more lavish. The main staircase was built with an inlaid handrail and carved lead balusters and the main rooms were given their outstanding painted decoration. The most sumptuous room is the ballroom or great saloon with its lofty painted and gilded ceiling over a deep gilded frieze.

Chandos was succeeded by his only child, Lady Anne, whose husband, Richard, Earl Temple of Stowe, became the 2nd Marquess of Buckingham. He was created Duke of Buckingham and Chandos by his friend George IV who stayed at Avington with Mrs Fitzherbert. The Chandos — Buckingham era ended in 1848 when the family's hereditary extravagance became ruinous and their son was forced to sell his estates. Avington was bought by Sir John Shelley, brother of the poet, and the family retained ownership until 1952 when Avington's contents were sold and the estate dismembered. Shortly afterwards the Hicksons bought the house and surrounding grounds.

BREAMORE HOUSE, *Fordingbridge*

Sir Westrow Hulse, Bt
Tel: 01725 512468

Off A388, 5 km (3 miles) north of Fordingbridge
Open: Easter; Apr, Tues, Wed and Sun; May, June, July and Sept, daily
except Mon and Fri; Aug, daily, 2–5.30
£4.50, children £3, concessions
Home-made teas

Breamore enjoys an imposing position on the western slopes of the Avon valley, with protective woodlands rising behind. An Elizabethan house with an austere gabled front, its deep-red brick is decorated with stone quoining but devoid of anything more fanciful. The carefully arranged symmetry of gables with mullioned and transomed windows creates the desired effect.

The house was built by William Dodington, whose duties as Elizabeth I's Chancellor were obviously too onerous; he threw himself off the tower of St Sepulchre's Holborn in 1600. The house passed by marriage to the Grevilles and then, in 1748, was bought by Sir Edward Hulse, 1st Bt. His father was physician to William III and son outdid father by holding the same office for the three subsequent monarchs.

A fire in 1856 destroyed the Tudor interiors – only fireplaces and overmantels survived. The plaster ceilings are nineteenth-century and the panelling was put in at the same time. Fortunately most of the contents were saved. Benefiting from a series of judicious marriages to heiresses, the Hulses built up exceptional collections. There is a rich variety of furniture, including high-backed Charles II dining-chairs, a set of Queen Anne chairs made with American walnut and a number of Dutch marquetry pieces. The pictures are the primary feature, however. The great hall, the most impressive room, contains a selection including the children of Charles I by Van Dyck, a full-length portrait by Cornelius Johnson of Sir Norton Knatchbull, the Holy Family by Benvenuto Tisio and an important Teniers, 'The Coming of the Storm'. The Teniers is one of a number of Dutch paintings in the house collected by virtue of the family's Dutch origins and the marriage of the 2nd Baronet to a Dutch wife. Those in the dining-room include four large still lifes by Peter Andreas Rysbrach.

The two drawing-rooms are eighteenth-century in style, both with giltwood Chippendale overmantel mirrors. Francis Cotes painted the two Edward Hulses, as well as pastels of the 1st baronet and his family. Sir Edward's grandson, Samuel, was ADC to the Prince Regent, was knighted and became a Field Marshal. Beech's portrait of the young Regent hangs in the west drawing-room, while Sir Samuel acquired the set of Napoleonic battle scenes by Napoleon's travelling artist, Beaufort, and the head of the Duke of Wellington by J. Lucas. The Hudson portrait of Samuel and his brother Edward as children hangs in the same room as the 'Boy with the Bat'. One of the earliest and finest portraits of a cricketer, it came to the Hulses with Catherine Hamilton who married the 5th Baronet.

Admiral Hulse was one of Charles I's sailors who harried the Spanish galleons. Among his plunder was the set of fourteen paintings called 'The Races of Mexico' destined for Philip IV of Spain but seized by Westrow en route. He also produced the Mexican fan which, with the English pile carpet dating from 1614 that hangs on the stairs, is one of a number of Breamore's rare specialities. Further variety is provided by the unusually evocative museum of rural life and old agricultural machinery.

PALACE HOUSE, *Beaulieu*

The Lord Montagu of Beaulieu
Tel: 01590 612345

In Beaulieu on B3056, 11 km (7 miles) south-east of Lyndhurst
Open: Easter to end Sept, daily, 10–6; Oct to Easter, daily, 10–5
Prices available on request

Beaulieu is famous for its motor museum and Lord Montagu has been in the vanguard of country-house opening since 1952. Palace House is an interesting candidate for the success story that followed for it is not a stately home of great rank, filled with fabulous collections, but a perfectly positioned building of medieval monastic origins that evolved gently into a family home, whose contents illustrate that family's often distinguished history.

The Cistercian abbey was founded by King John in an uncharacteristically fulsome gesture; surrounded by spreading estates it flourished until the Dissolution, following which it was bought by Henry VIII's future Lord Chancellor, Thomas Wriothesley, 1st Earl of Southampton. The last Southampton daughter married Ralph, 1st Duke of Montagu and thence Beaulieu passed with the glittering Montagu possessions to the Dukes of Buccleuch, the 5th of whom gave Beaulieu to his second son, Lord Henry Scott, as a wedding present. In 1885 Lord Henry was created the 1st Lord Montagu of Beaulieu.

He employed the architect Arthur Blomfield to remodel and extend the abbey Great Gatehouse into a home. It had in fact been extended earlier and the tall twin gables facing the river are Elizabethan. Blomfield's work expanded the house's friendly rambling appearance while preserving the most interesting of its surviving monastic features. These are the old gateway and the fourteenth-century vaulting in the inner hall. Portraits begin with Chancellor Wriothesley and include the Montagu dukes as well as the Marquess of Monthermer whose early death ended the male Montagu line, but who brought to Beaulieu the Italian views by Antonio Joli which are the house's outstanding paintings.

The present Lord Montagu's father was painted in uniform reflecting the position he held of Inspector of Mechanised Transport to the Government of India during the First World War – an early indication of his son's enthusiasm to found the now renowned National Motor Museum in his father's memory. The series is brought up to date by a John Ward conversation piece of the present Lord Montagu and his family in the snow outside the house.

STANSTED PARK, *Rowland's Castle*

Trustees of Stansted Park Foundation
Tel: 01705 412265

Off B2148, east of Rowland's Castle
Open: July to end Sept, Sun to Tues; also Bank Holiday Sun and Mon; 2–5
£3.50, children £1.50
Tea room

In 1983 the late Earl of Bessborough established the Stansted Park Foundation, to preserve the home that his father had bought in 1924. The purchase followed the destruction by fire of Bessborough, the family's eponymous seat in County Kilkenny, and Lord Bessborough was not put off by the fact that Stansted itself had been rebuilt in 1903 after a fire in 1900.

The rebuilding, carried out for the Wilder family by Sir Arthur Blomfield, carefully preserved the Georgian character and appearance of the house which had been built by James Wyatt, with assistance from Joseph Bonomi, for an Indian nabob, Richard Barwell. For the approaching visitor the house's red brick with stone dressing, the low roof disguised behind a stone balustrade with a central pediment above the one-storey balustraded portico, could be unchanged Georgian and is given stature by the view across the expansive cricket ground in front.

For Lord Bessborough, Stansted was an ideal house to display the family's important collection of pictures which were saved from the fire in Ireland and remain of major interest today. In the staircase hall hang Dutch bird pictures and beyond, the main hall contains portraits, among which the most interesting are by Angelica Kauffmann of the two Spencer sisters, Henrietta Frances (who married the 3rd Earl of Bessborough) and Georgiana who married the Duke of Devonshire). Henrietta, with her two small sons, is the subject of possibly the house's most delightful portrait and arguably Hoppner's best work, which hangs in the dining-room. A collection of late-nineteenth and early-twentieth- century portraits dominated by the full-length painting by Philpot of Loelia Ponsonby who became Duchess of Westminster and the more arresting Birley of Roberte, the French mother of the present Lord Bessborough, and her three children, give the music room an evocative period atmosphere.

The porcelain in the dining-room originates from the collection of Lady Charlotte Schreiber whose first husband Sir John Guest was South Wales's largest iron-making magnate. Their daughter married the 8th Lord Bessborough. Many other works of art contribute to the house's perpetuated air of classical Edwardian grandeur.

NUNWELL HOUSE, *Brading*

Colonel and Mrs J.A. Aylmer
Tel: 01983 407240

Off A3055, 1.6 km (1 mile) from Brading, 5 km (3 miles) south of Ryde

Open: July to end Sept, Mon to Wed, 10–5, and Sun, 1–5
£2.80, accompanied children under-12 60p, concessions
[As Nunwell is the only HHA house on the Isle of Wight open to the public
it is unable to offer free entry to HHA Friends.]

Sir John Oglander, the engaging Carolean diarist whose family accompanied the Conqueror and was established at Nunwell from the twelfth century until 1982, wrote to his son, 'Fear God as we did; marry a wife thou can'st love; keep out of debt; see thy grounds well-stocked; and thou mayest live as happily at Nunwell as any Prince in the World.' Sir John was proud of his home where in 1647 he entertained his beloved Charles I the night before the King's imprisonment at Carisbrooke Castle and subsequent execution. Its original shape and one wing remain, with enjoyable Queen Anne and Georgian additions.

His west wing lies on one side of the central block which was given a Queen Anne front with a handsome rusticated stone arched doorway, faced in mathematical tiles – an early example of their use. The other side was given altogther grander – but harmonious – treatment during the 1760s and its symmetrical façade with a central bow overlooks the garden. The addition of the dining-room in 1896 and the music room in 1906 have done nothing to upset the varied harmony of the house which is greatly enhanced by the gardens it overlooks and the splendid views across the Solent.

Although the Oglander family sold Nunwell in 1982, their connection is still evident as some of the house's contents remained to be mixed with those of Colonel Aylmer's family and that of his wife, Shaunagh. Together they make for an enjoyable ensemble. Victorian Oglander portraits hang in the dining-room along with John Aylmer driving his coach-and-four in 1821 and portraits of Colonel Aylmer and his son. There is Venetian furniture and glass in the panelled morning-room that was Sir John Oglander's library. The drawing-room in the centre of the Georgian wing benefits from the handsome bow and contains a sunflower painting attributed to Van Dyck, a fine Thomas Allen seascape of the English fleet leaving Harwich to collect George III's future bride and Queen, Charlotte, and French faience plaques from Castletown near the Guinness home in County Kildare. The library is the most impressively decorated room with mid-eighteenth-century plaster decoration and good mahogany bookcases of the period.

In the older part of the house a Jacobean oak-panelled staircase leads up to the bedrom where Charles I slept, and elsewhere the Aylmer family's distinguished recordof military service is illustrated in a series of exhibitions, while the Home Guard museum recalls the importance of this body for the small island which would have been in the front line of any threatened German invasion.

THE BISHOP'S PALACE, *Wells*

The Church Commissioners
Tel: 01749 678691

In Wells at end of Market Place

Open: Easter to end Oct, Tues, Thur, Sun and Bank Holidays; Aug, daily, 2–6

£2, children free, concessions

Restaurant

The Bishop of Bath and Wells has stood on one side of the monarch at coronations since Richard I was crowned in 1189. The historical seniority of the see of Bath and Wells is amply confirmed by the seat of successive bishops since first built by Bishop Jocelin Trotman in the early-thirteenth century. The only walled and moated palace other than arch episcopal York, the whole area covers 5.26 ha (13 acres) within the lozenge-shaped moat fed with millions of litres (gallons) of water a day by the springs or 'wells' which give the city its name. From the town the approach across Bishop's Green towards the bridge and gatehouse is the perfect cloistered introduction: from the gatehouse the expansive main court opens out, the palace buildings and chapel to the left, the ruined great hall and gardens in front.

The bishops live in the most modern, fifteenth-century wing that faces the cathedral across the moat. During the 1960s Bishop Henderson decided to open the other rooms which as a result bear his name. The vaulted entrance hall and undercroft are splendidly medieval. A Jacobean oak staircase leads up to the main rooms which were refurbished throughout – notably with plaster ceilings and panelling – during the nineteenth century. Pious prelates gaze down from one end of the long gallery to the other while Bishop Jocelin's solar and great hall have become the drawing-room and conference-room. The latter contains an impressive nineteenth-century Wilton carpet originally made for Windsor Castle and all rooms contain portraits of successive bishops.

Linked to the Henderson rooms is the bishops' private chapel whose intimacy is superbly balanced with its lofty vaulted roof and broad arched windows with fine tracery and stained glass which give the chapel almost radiant lightness. The pews are Victorian and were carved in various Somerset parishes and along the back rows runs a frieze bearing the bishops' arms from 1275 to the most recently translated, George Carey, Archbishop of Canterbury.

COMBE SYDENHAM HALL, *Monksilver*

Mr and Mrs W. Theed
Tel: 01984 56284

On B3188, 5 km (3 miles) south of Watchet
Open: Mar to Oct, daily except Sat; 10–5
£4
Restaurant/Home-made teas

Although just in Somerset, Combe Sydenham lies in a hidden valley within Exmoor's National Park. Sir George Sydenham's house was probably built to celebrate his knighthood in 1583, but the gatehouse through which visitors approach beneath its handsome tower belonged to an older house with defence an obvious priority. Sir George's house was built on the Tudor 'E'-plan and its character is best preserved in the elegant porch. The house was substantially rebuilt following the Restoration in 1660, although by this time it had been reduced to the surviving west wing which forms the main portion of the present house. Without doubt the four towers which marked the corners of Sir George Sydenham's courtyard are the most unusual feature; one survives with its gabled top to increase the hall's appearance of intriguing irregularity.

The estate is currently under a forty-year restoration plan, initiated by the Theeds after they purchased Combe Sydenham in 1964. The house contains reminders of Sir Francis Drake's marriage to Sir George Sydenham's daughter (only successful after he had previously been firmly rejected by the family as a lowly sailor). The Elizabethan court-room, originally a range of monastic cells, has been recently restored with a sixteenth-century style ceiling and heraldic stone floor. Work still to be carried out, especially in the west wing, will do more to unveil the surviving features of Combe Sydenham's Elizabethan and seventeenth-century past, as well as enhancing the house's inviting surroundings.

FORDE ABBEY, *Chard*

Trustees of Forde Abbey
Tel: 01460 220231

On B3162, 1.6 km (1 mile) east of Chard junction

Open: Apr to end Oct, Wed, Sun, and Bank Holidays, 1–4.30 (gardens daily)
£4.50
Restaurant

'Nobody that could stay here would go from hence. Nobody is so well anywhere else as everybody is here.' Jeremy Bentham's remark made in 1814 is as true today. Forde is a beautiful house set in a remote, fruitful valley south of Chard. The Cistercians who came here in the twelfth century, established a great abbey complete with church, cloisters and accommodation; it achieved its final monastic glory in the early-sixteenth century under Abbot Chard. He was responsible for the Tudor-Gothic architecture reminiscent both in style and quality of the chapel at King's College, Cambridge.

Unfinished at the Dissolution, the abbey estates were leased and the buildings plundered. All was not lost, however, and after a century, what remained was bought in 1649 by Sir Edward Prideaux, Oliver Cromwell's attorney-general. He made good the structure, retained some of the best early work and remodelled the remaining building in a rich cosmopolitan style. Prideaux's rooms are beautifully panelled and have lively plaster ceilings. His splendid staircase, richly carved with flowers, the tops punctuated with decorated urns, is a showpiece leading from the great hall to the great chamber or saloon. The visitor is still overwhelmed on arrival in the saloon, exactly as Prideaux intended, for here is the house's main treasure, the great set of Mortlake tapestries of Raphael's Acts of the Apostles, astonishingly little faded.

Abbot Chard and Prideaux left their mark on Forde's architecture and interiors. The Evans family and their descendants, the Ropers, have added significantly to the collection of furniture and paintings – notably an interesting group of Old Master paintings. More recently the eighteenth-century garden has been replanted and extended, including a luxuriant bog garden full of horticultural rarities, and in 1993 won the HHA/Christie's Garden of the Year prize. House and garden together have the appearance of a grand version of an Oxford college, a rarity among country houses.

HATCH COURT, *Hatch Beauchamp*

Dr and Mrs Robin Odgers
Tel: 01823 480120

Off A358, 10 km (6 miles) south-east of Taunton

Open: mid-June to mid-Sept, Thur, 2–5

£3

Home-made teas

Hatch Court is a rarity; an eighteenth-century architectural masterpiece recast in the 1930s. The house's fascination lies in the marriage of these two periods. The house was designed in 1755 for John Collins by his friend, Thomas Prowse, a remarkable gentleman all-rounder: Member of Parliament, lawyer, amateur artist and architect. He created a sophisticated Palladian villa with a central block topped by four towers, with an open arcade on the ground floor. The exterior is immediately reminiscent of Hagley Hall in Worcestershire, for which Prowse executed a design. His layout has remained unchanged apart from the delightful curved wings, one containing the orangery.

Inside the plan is assuredly Palladian, a spacious central hall with a spectacular double cantilevered staircase. The sequence of surrounding rooms contain good architectural fittings – bookcases and chimney-pieces. On the staircase hang the Shuckburgh portraits from Bourton in Warwickshire including two imposing full-length paintings by Sir Martin Archer Shee.

The house was acquired in 1931 by Brigadier Hamilton Gault and his wife. They carried out stylish redecoration and discerningly introduced a group of contemporary

works of art: portraits by Glynn Philpots; equestrian paintings by Munnings; and sculpture. The rooms evince a strong period mood; the characters in Noel Coward musicals would have felt at home in the drawing-room.

At the back of the house is a well laid out museum to Princess Patricia's Canadian Light Infantry. Gault came from Montreal and raised the regiment in seventeen days at the outbreak of the First World War. Adjacent to the museum is an eighteenth-century china room where the family collection of porcelain is still displayed. The other delight at Hatch is the spacious deer park through which one approaches the house perched on its eminence below a typical Somerset wooded hill, as well as the gardens, in particular the walled garden, recently restored by Dr Odgers and his wife, who is Mrs Gault's great-niece.

BOWOOD HOUSE, *Calne*

The Earl and Countess of Shelburne
Tel: 01249 812102

Off A43, 3 km (2 miles) west of Calne
Open: end Mar to end Oct, daily, 11–6
£4.80, children £2.60, concessions
Restaurant and tea room

Set in one of 'Capability' Brown's most superlative and largest parks and overlooking broad descending terraces added in the nineteenth century, Bowood's long, low classical façades complete a harmonious whole. Or so it seems; in fact the house has been called the grandest stable conversion in England and once formed two courtyards to one side of a palatial classical mansion, improved by Keene and Adam, whose size more truly fitted the surrounding landscape.

In 1955 the present Marquess of Lansdowne took the painful and unpopular decision that was necessary for the survival of Bowood as a viable estate. He demolished the big house and converted the twin courtyards built by Keene. Keene's work is best seen in the two-storey east front that stretches between matching pavilions, but the better-known front is Adam's south-facing range overlooking the terraces. Adam's range was originally built as an orangery to close the courtyards on this side. The third and fourth architects to make important contributions to the present house were C.R. Cockerell who built the chapel in the arm that divides Keene's courtyards early in the nineteenth century, and Charles Barry who built the dizzily high clock-tower over the chapel and the ornate Italianate entrance to the park with gilded gates.

It was important that the new house would be able to display the family's art collection – from Lansdowne House in London as well as the big house – and the success is immediately clear to visitors. Conversion work has continued in stages since 1955 and in recent years Lord Shelburne carried out work that has produced the sculpture gallery, shop and restaurant on the ground floor and exhibition rooms above.

Looking along Adam's orangery, or Diocletian wing as it is sometimes known, it is hard to imagine that after the 1st Marquess of Lansdowne's death most of his extensive art collection was sold. The remainder, including the busts and classical marbles that he assembled from Italy, today form one of Bowood's most important treasures. The orangery has become a picture gallery, its walls hung with fine family portraits and a rich variety of other paintings. It makes an absorbing introduction to the other main rooms, including the laboratory where Dr Joseph Priestley discovered oxygen in 1774, Cockerell's chapel, the Adam library and the new sculpture gallery. Family history is constantly evident and almost all Lansdownes from the 1st Marquess, who was a Prime Minister, have held public office. There are items collected by the 5th Marquess when

Viceroy of India and the chair and footstool used by Queen Victoria at her marriage when the 3rd Marquess attended as Lord President.

The house itself is only a part of Bowood's appeal. Outside are the Brown park with its expansive lake fed by a cascade at one end and overlooked by the Doric Temple, the larger gardens, the pleasure grounds and rhododendron walks, and — for younger visitors — a-state-of-the art adventure playground. On one edge of the rhododendron walks overlooking the Wiltshire countryside stands Adam's sombre mausoleum, his most distinguished contribution to Bowood. It was commissioned by the Dowager Countess of Shelburne in memory of her husband who purchased Bowood in 1754 and whose son became the 1st Marquess.

CORSHAM COURT, *Corsham*

James Methuen-Campbell
Tel: 01249 712214

In Corsham on A4, 6.5 km (4 miles) west of Chippenham
Open: Jan to end Nov, daily except Mon and Fri, 2–4.30; Good Fri to end Sept, also Fri and Bank Holidays 2–6
£3.50, children £2, concessions

Corsham's picture collection remains among the half-dozen best in an English house, its Old Masters with few rivals. A large number were assembled during the eighteenth century by Sir Paul Methuen, and inherited by his cousin, also Paul, who purchased the Elizabethan manor of Corsham in 1745. In 1844 Frederick Methuen married Anna, only child of the Rev John Sanford, whose collection she inherited and brought to Corsham to complete the assembly of Old Masters.

The house saw many architectural changes from 1745. Paul Methuen retained the inviting Elizabethan south front that faces the south avenue across its broad courtyard, but gave the north front a Palladian look. In 1760 he commissioned 'Capability' Brown to landscape the park and enlarge the house, which Brown did by doubling the size of the Elizabethan wings on the south side, and by making the east wing into a set of state rooms to display the pictures. In 1800 John Nash carried out ambitious further work, adding pinnacles, buttresses and battlements and transforming the north front into 'Strawberry Hill' Gothic. This did not last, however, and in the middle of the nineteenth century Thomas Bellamy replaced the north front with the present sombre, monumental design.

Brown's park was later altered by Humphry Repton who added the lake planned, but not executed, by his predecessor. Brown's Gothic bath house remains one of the best garden buildings that he designed. His major interior was the picture gallery, a triple cube with a coffered and coved plaster ceiling originally designed for Burton Constable in Yorkshire, but rejected. The room was planned with the major pictures in mind, this accounting for the powerful unity of the display. At one end Van Dyck's equestrian portrait of Charles I is central, on the main wall Van Dyck's 'Betrayal of Christ' to one side of the Scheemakers chimney-piece is balanced by a version of Guido Reni's 'Baptism of Christ' of similar size in a matching carved frame. Over the fireplace is 'The Wolf Hunt' by Rubens. These are the largest, but the other Old Masters that line the walls above the furniture are no less absorbing in quality and subject.

Brown's other state rooms are the cabinet room, the state bedroom and the octagon room. The first contains Filippo Lippi's 'Annunciation'; the highlight of the state bedroom is 'The Infant Christ' by Guercino; the octagon room contains forty paintings with a rare portrait of Elizabeth I in old age more than holding its own among works by Claude, Andrea del Sarto, Breughel the elder and Teniers. The collection extends into the hall – where Bellamy's cold and cavernous staircase temporarily dampens the spirits – and corridors, the music-room and dining-room on the south front, both of which Bellamy redesigned. Reynolds' vivacious quality at portraying children is superbly demonstrated in the two pictures of Paul Methuen's children in the dining-room.

The quality continues in the furniture: in the picture gallery Adam pier glasses over side tables – a set of four – and the enormous suite of Chippendale furniture covered in crimson damask to match the walls; best of all, the specially commissioned John Cobb marquetry commode with flanking torchères in the cabinet room and the Florentine *pietra-dura* cabinets that give the room its name; the Thomas Johnson mirrors in the state bedroom and others in the octagon room are a selection which alone would make Corsham a house of the highest distinction. The works of art include 'The Sleeping Cupid' attributed to Michelangelo, and porcelain is another arrow in an artistic quiver of seminal importance.

HAMPTWORTH LODGE, *Landford*

N.J.M. Anderson
Tel: 01794 390215

Off A36, 16 km (10 miles) south-east of Salisbury between Redlynch and Landford

Open: end Mar to end Apr, daily except Sun, 2.15–5
£3, children free

Hamptworth Lodge is an ideal example of the derivative quality of Edwardian architecture. The handsome house set in the far corner of Wiltshire, where the county runs into the New Forest, looks convincingly Tudor from a distance and the external brick and timber construction is equally impressive. The original house was built in 1620 and extensively altered during the nineteenth century; but the seemingly authentic building is, externally, pure reproduction, rebuilt by Sir Guy Dawber between 1910 and 1912.

Internally there are genuine Elizabethan and Jacobean overmantels removed from another house, but more important is the skilful arrangement of rooms around the spacious hall, which recalls the period of inspiration as well as being convenient – a high priority for Edwardians. Both Dawber and his client at Hamptworth, Harold Moffatt, were fervent admirers of the Arts and Crafts and every detail of the work on the house exemplifies the movement.

The great hall contains an impressive hammerbeam roof; other rooms have finely worked plaster ceilings. Moffatt's enthusiasm for Arts and Crafts is best shown in the fascinating selection of furniture that he carved himself in a rich variety of woods. The main rooms, facing south and west, look over the terraced gardens laid out to recreate the style of the seventeenth century and completing an important period piece with the house and its contents.

LACOCK ABBEY, *Nr Chippenham*

The National Trust / A.M. Burnett-Browne
Tel: 01249 730227

In Lacock off A350, 5 km (3 miles) south of Chippenham

Open: Apr to end Oct, daily except Tues, 1–5.30 (last admission 5)
£4.20, children £2.20

The abbey and delightful village of Lacock constitute a harmonious community which reflects the abbey's distant past when it was occupied by Augustinian nuns from 1232, the year Ela, Countess of Salisbury, founded the nunnery. Cloth manufacture made the village prosperous, but the nunnery met a predictable end at the Dissolution of the Monasteries and the property was handed to a typically avaricious Tudor courtier, Sir William Sharington. Sharington pulled down the nuns' church but converted most of the rest of their buildings into his home, and it survives as a leading illustration of such a conversion from monastic to domestic.

Sharington's work skilfully retained outstanding features of the nunnery, in particular the cloisters, while adding new features such as the first-floor gallery along the east range, the striking polygonal tower on the south-east corner, and a number of features inside and out that reflected his interest in classical architecture – an enthusiasm shared with his near-neighbour, John Thynne at Longleat. His financial wrong-doing eventually caught up with him, he was imprisoned and his estate at Lacock confiscated. Sharington bought his freedom by betraying Sir Thomas Seymour and was able to buy back Lacock for a vastly inflated price. It passed through marriage to the Talbot family and during the eighteenth century the antiquarian John Ivory Talbot employed Sanderson Miller to make alterations in a Gothic style that evoked the house's medieval origins. Between 1827 and 1830 William Henry Fox Talbot rebuilt the south range in Tudor-Gothic style, but he is best known as the pioneer of photography. His negative of the gallery's oriel window is the oldest in existence.

Sanderson Miller's hall is notable for the quantities of heraldry introduced by John Talbot, and for its series of terracotta figures. From here to the galleries in the south and east ranges, Sharington's muniment room in the south-east tower, and the dining-room, the mix of periods, and different medieval, classical and Gothic details piece together Lacock's centuries of history.

LONGLEAT HOUSE, *Warminster*

The Marquess of Bath
Tel: 01985 844400

Off A362, 10 km (6 miles) west of Warminster
Open: Easter to Sept, daily, 10–6; rest of year, daily except Christmas Day,
10–4 (days and times of opening may vary)
Grounds £2, children 50p; House £4.80, children £3
[prices may be subject to review during year]
Tea room

A select band of England's greatest houses have long been at the forefront of showing to the public, houses that are unquestionably national treasures as well as private homes. Immediately one thinks of Longleat which opened its doors in 1949, the very first to do

so on a commercial basis. The visitor's first view of Longleat, preferably from the wooded ridge known as 'Heaven's Gate', is impressive for even the most disinterested observer. For the enthusiast it is a magical revelation: the prototype great Elizabethan country house set in one of the most perfectly planted eighteenth-century parks.

Sir John Thynne was only interested in money and architecture and combined the two to spectacular effect. Assisted by Robert Smythson, the architect at the helm of Elizabethan country-house architecture, and a Frenchman, Allen Maynard, Thynne produced a house of palatial size that combined the most memorable English medieval style, Perpendicular, with Renaissance classicism. Perpendicular produced the towering mullioned windows through which light floods and which combine with the silver-toned walls to extraordinary effect. The classical symmetry of the house's external shape, the details of pilasters and regularly arranged projecting bays were displayed for the first time in an English country house. The roofscape with its classical balustrade and pepperpot turrets continues the sense of fusion to the house's upper limits.

The great hall shows that Thynne's arrangement of rooms was traditional (although they have been subsequently altered throughout); the classical composition of English interiors did not come until Inigo Jones. Maynard carved the amazing Mannerist stone fireplace – and was probably responsible for the exterior decoration as well. The most extensive interior alterations were carried out by Jeffry Wyatville after 1806 and, more lavishly, during the 1870s and 1880s in Italian style by John Diblee Crace for the 4th Marquess – an Italophile and important collector.

The manner in which the exterior blends a fundamental Englishness with breathtaking continental influences continues inside. Huge Woottons hang in the hall and portraits extend from the sixteenth to the twentieth centuries. Some of the best are the earliest, of canny-looking Thynnes and other important personages such as the Duchess of Richmond by Van Dyck. Gilded furniture dates from Wyatville's period.

These are balanced – or perhaps overshadowed – by lavish Italianate ceilings, doorcases and chimney-pieces, Venetian mythological paintings, and Venetian Baroque and French furniture.

Outside, Russell Page, who first worked for the late Lord Bath during the 1930s, was involved in the adaption and simplification of the formal gardens on the north side which extends beyond Wyatville's orangery to the Secret Garden. The design recalls the enormous parterres which were added around the house by London and Wise at the end of the seventeenth century, but removed by 'Capability' Brown when he began the park in 1757. Repton made a few subsequent alterations, joining the two lakes and removing some trees where they were too densely planted, but the setting remains Brown's and one of the outstanding landscapes of any period. In recent years the present Marquess established the world's largest hedge maze and has now planted a new Maze of Love with roses and box hedging.

MALMESBURY HOUSE, *Salisbury*

John Cordle
Tel: 01722 320727

In the cathedral close, Salisbury
Open: Apr to end Oct, Tues, Thur, Fri, Sat and Bank Holidays, 11–5
Prices available on request
Tea room

Malmesbury House presents two contrasting faces; beside Queen Anne gate into the close its old, originally medieval part is notable for a seemingly hanging oriel window, from inside the close the visitor approaches a serene Queen Anne façade of Chilmark stone. This was added by Sir Christopher Wren after 1698 to accommodate rooms displaying outstanding rococo plaster work, for the Harris family who occupied the house from 1660 until the early-nineteenth century. The house takes its name from James Harris, 1st Earl of Malmesbury, the unfortunate diplomat who produced the Prince Regent's wife, Caroline of Brunswick, and caused the celebrated remark on the Prince's first sight of his future spouse, 'Harris, I am unwell, fetch me a glass of brandy.'

Malmesbury's new front was built by the Earl's grandfather and the interiors done by his parents, who regularly entertained Handel in the house, as well as Reynolds, the historian Gibbon and – less popularly – Dr Johnson. Mrs Harris considered him 'beastly in his dress and person and he eats quantities most unthankfully' The undemonstrative exterior disguises ebullient Georgian decoration inside. The staircase hall, the drawing-room and dining-room all contain rococo-inspired plasterwork. In the hall niches draped with plaster swags and garlands contain busts of Milton, Shakespeare and Johnson.

The most surprising room is the upstairs library whose small space is literally crammed with Gothic decoration as lively as it is well-executed. Bookcases are surmounted by ogee-shaped canopies, as is the chimney-piece, and a Gothic bay window looks out over the garden to a little Palladian orangery. One bedroom has a ceiling painted by de Wit, another in the old part of the house is the Charles II room with the oriel window. The music room named in honour of Handel in the old part of the ground floor is an intimate contrast to the Georgian main rooms.

John Cordle, a Member of Parliament for 18 years, came to Malmesbury in 1968 and the pristine condition of the interiors is thanks to his restoration. He laid the stone floor in the hall, which is more suitable than the rotting wooden one that he found, restored the plasterwork and carried out the various decorative schemes such as the duck-egg blue hall and equally successful blue and white drawing-room. The furniture and pictures have been carefully chosen to be in keeping with the period and style of the rooms.

SHELDON MANOR, Chippenham

The Gibbs family
Tel: 01249 653120

Off A420, 1.6 km (1 mile) west of Chippenham

**Open: Easter Sun and Mon; then Thur, Sun, and Bank Holidays to
first Sun in Oct inclusive; 12.30–6
Prices available on request
Home-made lunch/tea**

Most visitors seem to agree that there is something special about Sheldon. There are no famous names associated with its architectural evolution from the thirteenth century on, medieval builders were usually anonymous craftsmen. Nonetheless the thirteenth-century porch which greets the visitor from behind two venerable yew trees is quite unique, a gem that only survives elsewhere in churches of the period. This was built by the crusader Sir Geoffrey Gascelyn, who acquired Sheldon in 1256 and established his family there for two hundred years.

In 1424 it was bought by the Hungerford family, at the time powerful and acquisitive Wiltshire landowners. They built the fifteenth-century wing to the right of the porch but their occupation was infrequent and it was sixteenth-century tenants who added the similarly gabled but taller wing to the left. By the late-seventeenth century the Hungerfords had shot their bolt, Sheldon was sold and slumbered as a farmhouse, for which the two barns were built during the eighteenth century, until 1917 when Henry Martin Gibbs bought it for his son.

Gibbs' taste was that of many late-Victorian romantics and ideally suited to Sheldon's atmosphere. No doubt he took great care to preserve the original water cistern in the buttressed porch whose vaulted ceiling supports an upper 'priest's' room. He would have approved of the linenfold panelling introduced by his predecessor, and studiously preserved the largely undisturbed layout of the rooms: the dining-room below a library (the original solar) in the fifteenth-century wing, and the hall in the sixteenth-century wing, beyond the oak staircase. The contents he brought were well chosen, in particular the furniture which includes four Elizabethan oak refectory tables, Lancashire chairs, 'seaweed' marquetry, and a pair of Dutch ebony cabinets. His enthusiasm for the aesthetic movement is demonstrated in the William de Morgan pottery, while surprising but no less suitable in its period romanticism, is the Tissot painting 'Marguerite à l'Eglise'.

Mrs Gibbs and her late husband, Martin, took on Sheldon in 1952. Following a series of tenants, the house once again had gone into decline, and required rejuvenation. This they carried out to great effect, at the same time as providing their own contribution in the garden with romantic planting on the terraces around the house, notably the collection of old-fashioned roses, a maze which provides endless delight for children, and, at a distance, a formal water garden concealed by clipped hornbeams.

WILTON HOUSE, *Nr Salisbury*

The Earl of Pembroke
Tel: 01722 743115

In Wilton on A30

Open: 3 Apr to end Oct, daily, 11–6 (last admission 5)
£6.20, children (5–15) £3.80, concessions
Restaurant

Wilton represents the apogee of English aristocratic patronage and connoisseurship. Its layers of artistic quality have been built up by successive generations of Pembrokes who commissioned, designed, purchased and entertained at all the right times in England's cultural development. In the four hundred and fifty years since Henry VIII granted the abbey and estates of Wilton to William Herbert in 1544, there appears to have been only one bad hat: the 7th Earl who ran up debts, was accused of murder, convicted of manslaughter and banished to Wilton, where he died in 1683. The present Earl's career as a film producer may be unconventional but he is no less devoted to Wilton than his scholarly father (who catalogued the collections), as confirmed by his imaginative additions to the gardens.

It is important to grasp the family's evolution. William Herbert's tenure of office through four Tudor reigns, and his Earldom awarded by Edward VI, propelled the family into political and social ascendancy which subsequent generations retained and built upon. His son married Mary, sister of Sir Philip Sidney; they ushered in the first of Wilton's halcyon periods as a centre of Elizabethan and Stuart court life, continued by their sons, the 3rd and 4th Earls. Mary's brother, as well as Spencer, Shakespeare, Isaac de Caus, Inigo Jones and John Webb were central characters.

With the inheritance of the 8th Earl in 1683 another golden era dawned, of scholarship, great collecting and the contributions by his son, the 'architect Earl'. His Palladian bridge across the Nadder beyond the lawns and cedars to the south of the house marked a watershed in the English landscape; it was copied at Stowe, Hagley Hall, Prior Park and by Catherine the Great at Tsarskoye Selo. The 10th Earl commissioned work by Sir William Chambers, the 11th Earl commissioned James Wyatt. Through the nineteenth and twentieth centuries successive Earls were soldiers, scholars and politicians, consolidating and caring for Wilton and its collections.

Enclosing a central courtyard, the square house retains evidence of all these developments. No two fronts are the same but the gentle Chilmark stone gives strong unity. Chambers provides the introduction with his 1755 Triumphal Arch before the forecourt. The 1st Earl's Elizabethan house is retained in the central portion of the east façade, and Wyatt built the Gothic cloisters that surround the courtyard on two levels.

But it is the south front that is of seminal importance and provides Wilton's most enduring image. Its simple but majestic proportions and detail proved as influential as any other single house to the development of English classicism. Its reputation heightens the lingering question of its authorship. Philip, the 4th Earl certainly commissioned Isaac de Caux around 1636 and a drawing by de Caux survives. But the subsequent fire in 1647 gutted Wilton's interiors and the façade may have been partially rebuilt by John Webb, advised by his uncle Inigo Jones, albeit reproducing de Caux's original.

It was the partnership of the aging Jones and his nephew which produced Wilton's interior *tour de force*, the Double Cube room, acknowledged to be both the most sumptuous and important seventeenth-century interior in England. The combination of the white and gold decoration, coved ceiling and painted *trompe-l'oeil* canvases, the marble chimney-piece, towering Corinthian doorcase at one end and the great Van Dyck portraits specially commissioned for their allotted spaces, is overpowering. The style continues in the adjacent Single Cube room.

In these rooms, the other Jones — Webb state rooms and throughout the house, the visitor soon appreciates the endless quality of the picture collection which has few private rivals anywhere in Europe, the furniture with eighteenth-century highlights in the quantities of work by Kent and Chippendale, and works of art such as the 8th Earl's collection of antique statues and busts. In such august company Scheemakers statue of Shakespeare that greets visitors in the entrance hall is a worthy addition and an immediate signal of the education in English culture that lies ahead.

EAST ANGLIA AND THE SOUTH EAST

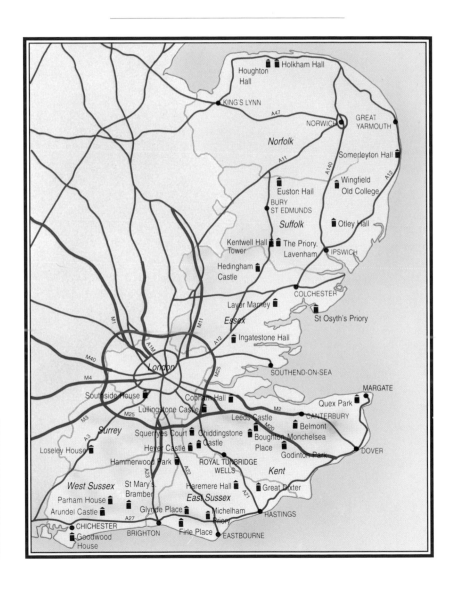

HEDINGHAM CASTLE, *Castle Hedingham*

The Hon Thomas and Mrs Lindsay
Tel: 01787 460261

Off A604, 8 km (5 miles) north-west of Halstead
Open: Apr to early Sept, daily; Sept and Oct, weekdays; 10–5
£2.75, children £1.75
Cream teas by arrangement

The strategic importance of Hedingham's position is clear as you enjoy the commanding views in all directions from the upper floors of the Norman tower. It was built around 1140 – one of the few Norman keeps to survive from that period – by Aubrey de Vere, whose family was among the most powerful in Norman England. In 1142 Aubrey was made Earl of Oxford, a title which the family held for twenty generations until 1703. Macaulay called them, 'the longest and most illustrious line of nobles that England has seen'. After the soldiers of the Middle Ages came scholars and aesthetes; Edward, the 7th Earl is widely believed to have been the author of Shakespeare's plays.

The keep remains an imposing edifice and its pale ashlar stone, quarried at Barnack near Stamford, shows an expense testifying to the de Veres' importance. One hundred and twenty spiral steps lead from the basement, where food was stored, past the ground floor guard room, and on up to the first-floor banqueting hall spanned by a Norman arch – reputedly the broadest in Europe. A gallery still runs around the banqueting hall and above is the dormitory floor. The rooms on each level are kept plain, encouraging the visitor to slip back in time; school children imagining arrow slits and pots of boiling oil account for a large percentage of the castle's visitors. Today the sloping lawns and lakeside walks that surround the castle present an altogether more peaceful atmosphere, condusive to picnics rather than warfare.

INGATESTONE HALL, *Chelmsford*

The Lord Petre
Tel: 01277 353010

In Ingatestone off A12

Open: April to end Sept, Sat, Sun and Bank Holidays
(also Wed to Fri, mid-July to 1 Sept)
£3.50, children £2, concessions
Tea room

After the royal palace of Hampton Court, Ingatestone boasted the first example of a long gallery in England, completed around 1543 and setting the house in the vanguard of Tudor fashion. Such prominence is not altogether surprising; William Petre was Thomas Cromwell's Proctor as the Dissolution of the Monasteries was initiated for Henry VIII. His post demanded that he visit abbeys up and down the land and so, in 1539, he was able to purchase the manor of Ingatestone from the lands of Barking Abbey which had been surrendered to the crown. He replaced the existing modest dwelling at Ingatestone with one, 'very fair, large and stately, made of brick and embattled' – substantially the house that survives today.

Petre carried on to be Secretary of State to Henry VIII and to enjoy the rare distinction of surviving in office through the reigns of both Edward VI and Mary Tudor; perhaps because he was, in the view of one contemporary, 'the man who said nothing.' He founded a distinguished dynasty and his son was made the 1st Lord Petre. The 4th Lord Petre suffered for the family's Catholicism and died in the Tower having been wrongfully imprisoned in 1678 for taking part in the Popish Plot, while a century later the 9th Lord was a leading figure in the move for Catholic emancipation. A less serious incident involved the 7th Lord Petre, who flirtatiously snipped a lock of hair from his cousin, Arabella Fermor, thereby causing the family feud that inspired Alexander Pope's most famous heroic-comic poem: 'The Rape of the Lock'.

From Ingatestone – which they continued to occupy occasionally – the Petres spread to Thorndon Hall nearby on their Essex estates, which James Paine transformed into one of the most sumptuous Palladian houses in England. In 1876 fire virtually gutted the great house and in 1919, following the death of the 16th Lord Petre as a young soldier in 1915, his widow returned to Ingatestone and set about a painstaking restoration, which removed almost all the mainly eighteenth-century alterations, and reaffirmed the house's Tudor character. Now visitors can easily recall the original description as they go through the arch of the clock tower range and approach the long U-shaped house built of warm brick, with crow-stepped gables, tall patterned chimneys and a delightful octagonal turret staircase in one corner.

The succession of panelled rooms continue to evoke a strongly Tudor mood. The panelling in some rooms is original while elsewhere, such as in the dining-room, the oak linenfold is period, but put in during the inter-war restoration. Portraits represent almost all generations of the family; many of the earlier sixteenth- and seventeenth-century figures, such as the 2nd Lord Petre and his wife by Cornelius Johnson are very arresting, while the troublesome Arabella Fermor hangs in the one main room left with its eighteenth-century decoration. The portraits mix with other leading sixteenth and seventeenth century figures – Essex, Buckingham and Monmouth – and Old Masters. The furniture similarly combines much from the seventeenth century, such as the fine Charles II 'Harlequin' chairs, with later eighteenth-century and Regency pieces originally at Thorndon. The dining-room contains three important tapestries. One of two from the Mortlake factory is a portrait of the factory proprietor Thomas Crane, while the third is seventeenth-century Flemish depicting the Siege of Troy.

LAYER MARNEY TOWER, *Colchester*

Mr Nicholas Charrington
Tel: 01206 330784

Off B1022, 10 km (6 miles) south-west of Colchester
Open: Apr to end Sept, daily except Sat, 2–6 (Bank Holidays 11–6;
July and Aug, Sun 12–6)
£3.25, children £1.75, concessions
Tea room

Layer Marney is a building of sparkling originality and could not disappoint the most expectant of visitors. Not only is it the tallest of the select group of Tudor gatehouses that survive in England, it is the most flamboyant, architecturally assured and decoratively avant-garde. The arrangement of the eight storeys of windows in the towers that flank the three storeys of the central block, and the diapered brickwork, together exemplify Tudor vigour. The most important detail is the terracotta decoration, used for window mullions and on the towers

where the initials M and C (for John Marney and his wife Christina) flank crestings. This decoration puts Layer Marney among a tiny select group of buildings that enjoyed this fleeting brush with the Renaissance.

Terracotta was only introduced to England by Italian craftsmen working for Wolsey and Henry VIII; the Dissolution terminated the condusive relationship with Italy. It is most likely that the work at Layer Marney was carried out by Flemish craftsmen who had learnt from the Italians, which explains the slight haziness over the classical vocabulary.

It was the last – and by all accounts – only flourish of the Marneys who had occupied the manor since the twelfth century. Henry Marney rose to prominence during the reigns of Henry VII and Henry VIII. Around 1520 he determined to build himself a suitably fashionable and grand house. He died as building was beginning and only six weeks after he had been made a peer; two years later, in 1525, his son died too and the family line was extinct. Henry Marney's house was left largely as it is today: the gatehouse with its wings which would have formed the first range of an expansive courtyard of buildings, and the separated building to the south, called the long gallery.

After the Marneys, Layer Marney was owned by another prominent Tudor family, the Tukes, thereafter changing hands successively and falling into considerable disrepair. After some restoration during the nineteenth century it was bought in 1904 by Walter de Zoete who carried out far more extensive restoration and gave the interiors their present appearance. He also restored the church which stands to the south-west of the house and contains the tombs of Henry and John Marney, each with canopies that are the most striking of all the terracotta work. In 1958 Mr Charrington's father bought Layer Marney and the family have continued Walter de Zoete's work and opened the house to the public.

ST OSYTH'S PRIORY, *Clacton-on-Sea*

The Lady Juliet de Chair
Tel: 01255 820492

Off B1027, 5 km (3 miles) west of Clacton
Open: Easter, also May to end Sept, daily except Sat, 11–4.30
£3.50, children £1

St Osyth's can justly claim to contain the finest monastic remains in England and is a surprising discovery hidden away on the edge of the Essex marshes. St Osyth's Priory (or Abbey, as it was known for the first eighty of its five-hundred-year existence as one of the great Augustinian abbeys of Europe), is within the boundaries of Constable country, 19 km (12 miles) from Willy Lott's cottage at Dedham. The earliest parts of the monastery are thirteenth-century while additions from successive centuries through to the nineteenth, link together around an expansive quadrangle. Most impressive is the fifteenth-century gatehouse; other highlights of the ensemble are the sixteenth-century

Lord d'Arcy's Tower in the south-east corner, and the remnants of Abbot John Vintoner's house built on to the abbey and remodelled during the nineteenth century.

Somerset de Chair, who died in 1995, bought St Osyth's in 1954 and first restored the gatehouse for occupation. The eighteenth-century range in particular now contains his art collection, and outstanding paintings inherited by his wife from her father, the 8th Earl Fitzwilliam, including a number of celebrated Stubbs's.

EUSTON HALL, Thetford

The Duke and Duchess of Grafton
Tel: 01842 766366

Off A1088, 5 km (3 miles) south-east of Thetford
**Open: June to end Sept, Thur, also last Sun in June and first Sun in Sept,
2.30–5**
£2.50, children 50p, concessions

Euston was rebuilt for Henry Bennet, 1st Earl of Arlington whose name supplied the first A of Charles II's cabal government. Although he was to lose popularity and power, posterity was secured when his only daughter Isabella married Charles II's son by Barbara Villiers, Henry, 1st Duke of Grafton. Arlington left nothing to chance; she was betrothed at five and married at twelve. The house was considerably altered for the 2nd Duke by Matthew Brettingham who removed Arlington's domes from the corner pavilions and replaced them with the more demure Palladian pyramid roofs evident today. In 1902 fire destroyed two of the three sides; they were rebuilt, but in 1950 the 10th Duke decided for practical reasons to reduce the house to the block that survived the fire, as it is today.

The reduced space accentuates the rich effect of the paintings, a superlative array, many of them collected by Arlington to hang either at Euston or Arlington House in London (on the site of Buckingham Palace). His collection of royal Stuart portraits is only rivalled at Windsor Castle. The reputation of many make them instantly recognizable: Van Dycks of Charles I and Henrietta Maria, the group of their five children of which an identical version hangs at Windsor and another group of the elder three, of Strafford and Barbara Villiers' father, Viscount Grandison; Lelys of Arlington himself, Charles II, Prince Rupert of the Rhine, James, Duke of York (James II) and his wife, and more than one likeness of Barbara Villiers. Others are of great historical interest, such as the painting of the ball at the Hague in 1660 the night before Charles II's triumphal return to England, showing him dancing with his sister, the Princess of Orange.

Arlington's daughter is shown with her son in one of Kneller's most sophisticated portraits and the eighteenth-century Graftons added to the collection. The 3rd Duchess is shown in haughty pose dressed for George III's coronation by Reynolds, while her Prime Minister husband's main contribution was to commission an incomparable Stubbs of his 'Mares and Foals at Euston'. His father had commissioned Brettingham's alterations having considered ideas from William Kent for a completely new house. These plans may have been rejected, but Kent designed chairs for Euston, landscaped the park (which John Evelyn had advised Arlington on), and built the octagonal Temple. 'Capability' Brown completed the landscape work in 1769.

HOLKHAM HALL, *Wells-next-the-Sea*

The Earl of Leicester
Tel: 01328 710227

Off A149, 3 km (2 miles) west of Wells-next-the-Sea
Open: end May to end Sept, daily except Fri and Sat, 1.30–5
(Bank Holiday Sun and Mon, 11.30–5)
£3, children £1.50
Tea room

For many people Holkham's austerity disguises the indisputable fact that it is as Robin Fedden confirmed, 'the ultimate achievement of the English Palladian movement'. The riches of the interior are more easily appreciated and present an unparalleled ensemble. The visitor is soon immersed with a sense of inevitability: that one perfectly proportioned, lavishly decorated grand room will lead effortlessly to another. One can hardly imagine anyone daring to make alterations to Holkham and it remains as built. The surrounding park by William Kent softens the coastal site which a contemporary of Holkham's builder called, 'a most unpleasant place'. Only a nineteenth-century *porte-cochère* on the entrance side intrudes, while on the garden front William Nesfield's Victorian parterre, with its monumental fountain group of Perseus and Andromeda, is a harmonious addition.

Young Thomas Coke spent six years between 1712 and 1718 on the grand tour in Italy. In 1744 he was created Earl of Leicester. The house that he began in 1734 and which was not completed until after his death in 1759 is the fruit of his education and collecting during those years, and his association with the high priest of English Palladianism, the Earl of Burlington and the latter's protegé, William Kent. Much of the work was carried out by Leicester's surveyor, Matthew Brettingham, but the plan and decoration were produced by Leicester, Burlington and Kent together.

Externally no decorative flourishes were allowed to distract from the precise Palladianism – emphasized by the blandly pale brick baked nearby and used throughout.

In the central block state rooms fill a *piano nobile* and four identical wings each join to a pyramid-roofed corner tower. On the garden side the spatial arrangement of the broad façade, the subtle minor differences in window style, and the central portico, is breathtakingly assured.

The marble hall is as overpowering a greeting as to be found in any house. Eighteen enormous pink fluted columns support the coved and coffered ceiling, and broad stone steps lead up from the basement level between walls faced in pink Derbyshire alabaster. Roubiliac's bust of Leicester surveys the scene from above the door leading to the saloon, the central state room on the garden front. Here the combination of the rich coved ceiling and doorcases, wall hangings of Genoese velvet and chimney-pieces of Sicilian marble, suggest the hand of Kent who designed the gilded furniture covered in velvet. The whole presents a picture to rival Kent's work at the more sumptuous neighbour, Houghton.

The paintings in the saloon more than complement the decoration, especially Rubens's 'The Return of the Holy Family'. In the south dining-room hang two full-length portraits of Leicester's great-nephew 'Coke of Norfolk', the farming entrepreneur, one as a young connoisseur on the grand tour by Batoni, the other as an English squire by Gainsborough.

The north dining-room leads to the sculpture gallery and its ante-rooms the tribunes, where Leicester's devotion to classicism and the arts of ancient Greece and Rome are celebrated. The drawing-room is overlooked by Gheeraerts portrait of Sir Edward Coke, the Tudor Lord Chief Justice who founded the family's fortunes. For most visitors the quality of paintings reaches a zenith in the smallest state room, the landscape room, hung with landscapes, among which are notable works by Claude and Gaspard Poussin. Such undiluted quality typifies Holkham.

HOUGHTON HALL, *King's Lynn*

The Marquess of Cholmondeley
Tel: 01485 528569

Off A148, 21 km (13 miles) north-east of Kings Lynn
Open: Easter Sun to end Sept, Thur, Sun, and Bank Holidays
(telephone for further details)
£4, children £2, concessions
Tea room

Blenheim and Stratfield Saye were gifts of a grateful nation to military heroes, Marlborough and Wellington. Houghton, however, a house of equal stature to both, was created out of the fruits of political office – the successes of England's first Prime Minister, Sir Robert Walpole. It was built in just thirteen years (1722 to 1735) to a design by Colin Campbell, adapted by James Gibbs, Thomas Ripley and William Kent. Externally its massive square plan is remarkably lightened by the satisfying Palladian proportions and by the cupolas that surmount the four corner towers, giving Houghton one of the most distinctive skylines of any English house. Inside the decoration is William Kent at his most brilliantly unrestrained, assisted by the plasterwork of Artari. The series of state rooms on the

piano nobile, encircling the central hall aptly convey the authority and wealth of the most powerful man in the land.

Kent's interiors demonstrate the clever reinterpretation of classical and Renaissance models, enhanced by the exuberance of Roman Baroque, which gave such early-Georgian houses their combination of elegance and vigour. Walpole's great picture collection – at the time without rival in England – was sold to Catherine the Great by his ungrateful grandson; but Kent's interiors and furnishings remain at Houghton as ample testament to its splendours. Particularly noteworthy are his sets of gilded chairs, the French and Italian sixteenth- and seventeenth- century bronzes, the tapestries including the famous Mortlake of the Stuart kings, and the state beds.

The survival of Kent's rooms was both an accident of history (the house was largely unoccupied for over a century) and the result of the energy and taste of George, 5th Marquess of Cholmondeley and his wife, Sybil Sassoon. Her considerable fortune enabled Houghton to be revitalized and she brought to the house new collections such as the exquisite French furniture, porcelain and Old Masters. Between the wars they restored both house and gardens and their work has been continued by the present Marquess.

In recent years the enormous collection of model soldiers assembled by the present Marquess's father has been brilliantly displayed; it is an absorbing addition, not just for schoolboys. On the walls around are more family portraits and – suitably – good eighteenth- and nineteenth- century military paintings, notably a splendid Reinagle of the local militia.

KENTWELL HALL, *Long Melford*

Mr and Mrs J. Patrick Phillips
Tel: 01787 310207

On northern edge of Long Melford, off A134

Open: late Mar to mid-June, Sun, Bank Holidays and other selected days/weekends; mid-June to mid-July, Sat, Sun and other selected days; mid-July to late Sept, daily; Oct, Sun; usually 12–5
(telephone for further details)
£4.75, children £2.75, concessions
Restaurant

The attractive village of Long Melford has the unique distinction of two important houses of identical style and period, the National Trust property Melford Hall, and Kentwell which is approached from the north of the village along a majestic 1.2-km (¾-mile) avenue of three-hundred-year old limes. At the far end the Tudor house with protruding wings flanking a generous courtyard is immediately welcoming, the combination of warm brick, tall gables and a pair of cupola-topped towers enhanced by the encircling moat crossed by a central bridge.

Patrick Phillips bought Kentwell in 1971 and has carried out admirable restoration to both the house and its gardens. Sir Thomas Clopton built the house and his mother's will of 1563 refers to 'the new mansion', and the interiors saw continual alteration thereafter. The main staircase is seventeenth-century, chimney-pieces and doorcases eighteenth-century, but the most substantial alterations came after a fire in 1827. The owner, Robert Hart Logan commissioned Thomas Hopper (who had previously been working at neighbouring Melford Hall) to carry out the work, which he did in rich Gothic and Tudor revival style. He worked on almost all the main rooms with varying treatment. The most impressive are the dining-room and great hall, whose towering bay window contains rare fifteenth-century armorial glass (of which there is more in the billiard room). In the library he introduced dazzling scagliola columns and, as in the drawing-room, a fine chimney-piece.

The daunting restoration by Patrick Phillips and his wife was carried out over a number of years and involved painstaking redecoration and the introduction of furniture. The overall effect has been to bring the venerable house to life, especially on the occasions of the 'Tudor Re-creations' for which Kentwell has acquired a reputation.

OTLEY HALL, *Ipswich*

Mr J.G. Mosesson
Tel: 01473 890264

Off B1078, 11 km (7 miles) north-east of Ipswich, west of Wickham Market
Open: Bank Hol weekends, 2–6; and by appointment for groups
£4, children £2.50, group rates
Tea room

Martha's Vineyard, the fashionable holiday island in Massachusetts, was named after the daughter of Bartholemew Gosnold, whose family lived at Otley from 1440 to 1674 and built the fifteenth- and early-sixteenth- century moated house with a later Jacobean wing, all of which survives remarkably unchanged five hundred years later. The combination of steep gables, herringbone brickwork, half-timber and pargeting, and vigorously tall brick chimneys makes for an immediately arresting picture while inside many medieval features can be discovered.

The great hall at the core of the house has an outstanding timber ceiling with carved joists and moulded beams, and retains its original screen and eight-light mullioned window. Equally important is the panelling in the linenfold room, used as a dining-room, while upstairs the banqueting room retains panels of delicate sixteenth-century wall painting incorporating coats of arms.

Dorothy Sherston, who lived at Otley from 1910 to 1950, was largely responsible for the preservation of the medieval character of the house and its major features, as well as carrying out judicious restoration. Architectural work was carried out by Morley Horder, while Francis Inigo Thomas (co-author with Reginald Blomfield of *The Formal Garden in England*) supplied a plan for the garden. A picture of Thomas's plan hangs in the house, and although it was not carried out to completion, the addition in 1987 of the canal and mount took up two of his ideas. Mr Mosesson bought Otley in 1976 and opened the house to the public, for whom it provides a rare example of medieval vernacular architecture. The house's attractions were recognized in 1994 when it was selected by the HHHA/AA/NPI as one of the top twenty historic houses in Britain.

THE PRIORY, *Lavenham*

Mr and Mrs A. Casey
Tel: 01787 247003

In Water Street, Lavenham on A1141

Open: Apr and May, selected days; late July to early Sept, daily; 1.30–5.30
(telephone for further details)
£2.50, children £1
Restaurant

It is fitting that one of the most important houses in Lavenham, renowned for its medieval buildings, has, since 1979, been restored from an advanced state of dereliction by Mr and Mrs Casey. Pevsner wrote, 'There is nothing in Suffolk to compare with the timber-framed houses of Lavenham,' and a return to the house of 1600 was the aim of the Caseys' restoration. From a thirteenth-century hall house belonging to the Benedictine order it passed through successive owners, some connected with the cloth trade which brought Lavenham its fortune, who made various additions and alterations, accounting for the house's rambling appearance.

The timberwork, much of it exposed during the restoration, is of primary interest, in particular the crown-post roofs of the solar and great chamber, and the Jacobean staircase. Decorative pargeting is preserved on the gables of the front facing on to the passing street, which also have finely embattled bargeboards. The great chamber has Elizabethan strapwork over the fireplace and parts of the Elizabethan wall paintings that once decorated the whole painted chamber survive. Equally important as the surviving decorative and structural features, the arrangement of the rooms well illustrates how they would have been during the house's heyday.

SOMERLEYTON HALL, *Lowestoft*

The Lord and Lady Somerleyton
Tel: 01502 730224

Off B1074, 8 km (5 miles) north-west of Lowestoft

**Open: Easter to end Sept, Thur, Sun and Bank Holidays; July and Aug,
Tues and Wed; 2–5 (house)
£3.75, children £1.75, concessions
Tea room**

Somerleyton was built by the fortune of one Victorian plutocrat and embellished by another. Such a combination brings a surfeit of riches both inside and out. Olive Cook wrote of the house, 'As an image it astonishes by the diversity of elements which the architect has managed to assemble under one roof.' The diversity is not only architectural: the gardens contain glasshouses by Paxton and a maze and parterre by Nesfield; the fabulous winter garden has, alas, gone but its loggia and the conservatory survive. Inside is lavish carving, a monumental staircase hall, and an array of fine furniture, porcelain and paintings.

Morton Peto, who bought the Somerleyton estate in 1843, was a meteoric entrepreneur – and a devotedly philanthropic one. From bricklaying in his uncle's firm – part of which he inherited – he rose to be the leading building contractor and railway constructor of the day, a Member of Parliament and, in 1855, a baronet. The pinnacle of his career was winning the contract for the new Houses of Parliament, and when he set about modernizing the existing Jacobean Somerleyton, his architect was John Thomas, a sculptor and mason who had assisted Charles Barry on the work at Westminster.

Peto's idea was Victorian Jacobean; the end result was ornately heterogeneous. The entrance front has a Jacobean feel with its advancing wings whose gables recall those of the old house, but in addition there is a tall Italianate tower at one end, a French flavour in the balustrated stone screen that stretches between the wings on the entrance front, and rich stonework everywhere: balustrades, towering porch, and statues along the parapets. The stable block is topped with a tower containing a clock by the royal maker Vulliamy which had been planned for Big Ben. A row broke out over the cost, Vulliamy withdrew, and Sir Morton bought it for Somerleyton.

Thomas's work continued inside. The pair of white marble chimney-pieces in the ballroom reveal him in his outstanding metier, as a craftsman carver. So too do the oak columns in the entrance hall, and the imposing staircase. His appreciation of a fellow craftsman's work enabled the existing panelling and carving – reputed to be by Grinling Gibbons – to survive in the oak room. The combination of rich oak and the glittering white and gilded woodwork and crimson hangings in the ballroom perpetuates a strong sense of mid-Victorian affluence.

Sir Morton's affluence did not last. Generosity – he guaranteed £50,000 towards his friend Paxton's Crystal Palace – and extravagance, of which Somerleyton's Winter Garden was probably the last fling, plunged him into debt and in 1861, ten years after his new house had been finished, he put the whole estate on the market. It was bought in 1863 by Sir Francis Crossley (perhaps to celebrate his baronetcy of that year), whose family fortune came from their carpet-making mills in Halifax.

When Sir Morton sold Somerleyton, the fittings and works of art were included and many remain at Somerleyton today, such as the two paintings from the Napoleonic Wars by Clarkson Stanfield which Sir Morton had commissioned, and the mirror from the Doge's Palace, which he bought at the sale of the Duke of Buckingham's Stowe in 1848. Sir Francis and his successors (his son Savile was made 1st Lord Somerleyton and was the grandfather of the present owner) have made outstanding additions, none more so than the wonderful Wright of Derby in the dining-room. The 1st Lord Somerleyton collected the 2,200 volumes in the library which was made out of Sir Morton's grand two-storey banqueting hall. Successive generations of Crossleys hang in the staircase hall, but the most delightful family likeness is the Carrara marble figure by Thomas Durham of Savile Crossley as a boy with a spade and a hatful of seashells. The 4.85 ha (12 acres) of gardens are maintained to the highest standard and today a feeling of establishment does not diminish the vigour which Sir Morton instilled in the place.

WINGFIELD OLD COLLEGE, *Eye*

Ian Chance
Tel: 01379 384505

Off B1118, 11 km (7 miles) south-east of Diss
Open: Easter to end Sept, Sat, Sun and Bank Holidays 2–6
£2.50, children £1
Tea room

Wingfield College presents a piece of architectural trickery. The demure eighteenth-century front is only a façade, built on to the rooms of the existing medieval college, many of which were retained but disguised with false walls, ceilings and plasterwork. The college, whose church stands adjacent to the house, was founded in 1362 by Sir John de Wingfield, a friend of the Black Prince. His daughter married a de la Pole whose family became Earls and Dukes of Suffolk and who were generous benefactors for the college. In 1542 it was surrendered during the Dissolution and the college buildings then became a private house, to which Squire Buck added the Georgian façade. Mr Chance bought Wingfield in 1971 and has uncovered much of the medieval fabric. The most impressive room is the great hall with a fine oak roof, linenfold panelling and a screen incorporating three carved Tudor portraits. The church contains a series of important tomb effigies including Sir John Wingfield and John de la Pole, 2nd Duke of Suffolk and his wife Elizabeth Plantagenet (sister of Edward IV). In 1981 Mr Chance founded Wingfield Arts and Music which has international arts events through the year.

FIRLE PLACE, *Firle*, *Nr Lewes*

Viscount Gage
Tel: 01273 858335

On A27, 8 km (5 miles) south-east of Lewes
Open: May to Sept, Wed, Thur, Sun and Bank Holiday Mon (including Easter), 2–5
£3.85, children £2, concessions
Restaurant/Tea room

A warm, unassuming eighteenth-century house of manorial proportions, Firle has a cloak of intimacy which initially disguises the quality and richness of its contents. Georgian over early-Tudor, the rooms are pleasingly unpredictable in their arrangement and in a sense reflect that it is a house built by great artisans and unknown architects.

From being recusant Elizabethan Catholics, the Gage family grew to eighteenth-century prosperity through conformity and marriage and in the process Firle became fabulously enriched with art treasures. Old Master paintings – largely from the Cowper Collection – by Van Dyck, Rubens and de Koninck, range alongside a fine collection of English portraits by Reynolds, Zoffany, Gainsborough and Lawrence.

Exceptional English and French furniture and Sèvres porcelain complete the astonishing collection. The visitor is left ruminating where, outside England, one would discover such treasures shrouded by such modest understatement. On departure the church with its brasses, and the unspoilt village, should not be missed.

GLYNDE PLACE, *Lewes*

Viscount and Viscountess Hampden
Tel: 01273 858224

In Glynde, off A27, 6.5 km (4 miles) south-east of Lewes

Open: June to Sept, Wed, Thur, Sun and Bank Holidays; also May, Sun only
(telephone for further details)
£3.25, children £1.50
Tea room

An Elizabethan flint house, built around a courtyard on the edge of the South Downs, Glynde has passed through three families on its way to the present occupants, the Brands, Lords Hampden. The atmosphere is a blend of the sixteenth and seventeenth centuries with an element of eighteenth-century tidying up. Only the nineteenth century is nowhere visible. Built by the Morleys, a Civil War family who inherited the house from the Waleys, it passed to the Trevors. The Trevors included a Bishop of Durham who lived in the house. He enriched and improved Glynde during the seventeenth and eighteenth centuries, notably adding the fine staircase and grand panelled portrait gallery. Full of good country-house furnishings and a score of fine Old Master paintings, Glynde is first and foremost a family home, inasmuch agreeably informal. The appearance of public visitors rarely disturbs the slumbers of the family dog who is usually ensconced on the drawing-room sofa.

Two major exhibitions to commemorate Colonel Harbert Morley and the Great Rebellion of 1637 to 1660, and Mr Speaker Brand (Speaker of the House of Commons 1872 to 1884), have recently been added.

GREAT DIXTER, *Northiam*

Christopher Lloyd
Tel: 01797 253160

Off A28, 0.8 km (½ mile) north of Northiam
Open: Apr to mid-Oct, daily except Mon (open Bank Holidays), 2–5
£3.60, children 50p, concessions

Great Dixter was bought in 1910 by Nathaniel Lloyd, architectural historian and Arts and Crafts connoisseur. At that time it was a medieval hall house with later alterations. Almost immediately Lloyd commissioned Edwin Lutyens to assist with restoration and improvement of the house. At the time Lutyens was at the zenith of his career in English domestic architecture; his most delightful houses were built and the grandeur of New Delhi and post-war commissions lay ahead.

The work at Great Dixter must have appealed to Lutyens and he carried it out with consummate skill and sensitivity. The oldest part of the house was built between 1450 and 1464, timbered and tile-roofed, entered through a gabled two-storey porch and containing a great hall with parlour and solar beyond in a tall bargeboarded gable. Floors and partitions had been inserted around 1595. Lutyens removed these to open up the hall to its two-storey height and reveal the timbered roof with the rare combination of king-posts and hammerbeams. On the other side of the entrance porch he built on a tile-hung addition and supervised the linking of a timbered yeoman's hall on to the back of the house. Nathaniel Lloyd had found the hall derelict in Benenden and moved it to Northiam.

The garden at Great Dixter was always an important priority for Lloyd. Lutyens restored the barn, oast and other farm buildings which became features of the garden and, with the detail of walls, paths and doorways, his work achieved the ensemble that so characterized the best Arts and Crafts houses. Client and architect did not always agree; where Lutyens suggested brick walls, Lloyd insisted on the yew hedges which, with the topiary, are now such a feature of Great Dixter's appearance. Lloyd's son, Christopher has brought fame to the Great Dixter garden and made it a mecca for rare plant enthusiasts.

HAMMERWOOD PARK, *East Grinstead*

David Pinnegar
Tel: 01342 850594

On A264, 5 km (3 miles) east of East Grinstead

Open: Easter Mon to end Sept, Wed, Sat and Bank Holidays, 2–5.30
£3.50, children £1.50
Home-made teas

David Pinnegar bought Hammerwood Park in 1982, when the house was in an advanced state of dereliction and had been unsympathetically divided into apartments. Evidence of decay remains in the unrestored parts of the house where ceilings are still eerily missing. But much was achieved with commendable speed so that in 1992 the house's bicentenary could be celebrated with pride.

Hammerwood is of considerable importance as the first major house designed by the Yorkshireman, Benjamin Latrobe. Four years later he emigrated to the United States where he was responsible for the White House, the Capitol and a selection of other major American buildings. Latrobe studied under S.R. Cockerell with whom he developed an enthusiasm for Greek revival architecture which he put into practice at Hammerwood for his client, John Sperling. The house was built as a hunting lodge, dedicated to the god Apollo and inspired by original details at Paestum which Latrobe had visited.

The main front faces south, a restrained composition of a five-bay central block with tall Doric pilasters and flanking lower wings which have one of the house's many architecturally innovative features, matching Greek Doric temple porches. Another innovation was the use of Coade stone for the limited amount of decoration, notably the Bacchic plaques above the doorways in the two porticos, their partying figures copied from the Borghese Vase. Any doubt about Latrobe's Greek inspiration is dispelled by an inscription in Greek on one of the Coade stone capitals: 'This is the first portico of John Sperling's mansion. The architect is B.H. Latrobe. He made it in the 1792 year of Jesus Christ and the second year of the 642nd Olympiad.'

Inside some of Latrobe's plaster cornices and ceilings have been restored and – with the exception of the huge dining-room and rooms above – most of the main rooms painstakingly redecorated and furnished. The most impressive flourish is the allegorical *trompe-l'oeil* mural which now decorates the entire staircase hall, completed for the 1992 celebrations. It is no surprise that the restoration has won a number of awards and David Pinnegar and his family have worked tirelessly, against considerable odds including hostile local opposition to the house being given extensive public access.

HAREMERE HALL, *Etchingham*

Jacqueline, Lady Killearn
Tel: 01580 819245

Off A265, 1.6 km (1 mile) from Hurst Green
Open: details available on request
Prices available on request

Where the land drops steeply from the edge of the Weald down to the Rother valley, Haremere Hall sits tucked underneath the escarpment with views over the gentle landscape beyond. No doubt this position was one of the attractions to Lord and Lady Killearn when they bought Haremere in 1948, after his retirement from a distinguished ambassadorial career. The two main fronts of the ragstone house are both handsome and immediately tell of their different dates. The 1616 main front, facing west, has two delightful projecting bays topped with Dutch gables of theatrical height. The south front has a nineteenth-century broad gable over an unusual two-storey mullioned bay window, but the neat symmetry of the rest of the range immediately suggests its 1682 period.

The panelling in the great hall is probably contemporary with this later period, but the ceiling is more likely to date from the earlier work. There are striking carved fireplaces and overmantels, some original, others introduced by different owners – of which Haremere has had a succession. The most colourful was the Regency Sir John Lade, who inherited a considerable fortune and spent a large amount of it entertaining his friend, the Prince Regent, or in various reckless schemes. His consuming passion was driving and he once steered his four-horse phaeton from Bath to London in eight hours. His lowly born wife Letty used such language that the Regent often commented, 'He swears like Letty Lade.'

Lampson – Lord Killearn's family name – portraits alternate with other decorative pictures recalling his succession of diplomatic postings such as Egypt, and the decoration and furnishing of the house is the Killearns' work, as is the attractive terraced garden.

MICHELHAM PRIORY, *Hailsham*

Sussex Archaeological Society
Tel: 01323 844224

Off A22, 1.6 km (1 mile) east of Upper Dicker
Open: end Mar to end Oct, daily, 11–5.30
£3.30, children £1.90, concessions

Michelham Priory comprises the surviving buildings from the Augustinian priory founded in 1229. After suppression during the Dissolution and subsequent sale, the priory passed through successive owners, the earliest of whom added to the buildings. By the beginning of the twentieth century, however, much of the priory was derelict. In 1924 it was bought by Mr and Mrs Richard Beresford-Wright who carried out extensive restoration, continued by their successor, Mrs Hotblack who, in 1959, bequeathed the property in trust to the Sussex Archaeologicial Society.

The expansive moat, which provides an ideally gentle atmosphere, gives an indication of the priory's former substance, four ranges of buildings enclosing a square cloister and incorporating a large church. This and much of another range has gone and the surviving buildings – occupied as a house after the Dissolution – comprise part medieval with Tudor additions. A bridge over the moat leads through the tall fourteenth-century gatehouse and, of the main priory buildings, the south range is the most intact with warm sandstone walls, mullioned windows and deep tiled roofs. In the remainder of the west range is the fine thirteenth-century undercroft through which visitors enter the house and many other rooms contain exhibitions of monastic life and museums. Detached from the priory buildings are a sixteenth-century barn with an impressive timber roof, a timbered water-mill and the gardens which have been extensively restored.

BELMONT, *Faversham*

The Harris (Belmont) Charity
Tel: 01795 890202

Off A251 (signed at Badlesmere), 6.5 km (4 miles) south-west of Faversham
Open: Easter to end Sept Sat, Sun and Bank Holidays, 2–4.30
£4.50, children £2.50
Tea room

Belmont's inaccessibility has contributed to its undeserving obscurity. Its architectural distinction is only one aspect of a rewarding ensemble with the splendid fortes of empire, cricket and clocks. The house boasts the finest private clock collection in the country, assembled by the 5th Lord Harris. His father was a figure whose importance in the history of English cricket is second only to that of W.G. Grace. Generations of the family served with distinction as imperial soldiers and administrators.

Belmont has been the Harris home since it was bought at auction by the 1st Lord – victor of Seringapatam – with the prize money from his Indian campaign. On the site of an existing eighteenth-century house, named Belmont because of its superb position overlooking the surrounding countryside, the present house was built for Colonel John Montresor by Samuel Wyatt between 1789 and 1793. It remains one of the most unspoilt examples of Wyatt's work, as the authority on the family of architects, John Martin Robinson, has noted. Samuel 'thought of himself as an engineer-architect rather than an artist-architect like his brother James and Belmont is a text-book example of his work.'

The entrance is through a long Ionic portico on the south side, with, adjacent to the west, an orangery that was a classical forerunner of the Victorian conservatory. The main façade faces east between symmetrical bows at either end topped with shallow domes and glassed look-outs. Floor-length windows to maximize the views combine with the bows and domes to give the house an attractively generous appearance while the look-outs are a good example of Wyatt's ingenuity. The house was built of similar red brick to the stable courtyard on the west side but the main fronts were covered in pale mathematical tiles, another Wyatt novelty, as were the Coade stone Ionic capitals and circular and square wall plaques that are the exterior's most attractive features.

Wyatt's restrained but impeccable neo-Classicism continues inside, in the broad axial corridor off which the main drawing-room, dining-room and library open along the east front. The splendid staircase hall rises the full height of the house to a central oval skylight, and contains a cantilevered stone staircase with a wrought-iron and lead balustrade and mahogany handrail. Both drawing-room and library have curving ends to match their bow windows and in all the rooms Wyatt's fittings are of unfailing quality.

The contents complement Wyatt's work. In the entrance hall three rare longcase clocks, including a Tompion and a Knibb, set the standard for the array that follow throughout the house and provide a symphony of chimes on every hour. Much of the furniture is Regency, added by the 2nd Lord Harris, but there are earlier English pieces and French furniture in the drawing-room. Among family portraits, many hanging on the various levels of the staircase hall, the outstanding work is the large group of the 1st Lord Harris and his family by Arthur Devis in the dining-room. The most engaging is the 2nd Lord Harris as a boy, vaulting a gate in Richmond churchyard, by W.R. Bigg in the drawing-room.

Fascinating memorabilia abounds such as the richly decorated sword presented to the 2nd Lord by his fellow officers, 'in testimony of their respect for his highly meritorious conduct at the ever memorable battle of Waterloo'; the exotic headdress of Tippoo Sultan who was defeated at Seringapatam; oriental bronzes and ceramics collected by the 4th Lord Harris who – among other positions held – was Governor of Bombay (his father governed Madras). For horological enthusiasts in particular the first floor clock museum is an absorbing place.

BOUGHTON MONCHELSEA PLACE, *Maidstone*

Charles W. Gooch
Tel: 01622 743120

In Boughton Monchelsea on B2163, 8 km (5 miles) south of Maidstone

**Open: Good Fri to early Oct, Sun and Bank Holidays;
also July and Aug, Wed (telephone for further details)
£3.25, children £1.25, concessions
Tea room**

Boughton Monchelsea enjoys a spectacular position on a south-facing ridge overlooking a vast expanse of the Kentish Weald. Not surprisingly, the site had been built upon for some time in 1551 when Robert Rudston purchased the manor and began the changes which produced the present house, substantially built after 1567. Rudston used local Kentish ragstone dug from a quarry in Boughton. The entrance front, with a distinctive two-storey porch and gables, is Rudston's work while other details came later, such as the battlements on all four sides, added at the end of the eighteenth century.

Most of the internal character dates from alterations by later generations of Robert Rudston's family. The impressive staircase was built during the 1680s; nearly a century later the hall and dining-room were given a Gothic appearance with vaulting and clusters of columns. Bold Regency furniture complements the Gothic decoration while the drawing-room retains the earlier combination of a delicate rococo giltwood mirror over a marble chimney-piece of the same period. Good Mortlake tapestries hang over the stairs and in the dining-room, while the parish church tucked into a corner where garden meets park should be visited for its unexpectedly splendid memorial to Sir Christopher Powell by Scheemakers.

CHIDDINGSTONE CASTLE, *Edenbridge*

Trustees of the Denys Eyre Bower Bequest
Tel: 01892 870347

In Chiddingstone, off B2027

Open: Apr, May and Oct, Wed, Sun and Bank Holidays; June to Sept, Tues to Sun and Bank Holidays; 2–5.30 (The Trustees reserve the right to close the castle for private functions)
£3.50, children £1.50
Tea room

The young architect, William Atkinson was working on Scone Palace near Perth when, in 1805, he supplied designs for Squire Henry Streatfield to update his Carolean home, Chiddingstone. The two Georgian Gothic buildings have intriguing similarities, but while Scone finished up a palace, one of the most prestigious commissions of Atkinson's career, at Chiddingstone his more humble client had been too ambitious. In 1807 building was stopped with only the north and south wings complete, the east range was left with its old dormer windows and when Streatfield's son continued the work, he was advised by the less competent Henry Kendall. In comparison to Scone's finished grandeur, Chiddingstone is characterized by a friendly, more modest picturesque atmosphere which extends to the grounds and lake, landscaped when the house was being remodelled.

Streatfields lived at Chiddingstone for four hundred and fifty years from Henry VIII's reign; by the turn of this century the castle was let, then sold in 1938. After a short spell as a school it was badly damaged during wartime occupation and then, in 1955, help arrived in the form of Denys Eyre Bower. From being a penniless bank clerk and collector, he became an art dealer and bought Chiddingstone to display his collections which are specialized and unusual: Stuart and Jacobite pictures and memorabilia; Egyptian antiquities; Japanese and Buddhist works of art.

Chiddingstone's most elegant room is the White Rose drawing-room hung with a rare collection of Stuart portraits. As well as more familiar faces there are Prince Charles Edward's brother, Prince Henry, Cardinal York, and Charles I's small children, Princess Elizabeth and the Duke of Gloucester, by Cornelius Johnson. Of similar quality is Samuel Cooper's miniature of Charles II. Most exotic – but in another room – is the portrait of Nell Gwyn, draped but nude, representing Venus with her son, the Duke of St Albans as Cupid. The picture is by Lely and Bower did not consider it suitable to hang with the royal Stuarts. Other rare items include Charles I's handkerchief and the letter from the Duke of Monmouth to his uncle, James II, written the night before his execution.

The Japanese collection contains superb lacquer pieces, including the Beckford cabinet which Bower discovered in 1940, and exquisite carved ivory and lacquer Japanese ladies. Among the Egyptian antiquities is a mummified cat. With plenty of such oddities, the various collections are an intriguing discovery; at the same time they reflect the connoisseurship of their creator, evident in his sensitive portrait by Dame Laura Knight.

COBHAM HALL, *Nr Gravesend*

Westwood Educational Trust
Tel: 01474 823371/824319

Off A2/M2 between Gravesend and Rochester

Open: April, July and Aug, most Wed, Thur and Sun, also other selected days (telephone for further details)
£2.50, children £2
Tea room

The fortunate pupils at Cobham Hall spend their time in surroundings few other schools can match. Three distinguished families in turn lived at Cobham: the Lords Cobham, the Dukes of Lennox and Richmond, and the Earls of Darnley, and each have left fine evidence of their occupation.

William Brooke, Lord Cobham was a powerful Elizabethan courtier and in 1584 set about transforming the old manor house into a sumptuous Tudor mansion. He did so by the addition of two wings, each gabled and surmounted with swirling chimney stacks, but most notably decorated with an octagonal turret on each corner, each topped with a lead dome. Cobham's wings survive, but between 1662 and 1670 the central block of the house was rebuilt by Charles, 6th Duke of Lennox and Richmond, with John Webb (Inigo Jones's son-in-law) as his architect.

In 1713 the 6th Duke's descendant, Lady Theodosia Hyde married Mr John Bligh who was awarded a number of peerages before, in 1725, being made Earl of Darnley. During the eighteenth century and up to 1830, many of the interiors at Cobham were extensively altered and redecorated for the Darnleys, mainly by Sir William Chambers and James Wyatt. Chambers was responsible for the decorative scheme that altered the two-storey banqueting hall in John Webb's central block (where Webb's lavish original decorative scheme had always been gilded) into the gilt hall or music hall, complete with its unique Snetzler organ in one of the two galleries that Chambers added at either end.

The ceiling is decorated with the arms of the Dukes of Lennox and over the chimney-piece hangs a copy of the double portrait by Van Dyck of Lord Bernard and Lord John Stuart, sons of the 3rd Duke and both killed in the Civil War.

Wyatt designed the furniture in the gilt hall and elsewhere he was responsible for the fine Etruscan decoration of the vestibule, as well as Gothic details in the entrance hall and the chapel, and the reconstruction of the Tudor gallery. This room was subsequently altered again as part of work by the somewhat less talented architect, George Repton, whose father, Humphry, in 1790, was commissioned by the 4th Earl of Darnley to landscape the park. Important restoration of the park has been carried out by the Cobham Hall Heritage Trust, especially since the extensive damage caused by the 1987 hurricane.

GODINTON PARK, *Ashford*

Godinton House Preservation Trust / Alan Wyndham Green
Tel: 01233 620773

Off A20, 1.6 km (1 mile) north-west of Ashford

Open: Easter Sat, Sun and Mon; June to Sept, Sun and Bank Holidays, 2–5
£2, children £1

Mellow brick gables beckon above yew hedges shaped to match as one approaches Godinton through its eighteenth-century park which disguises the house's proximity to Ashford. From around 1500 until 1895 it was home to the Toke family, Kentish squires who improved the house at different times – with the occasional flourish. Shortly after the turn of this century the then owner commissioned Sir Reginald Blomfield to lay out the present garden which so enhances the house's surroundings, and in 1919 Godinton was bought by Mr Wyndham Green's grandmother, the Hon Mrs Ward.

The various façades, all with the distinctive curved gables that reflect a Flemish influence on Kentish architecture, date from different periods. The east front is early-seventeenth century when the present house was built to the surviving square-plan around a small courtyard; the south front which also overlooks the garden is eighteenth-century, the north-facing entrance front is mainly early-nineteenth-century. The integration of periods continues inside to a degree that has often puzzled architectural historians. In the great hall the magnificent tie-beam and king-post are part of the fourteenth-century roof, most of which is concealed behind a later ceiling. Beyond the hall the staircase with heraldic beasts was described by Christopher Hussey as 'overloaded with enrichment' and although dated 1628, could be in part nineteenth-century.

The 1635 upstairs great chamber is the finest room; created by Captain Nicholas Toke, a rumbustious soldier who had five wives and died in 1680 when en route to London looking for a sixth. He was responsible for the room's superb carved chimney-piece and panels with a frieze of military figures reflecting his own enthusiasm. Downstairs the chimney-piece in the library carved with symbolic figures commemorates one of his marriages. Here, as in the great chamber and hall, the chimney-piece is of unusual local Bethersden marble.

Toke portraits and some furniture, notably the fine Chippendale dining-chairs remain at Godinton, but important additions have been made by both Mr Wyndham Green and his grandmother. The elegant white drawing-room hung with a collection of watercolours (including a group by Myles Birket Foster) was her sitting-room, outside which the garden hall is furnished and decorated with Chinese Chippendale chairs and Chinese ceramics. The library displays the majority of the house's important early-Worcester collection. Among many portraits, Wards in the dining-room, Tokes and suitable royal Stuarts in the great hall, the pick are in the great chamber and the adjoining gallery: works by Raeburn, Reynolds, Cornelius Johnson and Van der Helst. For most visitors Godinton's provincial, squirearchical history makes it easily enjoyed and disguises its wealth of contents.

HEVER CASTLE, *Edenbridge*

Broadland Properties Ltd
Tel: 01732 865224

Off B2026, 5 km (3 miles) south-east of Edenbridge
Open: early Mar to early Nov, daily, 11–5
Prices on application
Restaurant

The combination of Hever's appearance, its comet-like rise and fall during Henry VIII's reign and its transformation by one of the wealthiest of Edwardian plutocrats gives an air of unreality to the place; one might not be surprised to hear that it is all a lavish film set. But such hints of pastiche disguise important medieval architecture, absorbing history and restoration of almost unparalleled munificence and quality.

The moated medieval castle was bought in 1462 by Sir Geoffrey Bullen. His grandson, Sir Thomas was father of Anne Boleyn whom Henry VIII married, having tried her elder sister Mary as a mistress first. Boleyn supremacy was brief and ended with Anne's execution on Tower Hill in 1536. Their demise was emphasized when Henry VIII later granted Hever to his divorced fourth wife, Anne of Cleves. The castle was occupied by three successive families from 1557 until 1903, when it was bought by William Waldorf Astor, who had settled in England in 1890.

It is his Hever that the visitor sees today and it is fortunate that, when the Astor family sold the place in 1983, the major fittings and many contents remained. The unrivalled armour collection has gone, but Astor's series of immaculately precise and superbly worked Tudor interiors survive, notable in particular for their panelling and carving by W.S. Frith, as do much of the carefully chosen furniture and Astor's eclectic often fabulous collection of works of art and antiquities.

Astor made two major additions to Hever; the extraordinary 'Tudor village' which provided necessary extra rooms and service areas and continued the architectural quality of his work on the castle, and the Italian gardens. The latter, with its Pompeiian Wall displaying an astonishing array of antiquities, and classical architecture culminating in the loggia overlooking the lake created by damming the passing River Eden, is the most important Italianate garden in England.

LEEDS CASTLE, *Maidstone*

Leeds Castle Foundation
Tel: 01622 765400

Off B2163 (M20 exit 8), 6.5 km (4 miles) east of Maidstone

**Open: Mar to end Oct, daily, 10–5; Nov to end Feb,
daily (except Christmas Day), 10–3**

**£8, children £5.20, concessions [owing to its charitable status Leeds Castle
is unable to offer free entry to HHA Friends]**

Restaurants

Few castles can rival Leeds's reputation for antiquity and romance and its island position remains superb, evoking the times of the medieval kings and queens for whom it was a favourite haunt. The group of pale stone buildings confirm that it was a place for enjoyment rather than a defence; they present a cross-section of periods from Norman to the nineteenth century.

Among the oldest are the keep or Gloriette on its own small island, reached by corridors over an arched stone bridge and the revetment wall with two drum bastions. The main body of the castle which extends from the corridor bridge on to the larger

island was rebuilt as part of extensive restoration by Fiennes Wykeham-Martin during the 1820s. This had changed from the original medieval building to being Jacobean, then Gothic before he restored its medieval appearance. Facing across the castle's lawned courtyard at the entrance to the castle island is the largely thirteenth-century gatehouse.

In 1926, by which time Leeds was again in need of restoration, it was sold by the Wykeham-Martin family and bought by the Hon Olive Wilson-Filmer, who later became Lady Baillie. Her mother was the daughter and heiress of William Whitney of the

United States, and her father was the grandson of the 1st Marquess of Anglesey who led the cavalry at Waterloo. Lady Baillie restored the castle buildings and redecorated the interiors, mainly assisted by the French decorator, Stephane Boudin.

The finished work combines suitability to the castle's ancient origins with the comforts of a country house and involved the introduction of many important works of art. Old Masters such as Tiepolo's 'The Pulchinello's Kitchen' and modern paintings add distinguished variety to portraits of Leeds's royal occupants such as Henry VIII, and later non-royal owners, in particular the Culpeper and Fairfax families whose successive ownership spanned the seventeenth and eighteenth centuries. Other additions by Lady Baillie include the sixteenth-century newel staircase, and the fireplace in the Henry VIII banqueting hall, both French, the seventeenth-century panelling from Thorpe Hall near Peterborough, and an extensive collection of rare Chinese porcelain.

Lady Baillie's devoted custodianship of Leeds ended with her death in 1974, before when she had arranged for the property to pass into the ownership of a charitable trust, the Leeds Castle Foundation that would maintain Leeds.

LULLINGSTONE CASTLE, *Eynsford*

Guy Hart Dyke
Tel: 01322 862114

In Darenth valley via Eynsford on A225
Open: Apr to Sept, Sat, Sun and Bank Holidays, 2–6
£3.50, children £1.50
Tea room

North Kent, within walking distance of the M25 motorway, is not where one would expect to discover so secluded a piece of countryside as the small Darenth valley. Lullingstone Castle was recorded as Lullingstone Ros in Domesday with an estate of 48.5 ha (120 acres). Today it is the same size; in between the estate swelled to 2428 ha (6,000 acres) and Harts and Dykes occupied positions of power and entertained royalty.

Sir John Peche was one of Henry VII's most dashing jousting knights and set about transforming Lullingstone after being knighted at the Battle of Blackheath in 1497. He added the battlemented gatehouse through which the visitor approaches, possibly the earliest surviving brick gatehouse in England. The house itself, which lies across expansive lawns with St Botolph's church to the left, is deceptive. Remodelling for visits by Queen Anne disguises the Tudor construction. In the hall a 1725 view shows both the original moat and a second gatehouse.

The work in honour of Queen Anne was carried out at the beginning of the eighteenth century by Percival Hart. The portraits of his son-in-law, Sir Thomas Dyke and that of his son Sir John Dixon Dyke, are unusual full-length works by Domenico van Schmissen, and both hang in the entrance hall. The dining-room to one side was panelled during the remodelling, and the staircase inserted, with characteristic early-eighteenth-century balusters, the Peche crest of a lion's head at intervals, and deliberately shallow treads to assist the ascent of the portly Queen Anne.

Upstairs is Lullingstone's forte, the Elizabethan drawing-room. The barrel vault ceiling with sumptuous plasterwork incorporating medallions of Roman dignitaries is original but the panelling with pilasters and carved capitals was Sir Thomas's eighteenth-century work. Queen Anne in royal robes surveys the room from one end and a leather chest with her crown and monogram stands in the room.

St Botolph's Church should not be missed. It retains evidence of Norman origins and Edward III reconstruction, with contributions by successive owners. Its rood screen was inserted by Sir John Peche and the north chapel built for his splendid tomb. There are more tombs and wall memorials to Harts and Dykes, the plaster moulded ceiling is Queen Anne, the stained glass dates from the fourteenth to the eighteenth centuries and the altar rail was added in the late-twentieth century by Sir Oliver Hart Dyke who restored the gatehouse and much of the castle.

QUEX PARK, *Birchington*

Trustees of the Powell-Cotton Museum
Tel: 01843 42168

In Birchington, off A28

Open: Easter to end Sept, Wed, Thur and Sun, also Aug, Fri, 2.15–6
£2.50, children £1.80, concessions
Tea room

Quex Park is a curiosity among country houses. Marooned among cabbages and potatoes on the Isle of Thanet it hides surprises and treasures. A hint of what lies ahead comes as one approaches; from the woods that surround Quex a quaint white-painted metal tower points skyward. It surmounts a Gothic folly called the Waterloo Tower built by John Powell Powell to celebrate the great victory and to accommodate his enthusiasm for campanology; it contains one of the few secular peals of twelve bells in England.

John Powell Powell was responsible for much of Quex's present appearance. Inheriting from an uncle in 1808, he demolished the dilapidated old house, replaced it with the Regency one that largely survives, and planted the park that securely encloses it. From 1883 the house was extended by Henry Horace Powell Cotton and took on a Victorian appearance. His son, Major Percy Horace Gordon Powell-Cotton, made the most unusual – and distinguished – additions to Quex. Explorer, collector, hunter and naturalist, he was an authority on Indian and African fauna and ethnography and in 1896 begun the museum at Quex, adjoining the house, which now contains an astonishing array of dioramas, consisting of exhibitions of animals in their natural habitat.

Major Powell-Cotton also acquired the distinguished collection of Chinese Imperial and Taste porcelain which is the highlight of Quex's works of art, as well as the almost bewildering array of antiquities from many African and oriental countries and rare items of British archaeology. His collections are also displayed in the house where he decorated and furnished the drawing-room in oriental style. The panelling and other carved decoration is all Kashmir walnut, while much of the furniture is elaborately carved padouk wood from India. Three generations of Cottons served the East India Company and their portraits hang with other members of the family in the Armoury (whose weapons are now in the museum).

In addition to the main collections, notable curiosities abound throughout the house: in the boudoir a pair of tortoiseshell and satinwood card tables; in the gallery an Italian seventeenth-century marble bust of 'The Laughing Philosopher' which belonged to Henry, Lord Holland (who had a substantial house at Kingsgate near Broadstairs and who owned Quex for a time from 1767); and in the library the Congreve or rolling-ball clock, made for John Powell Powell by William Congreve, who made rocket batteries during the Napoleonic Wars.

SQUERRYES COURT, *Westerham*

J.St A. Warde
Tel: 01959 562345/563118

In Westerham, off A25

Open: Mar, Sun; Apr to end Sept, Wed, Sat, Sun and Bank Holidays; 2–6
£3.70, children £1.80, concessions
Home-made teas

Carolean in date, William and Mary in appearance and satisfyingly symmetrical, Squerryes is instantly enjoyable, the country house of many people's imagination. The house was built in 1680 by Sir William Crisp, replacing one that Evelyn had noted in his diary in 1658 to be 'old but convenient'. In 1700 Squerryes was sold to Edward Villiers, 1st Earl of Jersey, and, in 1731, to John Warde whose family has lived here ever since.

John Warde brought to the house much of the fine early eighteenth-century furniture, including the upholstered chairs and giltwood mirrors in the drawing-room. He also commissioned the splendid armorial service from Canton, about one hundred and fifty pieces in all, bearing the Warde arms impaling Bristow. He used to watch his racehorses exercising from the gazebo in the park and his sporting enthusiasm prompted the painting of him and his family at Squerryes by John Wootton.

His son, also John, was the family's most important collector and brought to Squerryes most of the distinguished paintings. In the drawing-room are Dutch cabinet paintings by Jacob Ruysdael, Van Goyen, Hondecoeter and Steenwyck, although the group by Van der Helst was acquired by the family at an earlier date. Other paintings acquired by John Warde II are a majestic still life by Peter de Ring, works by Luca Giordano and Rubens, and Van Dyck's 'Martyrdom of San Sebastian'.

John Warde I was responsible for the tapestry room. The three Soho arabesque

tapestries were specially woven around 1720 by Joshua Morris and incorporate the Warde arms, as do the settees and stools in the room. Very different is the Wolfe room, a sanctuary to the general who was born and brought up in Westerham and was a close friend of George Warde, for whom Benjamin West painted the arresting posthumous portrait of Wolfe as a boy.

The Warde sporting enthusiasm remained strong. John Warde II commissioned Stubbs to paint his Arab horse. His son, another John, holds the horse in Stubbs's painting, but achieved more lasting fame as the 'Father of Foxhunting'. He is credited with being the first man to keep hounds exclusively for fox-hunting, was master of the Pytchley for eleven seasons, founded the West Kent hunt and continued to ride to hounds when weighing well over 127 kg (20 stone). His picture by Barraud hangs in the dining-room, with the Wootton and other enjoyable family paintings, not least a Zuccharelli of Harleyford Manor near Marlow, the married home of a Warde daughter and Toad Hall in Kenneth Grahame's *The Wind in the Willows*.

SOUTHSIDE HOUSE, *Wimbledon*

The Pennington-Mellor-Munthe Trust
Tel: 0181 947 2491 / 946 7643

On B281, south side of Wimbledon Common

Open: Oct to end May, Tues, Thur, Sat and Bank Holidays, 2–5
£5, accompanied children £2

There is a stirring story that at the height of the London Blitz Mrs Hilda Pennington-Mellor-Munthe left Southside House after it had suffered a number of direct hits from German bombs and set off in the family carriage, the horses steered by an alcoholic Irish riding master, to the safety of her Herefordshire home, Hellen's. She and her maid clasped jewellery, silver and other valuables that they were able to carry to safety and which she returned after the end of the war when the War Damage Commission voted to assist the extensive rebuilding that was required at Southside.

The house has passed – via occasionally tortuous routes – by descent or marriage from Robert Pennington who developed a modest farmhouse into the present William and Mary house. It continued to be known as Holme Farm until the early twentieth-century when it became Southside House. Pennington had sent his wife and daughter to the house from the city of London after their son had died in the plague; his affection for his surviving family is shown by the two statues of 'Plenty' and 'Spring' set in niches on either side of the front door. Ensuing generations made considerable changes to the house's interiors. At one time it was divided into two dwellings, but the post-war restoration returned it as faithfully as possible to the late seventeenth-century original, the period emphasized by interior fittings such as large classical doorcases and deep carved friezes.

As at the family's home at Hellen's, Southside's greatest attraction is the distinguished picture collection which illustrates the lively family history and introduces the characters with whom they were associated. The dining-room contains an impressive number which include a full-length portrait of James Stuart, Charles I's nephew, attributed to Van Dyck, Hogarth's portrait of Sir Charles Kemeys-Tynte and St George by Edward Burne-Jones. A number of portraits in the house illustrate the family's close connection with the Dukes of Wharton and it was from the Whartons that Southside gained the collection of small portraits by Rousselle showing various relations of the 4th Lord Wharton.

117

LOSELEY HOUSE, *Guildford*

Mr and Mrs James More-Molyneux
Tel: 01483 304440

Via A3 and B3000, 8 km (3 miles) south-west of Guildford

Open: late May Bank Holiday to end Aug, Wed, Thur, Fri and Sat, also Aug Bank Holiday Mon, 2–5
£3.50, children £2, concessions
Tea room

Set in spacious parkland inhabited by its famous herd of Jersey cows, Loseley evokes the reigns of Elizabeth I and James I, both of whom visited the house. Sir William More was one of Elizabeth's most trusted advisers and he built the house between 1562 and 1568.

The Bargate stone came from the ruins of Cistercian Waverley Abbey and the sense of movement given to the entrance front by tall gables of varied width is emphasized by the chalk clunch window dressings and quoins.

The Tudor atmosphere is immediate as one enters the great hall, with panelling from Henry VIII's Nonsuch Palace. Decorative panels along the minstrels' gallery above one end of the hall were painted by an Italian artist, Toto del Nunziata, to adorn Henry VIII's banqueting tents. After James I visited Loseley, he presented the full-length portraits of himself and Queen Anne by John de Critz, but the most distinguished royal portrait is Edward VI wearing his father's royal collar; it is the first painting of the young boy after his accession. Family portraits in the hall are dominated by the splendid group by Somers of Sir More Molyneux, his wife and eight of their eleven children.

From the expansive hall the mood is immediately intimate in the small library, enclosed by bookcases and panelling with fine Elizabethan carving – not least the panel over the chimney-piece bearing the arms of Elizabeth I to commemorate her visits. Sir William More began the collection of books that was continued by later generations of the family.

The drawing-room beyond has a richly worked plaster ceiling inserted and gilded for James I's visit, as was the delightful frieze incorporating family emblems of the moorhen, cockatrix and mulberry tree. But the drawing-room's most astonishing decoration is the chimney-piece which is carved out of a massive single block of chalk.

Sir William More's portrait hangs in this room, a distinguished old man by Lucas de Here; as do his son's (whose daughter eloped with the poet, John Donne) and those of other descendants.

The Tudor atmosphere continues in the bedrooms, while throughout the house there is a rich variety of furniture. The most interesting piece is the sixteenth-century inlaid Wrangelschrank cabinet collected by Sir Poynings More which is in the drawing-room, along with an inlaid Queen Anne cabinet decorated with a seaweed pattern.

ARUNDEL CASTLE, *Arundel*

Arundel Castle Trustees Ltd
Tel: 01903 883136

In Arundel north of A27

Open: April to end Oct, daily except Sat and Good Fri, 11–5
£4.50, children £3.50, concessions
[Arundel is not able to offer free entry to HHA friends]
Restaurant

Arundel Castle is entirely suitable as a home for England's premier dukes; its walls encapsulate the vicissitudes of their progress. William the Conqueror granted lands in Sussex to Roger de Montgomery who built the original castle. His Fitzalan descendants (Earls of Arundel) extended the castle and were, like the Howards (Dukes of Norfolk), in the mainstream of English history throughout the turbulent medieval and Tudor centuries. Only years after the two families were joined in 1556 by the marriage of Lady Mary Fitzalan and Thomas, 4th Duke of Norfolk, the Duke was beheaded by Elizabeth I for plotting to marry Mary, Queen of Scots. Such brushes with royalty were commonplace and the family history is dotted with attainders, executions and martyrs.

Head of the peerage and Roman Catholic to boot, the Norfolks were a likely target during the Civil War; in 1643 the castle was sacked. For over a century the semi-ruined buildings were hardly occupied and the family lived in splendour at eighteenth-century Norfolk House in London and at Worksop Manor in Nottinghamshire. Occasional restoration was begun, but nothing serious until the late-eighteenth century when the 11th Duke restored some buildings around the quadrangle and laid out the park. (He retained the keep as a ruin for his rare breed of American owls.)

Nearly a century later, Henry, the 15th Duke, was largely responsible for the castle as it is today. He was advised by C.A. Buckler who fused architecture with genealogy and antiquarianism; between 1875 and 1914 Arundel was transformed into a celebration of Roman Catholic medievalism. At the same time the Norman gatehouse, keep and the medieval curtain wall were all carefully repaired.

119

The scale is impressive: the exterior of the house was given towers and turrets, and the walls were refaced with ashlar. Cavernous rooms were given church-like interiors – at times it seems that you are never out of a chapel. The dining-room was one, the private chapel is one of the two most exhilarating Gothic revival interiors along with the library, whose vaulted ceiling was designed to look like a church; while across the grounds from the main body of the castle, the Fitzalan chapel forms one end of the parish church. The vast proportions reach a climax in the barons' hall, 15 m (50 ft) high and 40 m (133 ft) long.

Family history is told by the sumptuous array of portraits that depict successive generations. The poet Earl of Arundel, beheaded by Henry VIII, was painted by Stretes; the poet's father, the ruthless 3rd Duke, by Mytens. (The Duke encouraged two successive nieces, Anne Boleyn and Katherine Howard, to become wives of Henry VIII and consequently lose their heads – a fate from which he was only saved by the king's death.) The collector 14th Earl of Arundel, many of whose treasures were destroyed by the parliamentary sacking, is shown twice painted by Van Dyck, once with his Talbot heiress wife and once with his son. The groups of works by Mytens and Van Dyck are outstanding, but the picture gallery as a whole rivals any in England for historical importance. Later additions came from Worksop Manor and Norfolk House which also provided much of the outstanding eighteenth-century furniture. While most houses have their particular 'keepsakes', few are of the importance of Mary, Queen of Scots's rosary, bequeathed by Mary to Anne Dacre, wife of St Philip Howard.

GOODWOOD HOUSE, Chichester

The Earl of March
Tel: 01243 774107

Off A27, 5 km (3 miles) north of Chichester
Open: 7 April, Sun and Mon to end Sept, Sun and Mon;
also Aug, Tues, Wed and Thur; 2–5 (Closed on event days)
Prices available on request
Tea room

The French spy, Louise de Kerouaille, Duchess of Portsmouth could claim the distinction of being Charles II's most beautiful mistress. Her son was made Duke of Richmond and given the usual fistful of additional titles. He bought Goodwood House as his hunting lodge. Its incomparable setting on the South Downs inspired the 3rd Duke to build the racecourse and during his long life he transformed both the lodge and its surroundings. William Chambers built the stables for him during the 1760s, demonstrating his mastery of pure classical architecture. Towards the end of the century the 3rd Duke turned to James Wyatt to execute a scheme of monumental grandeur: an octagon with a series of classical façades and a domed tower at each corner. The present house is the three sides of the octagon that were completed.

Only from the air does the house have a peculiar appearance; from the ground the combination of the flint walls, two-storey colonnade on the entrance front and the green-domed towers presents a harmonious whole. Inside Wyatt's marvellous tapestry room survives intact with its Gobelin tapestries of Don Quixote, rich neo-classical decoration and white marble chimney-piece. Here successive monarchs from Edward VII have held meetings of the Privy Council while in residence for Goodwood races.

Other rooms display the treasures acquired or collected by successive generations. Not surprisingly, there are outstanding royal Carolean portraits by Van Dyck, Lely, Wissing and Kneller which hang in the ballroom – planned as a gallery by the 3rd Duke. His patronage of the arts is constantly evident. The receipt of payment for his superb portrait by Reynolds is preserved in the house; his portrait by Romney is of similar quality. He also collected much of the French furniture and porcelain. Other highlights include paintings by Canaletto, the best being the famous commissioned pair of Whitehall and the Thames painted from the windows of Richmond House in London, and, as one might expect, a Stubbs of the 3rd Duke's horses training at Goodwood.

PARHAM HOUSE, *Pulborough*

Parham Park Ltd
Tel: 01903 744888 (information)

Off A283, 3 km (2 miles) west of Storrington
Open: Easter to end Oct, Wed, Thur, Sun and Bank Holidays, 2–6
(last admission 5)
£4.25, children £1, concessions
Home-made teas

Situated beneath the South Downs, Parham is a distinguished Elizabethan house. In 1922 it was acquired by Clive Pearson and his wife who restored and adorned it with fine works of art, notably Tudor and Stuart paintings. Their work was continued by their

daughter, Mrs Tritton, until her death in 1993 and the house is now the home of her great-niece, Lady Emma Guinness. Built in 1557, Parham was sold in 1601 to the Bysshopp family whose descendants lived in the house until 1922. Bysshopps became baronets and, in 1816, revived the ancient barony of Zouche. The 17th Baroness Zouche sold Parham, when it lacked water, drains or electricity and alarming amounts of the roof.

The 1577 house was built of local grey stone with Horsham 'slabs' on the roof. It remains satisfyingly faithful to its original period. The traditional 'E'-plan has gabled wings and a central porch while the entrance front's most striking feature is the towering mullioned and transomed windows of the great hall. Under the Pearsons the existing parkland setting was enhanced with replanted and extended gardens.

For many visitors it is the works of art at Parham, notably the historical portraits collected by Clive Pearson, that are the highlight. Tudor monarchs and leading members of their courts look down from walls, familiar faces such as Charles II (by Verelst) and some less familiar, such as Edward VI by Stretes, with the occasional flourish such as Robert Peake's large portrait of James I's eldest son, Henry Frederick, Prince of Wales, riding a white charger. His younger brother, Charles, was painted by Mytens when he became Prince of Wales. The royal figures are not only English. In the parlour hang Claude Deruet's double equestrian portrait of Louis XIII and his wife, Louis XIII's father, Henri IV, Elizabeth of Bohemia and her husband. There are many Bysshopp faces and Knatchbulls (Mrs Pearson's family). For variety from the portraits there are seascapes, a kangaroo painted by Stubbs and a mouth-watering view of Venice by Bellotto.

Needlework is second only to the paintings and is predominantly Jacobean and Stuart; the furniture is equally suitable, extending from fine Tudor oak to early-Georgian walnut and a few excursions into later eighteenth-century mahogany. There is much else besides, not least a room devoted to Sir Joseph Banks, connected to the Knatchbulls by marriage.

ST MARY'S, *Bramber*

Peter Thorogood
Tel: 01903 816205

In Bramber off A283, 16 km (10 miles) north-west of Brighton

Open: Easter to end Sept, Thur, Sun, and Bank Holidays; also July, Aug and Sept, Mon; 2–6
£3.50, children £2, concessions
Tea room

After wartime occupation, when the house was driven into by a tank, St Mary's seemed doomed, and was only saved by Dorothy Ellis outbidding a reclamation merchant who wanted the timbers and stone. She began the restoration which, in more recent years, has been carried on by Peter Thorogood, to celebrate the house's fifteenth-century origins and distinguished features.

The quality of the building with its roof of Horsham stone and closely timbered overhanging upper storey is easily explained; it originally formed one side of a courtyard built during the 1470s for William of Waynfleet, a cleric of substance, Bishop of Winchester and founder of Magdalen College, Oxford. St Mary's was built on a site that had been granted to the Knights Templar during the twelfth century, when Bramber was a thriving port on the River Adur.

Now the restoration has removed some of the more intrusive alterations that took place once St Mary's ceased to be a monastic hostelry and eventually descended to a rough farmhouse. The work has made the best of the panelled rooms, where highlights are carved oak doors and chimney-pieces. The Gothic stone chimney-pieces were introduced around 1896 by the Hon Algernon Bourke who restored the house at that time. In the parlour there is a Dutch-style wainscot with ebony panels, while the gilt and flower-painted leather wall-covering along the passage has been expertly restored, as have the arched panels of the painted room, each with a landscape or seascape. Probably early-seventeenth century, they represent a rare early example of *trompe-l'oeil*. Among Peter Thorogood's major additions is the unrivalled collection of work by the nineteenth-century comic artist and poet, Thomas Hood.

MIDLANDS AND WALES

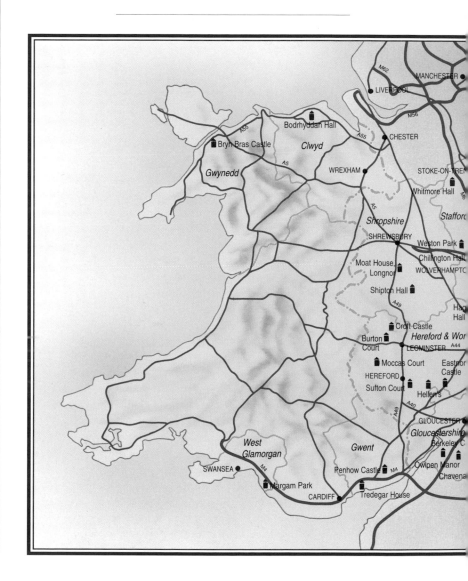

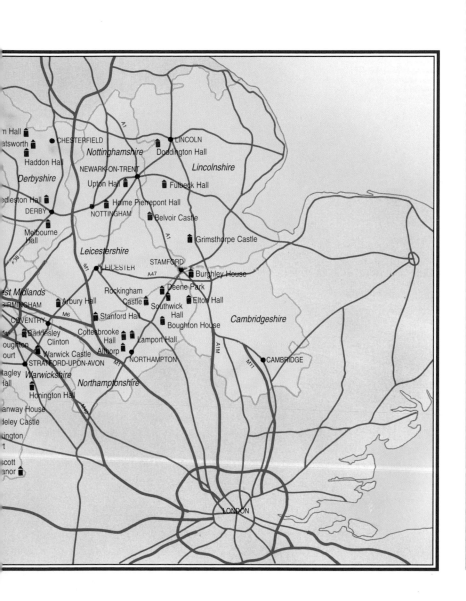

BURGHLEY HOUSE, *Stamford*

Burghley House Preservation Trust
Tel: 01780 52451

Off B1081, 1.6 km (1 mile) south-east of Stamford

Open: details available on request

Prices available on request

Burghley is for many people the greatest house built in the exuberant Elizabethan age. Completed in 1587, it is the place where Tudor becomes Renaissance, in a manner sophisticated and reflecting the status of its builder, William Cecil, 1st Lord Burghley,

the pre-eminent statesman of his time. Built around a central courtyard, with a series of adjoining state rooms on the first floor, the house continues to evoke the period of its construction and the personality of William Cecil – captured in his portrait by Marcus Gheeraerts. At the same time the contributions of subsequent generations over four centuries have made it a treasure-trove of collecting and patronage. English portraits from the sixteenth to the twentieth centuries, Old Master paintings, English and Continental furniture and Chinese and Japanese porcelain are fortes, but few areas of the decorative arts are absent.

Burghley's son was made Earl of Exeter and the 5th Earl, John, during the last two decades of the seventeenth century, was the next to have a dramatic influence on the house. Interiors were painted in rich Baroque style by Louis Laguerre and – in particular – Antonio Verrio – whose decoration of the Heaven Room is his masterpiece. Edward Marten provided ornate plaster ceilings and Grinling Gibbons exquisite wood carving. The 5th Earl travelled extensively on the continent collecting for Burghley. His acquisitions included Gobelin tapestries and furniture from France, paintings and works of art from Italy – all on a scale illustrated by a total of over three hundred important paintings. He also built up a notable library, now in the great hall.

His great-grandson Brownlow, the 9th Earl, effectively completed the decoration of the interiors at the same time as bringing to Burghley a second period of rich artistic additions. He commissioned a large quantity of the house's most important furniture, much of it from the leading firm of London cabinet-makers, Ince and Mayhew (who built two of Burghley's four magnificent state beds), and added the marble chimney-pieces when completing the decoration of the set of four 'George' rooms.

Like the 5th Earl, Brownlow collected extensively on the continent, as the further groups of Old Masters that he added testify. As important as any of his additions was his commission of 'Capability' Brown to landscape the park and give Burghley the superb setting it enjoys today. Brown also made a number of architectural alterations to the house, demonstrating to good effect this lesser known of his skills.

While there was no subsequent decoration or collecting on a comparable scale to that of the late-seventeenth and late-eighteenth centuries, each generation left its own important mark. Highlights of these later periods are the portraits of Brownlow's son, Henry (who was made Marquess of Exeter) and his wife and daughter by Lawrence; the pair of portraits by Gainsborough of Sir Christopher Whichcote and his wife (ancestors of the 4th Marchioness); the refurbishment of the George rooms for a visit by Queen Victoria and Prince Albert in 1844; the circular drum table on which Disraeli drew up his plans for the Congress of Berlin in 1878; and a selection of medals and trophies won by the 6th Marquess – famous as a gold-medal winning Olympic hurdler and painted in his Cambridge 'blue' blazer by Oswald Birley.

Today Burghley is the focus of a thriving estate and owned by a private charitable trust, for whom Lady Victoria Leatham (the youngest daughter of the 6th Marquess) and her husband and family occupy and care for the house, instilling an atmosphere whose liveliness softens the house's scale and richness.

ELTON HALL, *Peterborough*

Mr and Mrs William Proby
Tel: 01832 280468

On A605, 8 km (5 miles) south-west of Peterborough

**Open: Easter Mon, May and Aug Bank Holiday Suns and Mons;
July and Aug, Wed and Sun; also Aug, Thur
(telephone for further details)
£4, children £2 (under-fives free)**

The Proby family's occupation of Elton spans over three centuries, dating from Sir Peter Proby, whose grandson greatly extended the existing fifteenth-century tower and chapel, completing his work in 1666. During the late-eighteenth and early-nineteenth century further extensions gave the house a theatrically Gothic appearance, but during the mid-nineteenth century some of these were removed so that now the Gothic style is largely limited to the south-facing garden front.

The outstanding attractions are the library, furniture and paintings. Reynolds's friendship with the family is confirmed by his likenesses of them, as well as his self-portrait and another portrait of Kitty Fisher – banished to the housekeeper's room during the nineteenth-century on account of her loose reputation.

During the eighteenth century the family gained the title of Earl of Carysfort. In 1828 the 1st Earl's collection – excepting the Reynolds and other portraits – was sold. This dispersal partly inspired the 5th Earl to collect himself which he did with assured and varied taste. In addition to Old Masters, which are arranged with early portraits in the main dining-room upstairs, he collected the works of his Victorian contemporaries. In the lower octagon room are Henry Nelson O'Neil's 'Eastward Ho!' and Sir Lawrence Alma-Tadema's 'A Dedication to Bacchus'. Millais' 'The Minuet', showing the artist's daughter, hangs over the fireplace in the yellow drawing-room. Upstairs in the ante-dining-room a Constable of Dedham Vale and a Gainsborough landscape whet the appetite for the array in the main dining-room which includes works by Girolamo Genga, Hobbema, Poussin and Luini.

The 5th Earl purchased the magnificent pair of cabinets in the yellow drawing-room, made to order for William Beckford, and many other of the finest items of furniture at Elton. He was also able to make good much of the damage done to the library by fire in 1894, so that its twelve thousand or so volumes (especially strong in liturgical books and bibles, such as Henry VIII's *Prayer Book*), remain one of the finest private collections. Built up steadily from the time of Sir Thomas Proby, the library contains contributions from almost all generations of the family.

CHATSWORTH, *Bakewell*

Chatsworth House Trust
Tel: 01246 582204

On A263, 6.5 km (4 miles) east of Bakewell
Open: end Mar to end Oct, daily, 11–4.30
£5.75, children £3, concessions
[Chatsworth is unable to offer free entry to HHA Friends]
Restaurant

Chatsworth presents an unrivalled image of a ducal country seat: a great house, set in noble parkland, surrounded by impressive gardens, with splendid stables, quaint farms, and inside, endless evidence that it has been for centuries the home of an illustrious family. Most of these generations have left their mark and part of the appeal is the sense that far from being a period piece preserved with subsequent titivation, Chatsworth has evolved, accumulating steadily along the way. Today a good deal of the accumulation is from other Devonshire houses (the absent-minded Victorian statesman, the 8th Duke, could never remember how many homes he had), in particular Devonshire House in London, Chiswick villa (the home of Lord Burlington whose daughter married the 4th Duke), and Compton Place in Eastbourne.

Bess of Hardwick's Tudor house was replaced at the end of the seventeenth century by the 1st Duke of Devonshire in a building programme of twenty years that was just completed when he died in 1707. The Duke was closely involved and may himself have designed the west front that greets visitors looking across the park; a first view few ever forget. Prior to this, William Talman designed the south front facing the long canal and the east front looking across gardens to the wooded hill beyond. The west front came next, then, in 1705, after the architect Thomas Archer had already given Chatsworth the most exciting garden building in the country – the cascade house – he rebuilt the north front.

Just over a hundred years later Jeffry Wyatville rebuilt the east front and added the north wing. In between the periods of building activity at the house the 4th Duke commissioned James Paine to build the suitably ducal stable block, and the new bridge over the River Derwent whose course had been altered in 'Capability' Brown's landscaping of the park.

The 1st Duke employed a team of craftsmen who together gave Chatsworth some of the finest Baroque interiors in England. Walls and ceilings were painted by Verrio and Laguerre and later Thornhill, Tijou provided ironwork, and Cibber executed designs for rich carving. Much of this was executed by Samuel Watson who was born a few miles from Chatsworth. Despite humble origins Watson produced quantities of work of unrivalled quality, an interesting parallel to the degree to which house and estate are proudly self-sufficient today. The chapel is Chatsworth's Baroque highpoint and Watson carved the memorable alabaster altarpiece. Thornhill's later painting of the Sabine Room provides another rich spectacle.

Much of Wyatville's work for the 6th Duke aimed to make Chatsworth convenient to live in, while his more substantial internal alterations included the series of libraries for his employer's ever-increasing quantity of books. Outside, the Duke's gardener, Paxton, was ever busier constructing and planting. Even if his great conservatories have gone, his Emperor fountain – planned for a visit by the Emperor of Russia that never took place – glass wall-cases, cascades and rockeries, pinetum and arboretum all survive to celebrate this tireless polymath.

Both house and garden – as well as all other estate enterprises – have been energetically and lovingly attended to by the present Duchess and it is her contribution that has added a vital element for visitors. The works of art testify to the discernment of family collectors such as the 2nd Duke and few houses rival their quantity. But such is the atmosphere that has been instilled in recent decades that a tour of the house is not overpowering and indigestible. If to 'do' Chatsworth comprehensively in and out should take a week, a majority of visitors would be happy to stay the distance.

EYAM HALL, *Eyam*

R.H.V. Wright
Tel: 01433 631976

In Eyam off A623, 19 km (12 miles) west of Chesterfield
Open: end Mar to early Nov, Wed, Thur, Sun and Bank Holidays, 11–4.30
£3.25, children £2.25, concessions
Tea room

The spectacular countryside of the Derbyshire peak district is justifiably among the most popular in England and heading from the sprawling metropolis of Sheffield to Eyam, a mere 24 km (15 miles) to the south-west, one is reminded why. But of the thousands of annual visitors to the area, few have yet discovered Eyam Hall, which first opened to the public in 1992. The village gained a reputation for self-sacrifice during the plague of 1665, when having suffered an outbreak via a parcel of cloth from London, it imposed its own quarantine to prevent the disease spreading.

A few years later, in 1671, Eyam Hall was rebuilt and extended by Thomas Wright for his son, John, who had married a local heiress, Elizabeth Kniveton. The family have occupied the house ever since. John's house was built with local millstone grit and its low, gabled entrance front with mullioned windows, looking on to a protective courtyard seems to reflect the tough but impressive peak landscape that surrounds it. Inside, the house retains a small-scale intimacy; the succession of rooms are full of interest but never imposing. An extensive collection of family portraits illustrate the characters of successive generations, while good English furniture – an unusual pair of settles and a fine tester bed contemporary with the house, and George I chairs – make an enjoyable ensemble. The collection of toys and dolls in the nursery dates back to 1850 and is in keeping with this welcoming family home.

HADDON HALL, *Bakewell*

The Duke of Rutland
Tel: 01629 812855

On A6, 3 km (2 miles) south-east of Bakewell

**Open: Apr to end Sept, daily (closed Sun, July and Aug, except Bank
Holiday weekend), 11–5.45**
£4.50, children £2.80, concessions
Restaurant

Haddon has an air of romance that comes from its position on a wooded hillside above the Derbyshire Wye, its castellated stone walls and towers around two courtyards and hanging terraced gardens, its ancient establishment, neglect for nearly two centuries and, not least, its heroine Dorothy Vernon whose elopement with John Manners and their subsequent marriage gave the house to the Manners family who have owned it ever since. By 1703 when their earldom became the dukedom of Rutland they were based at Belvoir Castle and Haddon was maintained empty. In 1912 the 9th Duke began the restoration that became his life's work, preserving the house's architecture and features built up over five hundred years, while once again making it habitable.

William the Conqueror's illegitimate son, Peveril of the Peak, owned Haddon but the house dates from the twelfth century. It remains superbly medieval, a link between defensive castles which produced the west front rising from Norman walls, and later country houses. From its Norman beginnings Haddon evolved principally during the two centuries after 1370, the year when Sir Richard de Vernon IV built the great hall which divides the house's two courtyards. Later highlights were Sir Henry Vernon's completion of the dining-room and great chamber and finally, around 1603, the decoration by John Manners of the Elizabethan long gallery on the south side overlooking the gardens.

Architecturally and in their decorations, all the main rooms are of considerable importance. The hall retains much of its original timber structure. The dining-room has panelling surmounted by carved heraldic emblems and portrait medallions, and bright heraldic paintings in ceiling panels. The great chamber above and the long gallery with Renaissance-

patterned panelling are equally fine. The chapel has contributions from most of the building generations of which the medieval wall paintings are the chief glory. Suitably in a primarily medieval house, tapestries are of foremost decorative importance. The oldest is French, dating from around 1460 and carries the English royal arms. It may have been a gift from Henry VIII's older brother, Prince Arthur, to whom Sir Henry Vernon was Treasurer. The most striking tapestries are a seventeenth-century Mortlake set (probably owned by Charles I), depicting the senses, the borders decorated with scenes from Aesop's fables. Furniture includes an absorbing range of sixteenth- and seventeenth-century chairs.

Hanging over the gallery fireplace is a painting of Haddon by Rex Whistler, done in 1933, which captures the place's alluring atmosphere. For most visitors the series of stone-terraced gardens that descend beneath the rose-clad walls of the south front are integral to this atmosphere, their different size and levels given uniformity by balustraded walls and continuing the theme of variety so noticeable in the house itself.

KEDLESTON HALL, *Derby*

The National Trust / Viscount Scarsdale
Tel: 01332 842191

Signed from A38, 6.5 km (4 miles) north-west of Derby
Open: Apr to end Oct, Sat to Wed, also Bank Holiday Mon,
1–5.30 (last admission 5)
£4.20, children £2.10
Tea room

Arguably the National Trust's most important country house acquisition in recent years, Kedleston ranks high among the architectural achievements of the eighteenth century. It had been the home of Curzons for centuries before Sir Nathaniel Curzon inherited in 1758 and immediately decided to replace the existing house. Initially he consulted Matthew Bettingham, who had been working on Holkham Hall, the Palladian seat of the Earl of Leicester (who died in 1759), before turning to James Paine for further advice and designs. In turn Paine had to bow out to the ambitious young luminary of British architecture, Robert Adam, fresh from a tour of Italy and determined to secure the major commissions of the day.

All three architects had a hand in the house's external appearance which is utterly memorable, whether looking towards the porticoed north (entrance) front principally by Paine, the central block joined by colonnades to two side pavilions, or the south (garden) front. This is Adam's work, and exemplifies his idea of 'movement'. Twin balustraded flights of steps sweep up from ground level to the *piano nobile*. Free-standing

from the façade are the Corinthian columns that recall a Roman triumphal arch and the house is surmounted by a dome inspired by the Pantheon in Rome. Adam planned colonnades leading to a pair of side pavilions on this front, to match the existing ones on the north side, but Lord Scarsdale's funds seem to have been exhausted and the south pavilions were never built.

In 1761, during the completion of the house, Curzon was ennobled as the 1st Lord Scarsdale, and was able, to commission the series of interiors by Adam which more than complement the house's exterior. From the central hall, with its peristyle of local alabaster columns and statues in niches, and circular saloon beyond with its coffered dome, and the succession of state rooms on either side, the decoration is extraordinarily assured when one considers that this was Adam's first major commission in England. Chimney-pieces, doorcases, coved ceilings and the apse at one end of the dining-room, all balance magnificence with a supreme delicacy of craftsmanship in a way that was to become the hallmark of Adam's interior work.

The rooms were planned to display Scarsdale's collection of Italian and Dutch Old Master paintings and most still hang as he and Adam planned. They include Giordano's 'Triumph of Bacchus' in the music room and Cuyp's 'Landscape in the Rhine Valley' in the drawing-room, but the collection as a whole is as distinguished as the individual works. The quality is matched by furniture, including gilded sofas made by John Linnell, and the state bed by James Gravenor.

Lord Scarsdale's and Adam's ensemble, including the park which they landscaped together, moving the passing road in the process, and which with its lake spanned by a triple-arched bridge, gives the house a suitable setting, has been left virtually untouched by successive generations of Curzons. But the house contains their portraits and mementoes, in particular those of George Nathaniel, Marquess Curzon of Kedleston and Viceroy of India between 1898 and 1905.

MELBOURNE HALL, *Melbourne*

The Lord Ralph Kerr
Tel: 01332 862502

In Melbourne on B587, 14.5 km (9 miles) south of Derby off A453

Open: Aug, daily except Mon, 2–5
£4.50, children £2.50
Tea room

Melbourne is an engaging country house. Once the home of Queen Victoria's favourite Prime Minister, Lord Melbourne, it stands in the manner of a French *petit château*, on the edge of its eponymous village and beside a beautiful Norman church. In addition to the enduring attraction of the overall scene, Melbourne is of great importance for its formal garden in the manner of André le Nôtre. Laid out by Thomas Coke, it is a rare survivor from the early eighteenth century and rivalled by only one or two gardens from the period. From the sweep of lawn descending to a sheet of water in front of the house, radial avenues and walks between clipped hedges lead off into woodland on one side. There are waterworks and superb ornaments including the delightful 'Birdcage Arbour' made of wrought iron by Robert Bakewell, whose smithy was in Melbourne village, and the lead 'Four Seasons' urn by Jan van Nost. These two are the finest work of their kind in any English garden.

The architecture of the house is irregular, seventeenth-century at the back, with a fine provincial eighteenth-century façade by William Smith of Warwick looking over the sloping garden to the arbour. The colourful interiors are full of elegant furniture and the distinguished collection of seventeenth-century English portraits includes Lely's double portrait of Lord and Lady Chesterfield (Coke's parents-in-law), and Jacob Huysmans' masterpiece of Thomas Coke's children.

BELVOIR CASTLE, *Grantham*

The Duke of Rutland
Tel: 01476 870262

Between A607 and A52, 11 km (7 miles) south-west of Grantham

Open: Apr to Oct, Tues, Wed, Thur and Sat, 11–5 (Sun and Bank Holidays 11–6; Oct, Sun, 11–5)
£4, children £2.50, concessions
Restaurant

Belvoir should be approached from the Grantham to Melton Mowbray road. Dropping down into the village of Woolsthorpe, the castle appears proudly surmounting its wooded eminence, the realization of Victorian picturesque medievalism. From this distance the whole is satisfyingly harmonious and the continued approach offers a shifting picture of turrets, towers and battlements. Inside, cavernous rooms date from the rebuilding of the castle carried out by the 5th Duke and, more especially his Duchess Elizabeth, who hailed from Castle Howard. In 1801 James Wyatt was commissioned and continued work until his death in 1813, by which time two of the main fronts and many interiors were complete. Three years later fire destroyed most of his internal work and reconstruction was carried out by the Duke's chaplain, the Rev Sir John Thoroton with the amateur-architect Duchess closely involved.

In the Elizabeth saloon the Duchess commissioned Matthew Cotes Wyatt to create a sumptuous room with white and gilded wall panels. Wyatt painted the rich ceiling panels depicting Juno and Jupiter and arranged the red damask and gilded Louis XV-style furniture made for the room. He also sculpted the Duchess full length in white marble to stand at one end.

The one marvel of the fire was the survival of Wyatt's Regent's gallery, named in honour of a royal visit in 1814, which is the most splendid room in the castle. The central bow perfectly offsets the room's great length, the rose-red ground of the Gobelin tapestries illustrating the adventures of Don Quixote complements the damask shade of the original curtains, and carpet woven with a pattern of arum lilies. Maplewood doors and a variety of grand Regency furniture add to the overall composition. Gilded rococo pier glasses and portraits alternate with the tapestries, while a succession of busts by Nollekens on pedestals give continuity from one end to the other.

In the picture gallery the 4th Duke's contribution to Belvoir is clear; although most of the Old Masters that he collected were destroyed in the 1816 fire, there remains ample evidence of his connoisseurship: five Poussins depicting the seven sacraments, works by Teniers and van Steen, and three Gainsborough landscapes being a selection of the best.

STANFORD HALL, *Lutterworth*

The Lady Braye
Tel: 01788 860250

Off A14, 11 km (7 miles) north-east of Rugby, 3 km (2 miles) from M1 exit 19 (from north only) and M6 junction

Open: Easter Sat to end Sept, Sat, Sun and Bank Holidays (also Tues, following), 2.30–5.30 (last admission 5)
£3.50, children £1.70, concessions
Home-made teas

Robin Fedden described Stanford's south front as 'a textbook example of the William III style' and the visitor has to agree. Immaculately proportioned and faced in grey ashlar, its hipped roof with dormers over two storeys, with tall sash windows and side projections, it exemplifies the elegant style of the period. Part of Stanford's charm, however, derives from the balance of its different faces. From the park which extends to the River Avon the south front can be enjoyed at the same time as the similar one facing east, similar but different in period.

Around 1690 Sir Roger Cave, whose family had been at Stanford since the fifteenth century, commissioned the architects, Smiths of Warwick to build a new house. The estimate for £2,137.10.0 for demolishing the old house and building a new one is preserved in the library. William Smith executed the south front; his son Francis built the stables whose juxtaposition to the house is so integral to Stanford's charm. He probably also built the east front looking towards the stables and river at the same time, forsaking the expensive ashlar for mellow red brick.

The impressive double-balustraded stairway leading up to the entrance on the east front was added during the 1880s but otherwise, since the removal of a Victorian addition, Stanford is the work of the Smiths. This is also true of the interiors. William Smith planned the grey drawing-room and east staircase; his son Francis added the fine main staircase, and his son, William the younger, remodelled the original hall into the present ballroom with its lofty coved ceiling and impressive pedimented doorcase and chimney-piece.

Sir Roger Cave's son, Thomas, married Margaret Verney, who brought the ancient barony of Braye to the family – albeit in abeyance, which it remained until revived in 1839 in favour of Sarah Otway-Cave who became the 3rd Baroness. Family portraits bring together the stories of Cave and Verney and testify to the latter family's devoted royalism. There are portraits after Van Dyck of Charles I and his wife Henrietta Maria, and of the King's standard-bearer, Sir Edmund Verney, who was killed

grasping the royal standard at Edgehill and whose hand had to be cut off to release the standard. Exactly two hundred years after the battle, Sarah Otway-Cave, who had become Lady Braye, purchased in Rome the collection of pictures and Stuart relics that had belonged to Henry Stuart, Cardinal Duke of York. Most of the portraits hang in the ballroom providing a rare and fascinating insight into royal Stuart history.

The visitor should not leave without paying tribute to the earlier generations of the Cave family who are preserved in spectacular tombs in the adjacent church of St Nicholas. An unexpected discovery is the aviation museum in the stables which honours the friend of the 6th Lord Braye, Percy Pilcher, the first man to fly in England. Pilcher was killed in 1899 when his glider crashed in the park at Stanford. A replica of his machine 'The Hawk' is the museum's main exhibit, having been presented by the Royal Aeronautical Society.

DODDINGTON HALL, *Doddington*

Mr and Mrs A.G. Jarvis
Tel: 01522 694308

On B1190, 8 km (5 miles) west of Lincoln
Open: May to end Sept, Wed, Sun and Bank Holiday Mon, 2–6
£3.70, children £1.85, concessions
Restaurant

Doddington Hall was designed by Robert Smythson and makes an intriguing comparison to earlier, more theatrical masterpieces of this most distinguished Elizabethan architect: Longleat, Wollaton and Hardwick. Only its trio of cupolas lighten the unfussy, confident symmetry of the stone-quoined brick exterior which is reminiscent of Burton Agnes in Yorkshire, where Smythson began work in 1601 – the year after he finished at Doddington. Like Burton Agnes (see page 222), Doddington is approached via a delightful gatehouse (Dutch-gabled Elizabethan as opposed to Burton Agnes's later Jacobean one) and a square walled courtyard.

During the eighteenth century extensive interior work was carried out by Sir John Delaval, one of the more sober members of the notorious Delaval clan, who inherited from his grandmother. The hall – recently redecorated to its original Delaval colour scheme, parts of which survived under layers of white paint – sets the tone for the succeeding rooms with its cool Palladianism. Sir John was careful to preserve the structure of the main rooms, especially the long gallery which fills almost all of the top floor along the west front. His most noticeable change was the staircase, replacing the old Elizabethan one with the present one of restrained elegance with double flights.

Despite the various changes in name through marriage, the family succession of Doddington has been unbroken for four hundred years and this is reflected in the contents, notably the paintings. Smythson's patron, Thomas Tailor, is shown; there are Husseys by Michael Dahl, and many Delavals – two groups of children by Arthur Pond, Sir Francis Delaval, dashing in uniform, by Reynolds who also painted the important group that has always hung at the end of the gallery of Sarah Delaval, her husband Lord Pollington (later Earl of Mexborough) and their son dressed for George III's coronation. A beguiling likeness by Lawrence is one of two portraits of Sarah Gunman who, in the early nineteenth century, left Doddington to her lover, Captain George Jarvis, from whom the present owner is descended. The close connection with the Delaval's main seat at Seaton Delaval is emphasized by two views of the great Vanbrugh palace.

There is much good porcelain in the house – English, continental and oriental – some collected by the Delavals and most of the rest, notably the collection in the gallery, by Edwin Jarvis during the nineteenth century. The furniture is similarly varied: a rare set of Cromwellian bobbin chairs, Venetian and Dutch marquetry chests, an impressive pair of Naples ebony cabinets with painted glass panels and an 1805 Broadwood satinwood grand piano. The glorious bed in the Tiger room came from Seaton Delaval where it had been slept in by the Duke of Cumberland on his way to Culloden – when he weighed 146 kg (23 stone).

The enjoyable mixture was not all there in Sir John Delaval's day but he was so fond of Doddington that, when his ownership was disputed by his brothers on his inheritance of Seaton Delaval – the terms of his grandmother's will had precluded ownership of both properties, he cut down all the trees on the estate in rage and, as Antony Jarvis says, when a compromise was reached, 'lived out his life in a treeless and windswept parish'.

FULBECK HALL, *Grantham*

Mr and Mrs Michael Fry
Tel: 01400 272205

On A607, 18 km (11 miles) north of Grantham
Open: Easter, May and Aug Bank Holidays, also daily in July, 2–5
£3, children £1, concessions (1995 prices)
Tea room

The Fane family have owned Fulbeck since 1622 when Francis Fane (created Earl of Westmorland two years later) acquired the property from his cousin, Sir George Manners. The family have survived at Fulbeck despite various calamities. In 1731 a fire destroyed the house all but the service wing; the owner went bankrupt in 1887, but the property was bought by a Fane cousin; and the house was nearly ruined by the military after it was requisitioned for the Second World War. The present owners, Mary (née Fane) and Michael Fry, are still restoring parts of the house damaged during the war. One legacy of interest from the war years, however, is the Arnhem Museum, opened in the house since 1994. In 1944 Fulbeck was headquarters for the 1st Airborne Division who fought at Arnhem and the original operations' room is now the museum.

Elegant wrought iron gates lead, via an avenue of ancient limes, to the handsome Georgian house. The 1730s rebuilding was carried out by a local Stamford architect and his work predominates, with additions from later in the eighteenth century. The most prominent of these is the bowed north extension which was added in 1784. It offered welcome extra space to the then owner, the Hon Henry Fane, his wife and their fourteen children. The last addition was completed in 1902 by William Vere Reeve Fane.

In the interior the 1730s panelling has survived in the hall, staircase and landing. Pilasters, such a distinctive feature in stone on the exterior, reappear flanking the front door inside the hall doorway, across the hall, on either side of the staircase arch and, in reduced scale, in the oak panelling of the stairs. The drawing-room and morning-room are both of the 1840s, remodelled for General Sir Henry Fane. The dining-room dates from his parents' additions of 1784, and the library was created by William Dashwood Fane in 1894.

Fulbeck has connections with the 1st Duke of Wellington. Harriet, twelfth child of the Hon Henry Fane, became the Duke's closest female friend and intimate confidante from 1820 to her death in 1834. The family stress that she was not his mistress; the relationship was based on their mutual passion for politics. Harriet's cousin, Lady Georgina Fane, daughter of the 10th Earl of Westmorland, had rather different intentions, as a letter preserved in the drawing-room explains. It is from the eighty-year-old Duke to Lady Georgina's mother, asking the Dowager Countess to use her influence on Georgina to cease molesting him with 'daily vituperative letters'. She had mercilessly pursued the great soldier-statesman for decades, following a brief romance. She threatened to publicize his love letters to her and sue him for breaking a promise to marry her.

GRIMSTHORPE CASTLE, *Bourne*

Grimsthorpe and Drummond Castle Trust
Tel: 01778 591205

On A151, 6.5 km (4 miles) north-west of Bourne

**Open: Easter Sun to end Sept, Sun, Thur and Bank Holidays;
also Aug daily 2 – 6 (last admission) except Fri and Sat
£3, concessions
Tea room**

Grand and remote, Grimsthorpe sits improbably and dramatically on the edge of a Lincolnshire plateau. The long, straight approach is almost continental in its formal grandeur and much as Sir John Vanbrugh intended when he transformed the existing Tudor castle. The scale of the park, laid out later by 'Capability' Brown, including the enormous lake, increases the impressive nature of the scene.

It was a Duke of Suffolk who began the castle in the sixteenth century, and Dukes of Ancaster who commissioned Vanbrugh and Brown in the eighteenth. The ancient Willoughby de Eresby title dates from 1313 and can be held by a female, while the dukedom of Ancaster (created in 1715) became extinct in 1809 and the later earldom of Ancaster (created in 1892) similarly disappeared on the death of the present Lady Willoughby de Eresby's father in 1983, there being no male heir.

Hidden behind Vanbrugh's brooding facade, is a sixteenth-century quadrangle of great charm. Internally the house is romantic and exotic, with ceilings painted by the Italian Francesco Sleter, grand continental furniture and tapestries. The hall is considered by some to be Vanbrugh's noblest interior. Despite its size the house has an air of considerable privacy which complements the unspoilt remoteness of its position.

ALTHORP, *Northampton*

The Earl Spencer
Tel: 01604 770107

Off A428, 10 km (6 miles) north-west of Northampton

Open: Aug, daily, 2–5
£5, children £2.50, concessions
Tea room

Althorp remains brimming with evidence of generations of Spencer connoisseurship. Wealth from wool was the basis for the family's political and social supremacy as Earls of Sunderland. When the 5th Earl inherited the Marlborough dukedom in 1733, his younger brother, John, inherited Althorp. John's son was created Earl Spencer in 1765 and the house has passed in male descent to the 9th Earl who inherited on the death of his father in 1992.

The present house is principally the work of Henry Holland. In 1772 a section of the house's roof collapsed and Holland was commissioned by the 2nd Earl to transform the old building, part Tudor and part as altered during the seventeenth century. Holland's exterior, covered in grey mathematical tiles, is impressive but austere; the warm stone façades of Roger Morris's 1730 stables are more appealing.

The Wootton Hall, named after the series of pictures by John Wootton, was commissioned by the 5th Earl of Sunderland before he departed for Blenheim. The series of canvases, all ordered to fit the walls, illustrate his favourite horses. The house's centre is filled by the vast staircase

141

hall, or saloon (an open courtyard in the old house), where the walls are densely covered with portraits of unfailing quality. The collection reaches its zenith, however, in the picture gallery which survives from the old house. At the far end is one of Van Dyck's greatest pictures, the double portrait entitled 'War and Peace' depicting Lords Digby and Russell. Ranged along one wall are the Hampton Court beauties by Lely, all in the Sunderland frames named after the 2nd Earl who commissioned them. The ensemble is a rare experience.

The Marlborough room is hung principally with consummate works by Guercino, as well as others by Rubens and Salvator Rosa. These and many other Old Masters were collected by the 1st Earl Spencer. Throughout the house the rooms bear witness to the contributions by successive eighteenth-century craftsmen including Rysbrack, Vardy, Scheemakers and James 'Athenian' Stuart. Decorative highlights are in the South Drawing-Room, the Billiard Room and the Library, which is now hung with the house's unique collection of portraits by Reynolds, as well as works by Stubbs and Gainsborough. After the sale of Spencer House during the 1920s, the richness of Althorp's contents was increased.

Among such a quantity of artistic riches most people would be daunted by the challenge of making their own contribution, but in the short period of his occupation the present earl has achieved an impressive amount. A substantial programme of redecoration has encompassed every principal room and modified the richness of redecoration carried out for his father and stepmother. As well as restoring the chapel to its status, he has re-hung a number of the major pictures to present them to their best advantage, and Althorp is now restored to a state that would no doubt please his fastidious grandfather, the 7th (curator) Earl.

BOUGHTON HOUSE, *Kettering*

The Duke of Buccleuch and Queensberry and the Living Landscape Trust
Tel: 01536 515731

On A43, 5 km (3 miles) north of Kettering

Open: Aug, daily, 2–5
£4, concessions
Tea room

Approaching Boughton for the first time, a visitor might be forgiven for dreaming he was in France. No other house in England looks so authentically like a château. The effect is as intended by Ralph, 1st Duke of Montagu, who returned in 1678 from spending a decade as ambassador at the court of Louis XIV, to introduce England to French architecture and decoration. The mansard roof, arched colonnade and style of window are all in the French classical tradition. And yet the surprise of Boughton is that behind this elegant façade lies the Tudor building extended from a monks' hall by Sir Edward Montagu, Lord Chief Justice to Henry VIII.

Ralph Montagu's additions were married to the existing building so that many of the interiors retained their relative simplicity, small scale and low ceilings to a degree completely disguised by the grandeur of his north façade. Decorative changes were most noticeably applied to the great hall which lies at the centre of the village-like group. Its ancient hammerbeam roof is concealed above a richly painted barrel ceiling. The French flavour of the painting of the staircase hall by Louis Cheron and the 'Parquet de Versailles' floors extends to the furniture (including many exquisite gifts from Louis XIV himself), but not to the exclusion of English craftsmanship. There is rich evidence of Ralph's patronage of the Mortlake tapestry factory that he bought in 1674 and ran until 1691.

His collection of paintings was added to by his successors and today the array is the equal of the other Buccleuch houses. Ralph's son, the 2nd Duke, known as 'John the Planter', added 113 km (70 miles) of avenues to Boughton's estate. John's daughter, Mary married the Earl of Cardigan from neighbouring Deene Park who was created Duke of Montagu. When their son, the Marquess of Monthermer died aged thirty-five, Boughton was inherited by their daughter, Elizabeth who had married the Duke of Buccleuch.

The Buccleuch match meant – given they were mainly in Scotland or London – that Boughton was little used by the family for long periods, absence which preserved the atmosphere of the house's formative periods. Today Boughton is very much occupied by the family, its estates run with the admirably forward-thinking custodianship that they bring to all their extensive properties, and its works of art are readily available to both scholars and the more casual visitor.

COTTESBROOKE HALL, *Northampton*

Captain and Mrs John Macdonald-Buchanan
Tel: 01604 505808

Off A50 at Creaton, near A14, 16 km (10 miles) north of Northampton
Open: mid-Apr to end Sept, Thur and Bank Holiday Mon; also Sept, Sun;
gardens only, Wed and Fri; 2–5.30 (last admission 5)
£4, gardens only £2.50, children half-price
Tea room Plants for sale

A rose-brick house is a surprise in Northamptonshire, a county blessed with one of the best English building stones. Otherwise Cottesbrooke effortlessly joins the ranks of the county's most distinguished houses. Aligned on an axis with the spire of Brixworth church, 5 km (3 miles) away, it stands surrounded by gardens and eighteenth-century parkland. One can well imagine why Jane Austen was possibly inspired to use it as a model for *Mansfield Park*.

Completed in 1713 for Sir John Langham, Bt., and now generally attributed to Francis Smith of Warwick, the plan of a central block and flanking pavilions facing a courtyard exemplifies the architecture of that period. The outstanding internal addition was the mid-eighteenth-century rococo papier-mâché decoration by John Woolston of Northampton, carried out in the hall which retained its original marble cantilevered staircase.

Captain Macdonald-Buchanan's parents came to Cottesbrooke between the wars and made it a house of rare distinction. His mother was the only daughter of James Buchanan, Lord Woolavington, who used the fortune derived from his family's whisky business to build up the finest private collection of British sporting paintings in the world – rivalled only by the Mellon collection. The upper and lower curving corridors that link the west wing with the central block are both galleries giving a representative idea of the collection's quality. Outstanding in the china corridor is the Ferneley of Lord Craven's hunters at grass. Below is the comprehensive collection of Munnings's, many depicting Lord Woolavington's and his descendants' winning horses, as well as paintings of the Pytchley hounds and their huntsmen.

Ben Marshalls hang in the entrance hall with the Barraud brothers' painting of the

Beaufort Hunt, while the dining-room contains Marshall's masterpiece, 'Thomas Oldaker on Pickle', and 'Gimcrack on Newmarket Heath' by Stubbs – two of the most famous English sporting pictures. In the drawing-room an equestrian bronze of Empress Elizabeth of Austria recalls the period during the nineteenth century when she rented Cottesbrooke for hunting with the Pytchley. In addition there are collections of English, continental and oriental porcelain; and English and continental furniture includes a large Chippendale desk, Louis XV *fauteuils* and a Flemish cabinet-on-stand. Mainly gathered together during the last hundred years, the ensemble is an example of English connoisseurship in the best tradition.

DEENE PARK, *Corby*

Mr Edmund and the Hon Mrs Brudenell
Tel: 01780 450223/450278

On A43, 10 km (6 miles) north-east of Corby
Open: June, July and Aug, Sun and Bank Holidays, 2–5
£4, children £2 (under-10 free) concessions
Tea room

The intimate, mainly Elizabethan courtyard through which the visitor enters Deene would seem to set a tone; further progress reveals that it is only one flavour of the intriguing whole which Brudenells have added to since 1514. A tour of the outside moves from Elizabethan to Jacobean and then, along the south garden front, Tudor is extended by matching Georgian Gothic windows to give great length repeated in the gardens beyond, and canal and lake.

Seventeenth-century Brudenells were fiercely Royalist and Catholic. Their loyalty was rewarded in 1661 when Thomas Brudenell was made Earl of Cardigan. More settled times came in the eighteenth century, reflected in the set of three gracious rooms added along the south front sometime between 1750 and 1800, the Bow Room, Drawing-Room and Dining-Room.

The Bow Room's library reflects the scholarly leanings of generations of the family – the 1st Earl was especially upset when his books were removed from Deene by Cromwell's troops during the sacking of the house in 1643. Over the fireplace hangs Reynolds's sensitive portrait of Lady Mary Montagu, daughter and heiress of the 2nd Duke of Montagu. In the Drawing-Room family portraits mix with members of the Stuart royal family on account of the marriage of Anne Brudenell to Charles II's illegitimate son, the Duke of Richmond.

An unexpected change comes in the Dining-Room, where the most flamboyant member of the family, the 7th Earl of Cardigan who led the Charge of the Light Brigade, is introduced. Over the fireplace is his dashing portrait by de Prades leading the Charge. The artist's equestrian portrait of his second wife, Adeline de Horsey, hangs among Victorian Brudenells on the main staircase, part of the 5th Earl's additions. In the hall below is James Sant's group of the Earl describing the Battle of Balaklava to Prince Albert and the royal children. The Earl did not marry Adeline until 1858 and their subsequent behaviour scandalized society; not least the Queen who had originally been in the group but insisted on being removed when she heard of their goings-on.

Mr and Mrs Brudenell have carried out spirited restoration and a note of their gratitude to many helpers is to be found in the group of small portraits of members of the Deene staff by Richard Foster which hang in one of Deene's most intimate rooms, the Octagon.

LAMPORT HALL, *Northampton*

Lamport Hall Trust
Tel: 01604 686272

On A508, 13 km (8 miles) north of Northampton

Open: Easter to end Sept, Sun and Bank Holidays; also Aug, Mon to Sat; one tour at 4.30; 26 and 27 Oct, 2.15–5.15
£3.50, children £2, concessions
Home-made teas

Lamport's long, low façade looking out over parkland is easily enjoyed. It is also important, for the central block is a rare example of the architecture of John Webb, Inigo Jones's son-in-law. Webb was commissioned by Sir Justinian Isham, whose father had been given a baronetcy and whose family could boast settlement in the area from at least the Conquest.

Webb was commissioned to add to the existing house in 1654, but the troubles of the time often intruded; on occasion his patron sent instructions from prison. Sir Justinian's royalist sentiments were confirmed by his purchase of Van Dyck's huge

painting of Charles I on horseback which he hung in the High Room built by Webb. This caused Parliamentary displeasure, and his subsequent arrest was hardly surprising. The family's royal enthusiasm also accounted for the full-length portrait of Anne of Denmark by Van Somer and another similarly sized Van Dyck of Charles I with his horse, the original of which hangs in the Louvre. Sir Justinian's connoisseurship was continued by his son, Sir Thomas, as evidenced by the two magnificent Venetian cabinets that he collected on the grand tour, and his portrait by Maratti, but he died on the eve of his wedding aged twenty-four.

The 5th Baronet commissioned Francis Smith of Warwick to continue Lamport's changes, adding the wings that now flank Webb's central five-bay block. The library is the scholarly 5th Baronet's and the eighteenth century witnessed Lamport's elevation to a house of rounded quality with distinguished family portraits adding to Old Masters and the accumulation of good furniture, porcelain and other works of art.

It is sad that the 10th Baronet's collection of gnomes was almost entirely destroyed; now only one original survives in the china passage and the quaint figures that adorn the rockery are replicas. Visitors should cross the road to the adjacent church to admire the superb monument to the 5th Baronet, by Scheemakers. They should also acknowledge their debt to Gyles, the 12th Baronet, who bequeathed Lamport and its estate to an endowed trust to preserve it for public enjoyment.

ROCKINGHAM CASTLE, *Corby*

Commander Michael Saunders-Watson
Tel: 01536 770240

Off A6003, 3 km (2 miles) north of Corby

**Open: Easter to end Sept, Thur, Sun, Bank Holidays and Tues following;
also Aug, Tues; 1–5
£3.80, children £2.40, concessions
Tea room**

The year 1994 witnessed the nine-hundredth anniversary of Rockingham Castle, a span which divides with distinguished symmetry into two identical periods: four hundred and fifty years as a royal fortress and four hundred and fifty years as home of the Watson family. The views from the castle's pre-eminent position overlooking the broad Welland valley would have been equally commanding when William the Conqueror grasped the site's strategic importance and built one of the network of formidable castles from which he was able to subdue the native English. Successive monarchs used Rockingham for the next four centuries; King John was a frequent visitor and Edward I made substantial alterations to improve the secure but uncomfortable Norman castle for his queen, Eleanor. But towards the end of the fifteenth century the castle had lapsed into disrepair, Henry VIII leased it to Edward Watson and in 1619 his grandson, Sir Lewis Watson, bought the property from James I.

Edward I's gate with round towers was retained, as was the walled enclosure of the Norman outer bailey, but Edward Watson began the transformation from castle to house which his successors continued into the seventeenth century (especially after extensive damage by parliamentary forces during the Civil War who captured Rockingham, destroyed the Norman keep and retained the castle until the end of the war). Edward Watson added buildings to both ends of the thirteenth-century great hall and this range has steep Elizabethan gables. At one end is a long gallery wing, part Tudor but largely rebuilt after the Civil War, and altered again during the nineteenth century, when Anthony Salvin was commissioned to carry out both internal work and external additions, most prominent of which is the flag tower on the outside of the gallery wing.

Sir Lewis Watson was made Lord Rockingham, his grandson became an earl but those titles died out in 1746. Marriage to the daughter and heiress of Sir George Sondes of Lees Court in Kent meant that the family only used Rockingham as an occasional home during the eighteenth century, although some of its artistic highlights date from this period, when the Watsons were Lords Sondes. Eventually the Sondes family remained in Kent and a Watson brother continued the family's occupation of Rockingham.

The medieval character of Rockingham is best preserved in the cobbled 'street' of

service rooms and buildings. The old great hall was divided by Edward Watson into the present hall and adjacent panel room. The hall contains Tudor portraits in keeping with its period and including an important picture of Francis I of France by Joos van Cleeve. The elegant library has an eighteenth-century feel to it and the fine collection of books were largely assembled by the Sondes. But Rockingham's most memorable interior is the long gallery, successively remodelled until given its present form during the late-1830s when the bay window of Salvin's flag tower became a major new feature of the gallery. Charles Dickens immortalized the room when he used Rockingham as the model for Chesney Wold in *Bleak House*.

Generations of the Sondes family are represented in a series of outstanding paintings: single portraits by Lely, Reynolds and Angelica Kauffmann, and a family group by Dahl. Most memorable are two period pieces of rare quality: the children of the 1st Lord Sondes playing cricket by Zoffany, and the four sons of the 2nd Lord Sondes with their hounds by Ben Marshall. Few other rooms can boast two such pre-eminent, different sporting paintings.

SOUTHWICK HALL, *Oundle*

Christopher Capron
Tel: 01832 274064

Off A427, 5 km (3 miles) north-west of Oundle
Open: May to end Aug, Wed, Bank Holiday Sun and Mon, 2–5
£3, children £1.50, concessions
Tea room

Surrounded by some of the most palatial houses in the country, Southwick is refreshingly modest, its gables typifying the lesser manor houses of this area. Modesty does not mean lack of distinction and interest, nor of long establishment; of the original Knyvett family, Sir John was Edward III's Lord Chancellor and the house passed from them to the Lynns after the financial constraints of raising a ransom in the Hundred Years War.

Much of the medieval house remains, notably the fourteenth-century turreted tower overlooking a small courtyard, a vaulted room with distinctive doorways with shouldered heads and a circular stair turret, but the Lynns made considerable extensions during Tudor times and again during the eighteenth century. The oak panelling in one bedroom survives from the former, while the hall, study and parlour – with a fine Gothic bay window – date from the latter. In 1841 the house was bought by the Caprons and they rebuilt the east wing into two storeys. In 1909 they made an new entrance through the original undercroft.

The three families are best commemorated in the hall, originally the Knyvetts' great hall, remodelled by the Lynns during the eighteenth century and now hung with portraits of three generations of Caprons. There are enjoyable exhibitions of Victorian dress and Victorian and Edwardian children's clothes and nursery paraphernalia while the stables contain a more eclectic museum of rural life. One of the most distinguished occupants of Southwick was the eighteenth-century George Lynn, who observed the eclipses of Jupiter from a 4-m (13-ft) telescope erected on the main tower. His moving monument in the church next to the garden, depicting his wife mourning beneath a classical urn, is attributed to Roubiliac.

HOLME PIERREPONT HALL, Nottingham

Mr and Mrs Robin Brackenbury
Tel: 01602 332371

Off A52, 5 km (3 miles) south-east of Nottingham
Open: June, July and Aug, Tues, Thur and Fri, 2–6
£2.75, children £1
Home-made teas

Holme Pierrepont Hall is a surprising discovery beyond the outskirts of modern Nottingham. Despite the city's proximity, the ancient house has an undiscovered feel, encouraged by the knowledge that it was for centuries a subsidiary home for the Pierreponts of Thoresby Hall, although it had also been their original home. The house evolved from a medieval one built around an internal courtyard which survives as a charming enclosed garden, surrounded on three sides by the house, with the churchyard wall along the fourth. The entrance front retains much of its original early-Tudor character and brickwork dates from 1510. Inside the survival of the medieval lower and upper lodgings intact is a rare distinction; the superb roof timbers in the upper one contain the only cusped wind braces in eastern England and run the whole length of the building. Later alterations saw a seventeenth-century north wing go up, only to be pulled down in 1730; the florid Charles II oak staircase with carved panels was almost certainly moved from the demolished wing.

During the seventeenth and early-eighteenth centuries the Pierreponts were Earls and Dukes of Kingston. These titles became extinct after the 2nd Duke and his bigamous wife, Duchess Elizabeth Chudleigh, failed to produce a son, and in 1806 the nephew who had inherited was created Earl Manvers. Kingston and Manvers portraits are one of the chief attractions at Holme Pierrepont. The most impressive is the painting of Robert, 3rd Earl of Kingston, attributed to Gascard, in an elaborate carved frame. Manvers's hang on the staircase, including the 3rd Countess who lived here with her husband while Thoresby was being built by Salvin, and who added the colonnade around the courtyard. A fine portrait of her ancestor, Count de Coigny hangs in the long gallery.

Holme Pierrepont suffered badly from requisition during both World Wars, but brave restoration was begun by Lady Sibell Argles, daughter of the 4th Earl Manvers. Mr and Mrs Brackenbury bought the house in 1969 because she is descended from the 3rd Earl Manvers, and they have continued the work, including developing the gardens which are a major attraction for many visitors. The wide-ranging furniture includes many peculiarities such as the pairs of unusual Yorkshire and Derbyshire chairs and the Victorian bed made of Ceylonese rosewood. Brackenbury additions blend in happily, such as the self-portrait of the talented artist, Georgina Brackenbury.

UPTON HALL, *Nr Newark*

British Horological Institute
Tel: 01636 813795

In Upton, on A612, 11 km (7 miles) west of Newark

Open: details available on request
Prices available on request

Since 1972 Upton Hall has been the headquarters of the British Horological Institute. It was built in 1828 by W.J. Donthorne, a founder member of the Royal Institute of British Architects, for Thomas Wright, a Nottinghamshire banker. A small portion of the earlier Elizabethan house was incorporated by Donthorne, but his house is a characteristically chaste neo-classical building. In 1895 the house was bought by a Newark brewer, John Warwick, and he added the west wing which inevitably upsets the proportions of Donthorne's exterior when viewed from the south.

The hall became the home for various institutions during the twentieth century and was, from 1945 until 1972, St Joseph's Roman Catholic Theological College. The interiors have been substantially altered since Upton Hall was a private house, but now the Horological Institute's displays are full of interest for the clock and timepiece enthusiast. There are a number of historically important items on display such as the original mechanism from the Greenwich Observatory and the second-ever speaking clock. The two Sundays that mark the start and finish of British Summer Time are celebrated with special open days when visitors can take along their own clocks for discussion with experts.

BERKELEY CASTLE, *Bristol*

Mr and Mrs R.J. Berkeley
Tel: 01453 810332

Off A38, 26 km (16 miles) south-west of Gloucester

**Open: Apr to end Sept, daily except Mon, 11–5 (Apr and Sun, 2–5); also
Bank Holiday Mon, 11–5, Oct, Sun, 2–4.30
£4.50, children £2.25, concessions
Tea room**

If ever there was a castle that should be better known, it is Berkeley. It offers the visitor all the excitement of a medieval castle together with works of art from a cosmopolitan and discerning family. Just a few miles off the M5 between Bristol and Gloucester, it stands proudly in its gardens and landscape, still looking out over the Severn estuary which it was built to protect in the mid-twelfth century. A great deal of medieval grandeur remains in a series of towers, castellated walls and courtyards. A great hall, chapel, twisting stairs and narrow corridors all add to the excitement.

The potent medieval qualities which make the murder of Edward II at Berkeley quite in keeping were enhanced during the second quarter of this century, when nineteenth-century additions were done away with to return both the fabric and atmosphere of a medieval castle. At this time the pictures and other works of art were swelled with additions from other family houses. Sometimes the result was an embarrassment of riches, why else Old Masters in the kitchen other than shortage of space? Overall Berkeley affords a charming and intimate sequence of rooms where visitors can admire paintings by Stubbs, Van der Velde, Gainsborough, Reynolds, Batoni and many other artists. The pictures are accompanied by similarly distinguished works of art including bronzes and sumptuous tapestries.

CHAVENAGE, *Tetbury*

David Lowsley-Williams
Tel: 01666 502329

Off B4014, 3 km (2 miles) north of Tetbury
Open: Easter Sun and Mon; May to Sept, Thur and Sun; 2–5
£2.50, children £1.25
Teas by prior arrangement

The view of grey-stone Chavenage from the gateway before its forecourt has hardly changed since Edward Stephens rebuilt the house in 1576, having purchased the property in 1561. Stephens's house was typical Elizabethan, an 'E'-plan of two long side wings extending forward from the central block with a two-storey gabled porch. The Stephens family remained at Chavenage for some three hundred years and then, after a short period when the house was let, in 1891 it was purchased by George William Lowsley-Hoole Lowsley Williams, whose descendants have lived here ever since.

While long continuity is preserved in the entrance front, the house's garden front reveals a number of successive additions to the house, from the battlemented Gothic revival window at one end to the bow window of the dining-room which forms part of an Edwardian wing added in 1904.

The early Stephens's were responsible for many of the house's most interesting interior features, such as the imposing carved stone chimney-piece in the hall and the delightful Renaissance panelling in the oak room, decorated with carved allegorical figures and gilding. Upstairs two bedrooms hung with tapestries are called the Cromwell and Ireton rooms and record the house's close Parliamentarian connections during the seventeenth century. Nathaniel Stephens supported the Parliamentary cause, and when Cromwell's son-in-law, General Ireton, visited Chavenage at Christmas 1648, Stephens agreed to support the Impeachment of King Charles I. Among the many additions to the house brought by the present owner's family is the charming Victorian portrait of the Hoole boys at Ravensfield Park in Yorkshire, including the present owner's great-grandfather, William Wright Hoole.

KELMSCOTT MANOR, *Lechlade*

Society of Antiquaries
Tel: 01367 252486

Off A417, 3 km (2 miles) south-east of Lechlade
Open: Apr to end Sept; Wed, 11–1 and 2–5 (last admissions 12.30 and 4.30);
3rd Sat in each month, 2–6 (last admission 5.30);
Thur and Fri by apppointment
£6, children £3

Kelmscott is an unspoilt manor house that typifies the warm stone architecture of the Oxfordshire–Gloucestershire part of the Cotswolds. Most of the gabled house was built around 1570, by Richard Turner, and then a century later the tall block was added to the north-east side. The architectural style, internal timberwork and stone chimney-pieces are full of quality, but more important for Kelmscott's history was their attractiveness to William Morris, for whom the house was his country home from 1871 until his death in 1896. Morris rented the house, but after his death it was bought by his widow in 1913. Eventually, in 1962, it passed to the Society of Antiquaries, as set out in the will of the Morris's younger daughter Mary (May), who died in 1938.

Items from Morris's own house and his daughter May's, both in Hammersmith, have been brought to Kelmscott to make it a fascinating treasure-trove of the artist/craftsman and his circle. He shared the lease of the house first with Dante Gabriel Rossetti, and then with his publisher, Frederick Startridge Ellis. There are many tapestries, embroideries and carpets designed by the Morris's and produced at their Morris company, and many pieces worked by the family themselves, such as the 'Cabbage and Vine' tapestry woven by Morris in 1879 and the embroidered hangings of his oak four-poster bed, by his wife and daughter.

Before they came to Kelmscott, Rossetti had been long struck by Jane(y) Morris's beauty, and his four drawings of her (including two studies for the Virgin in his altarpiece for Llandaff Cathedral), and portrait in oil, 'The Blue Silk Dress', are pre-eminent among the pictures, along with his two chalk drawings of the Morris girls, Jenny and May when they were aged ten and nine. The manner in which the house's pictures illustrate the Morris circle and their lives is shown perfectly in the drawing of Morris on his death-bed by Charles Fairfax-Murray, who was sitting with Morris at the time of his death. Their own work mixes with the older pieces, such as Brussels tapestries and Dürer woodcuts, that they admired and the arrangement throughout the house – extensively restored by the Society of Antiquaries between 1964 and 1967, and redecorated in many parts with modern Morris wallpapers and textiles – presents visitors with an absorbing illustration of the Morris circle's lives and achievements.

OWLPEN MANOR, *Dursley*

Mr and Mrs Nicholas Mander
Tel: 01453 860261

Off B4066, (M5 exits 13 and 14), 5 km (3 miles) east of Dursley,
0.8 km (½ mile) east of Uley

Open: Apr to end Sept, Tues, Thur, Sun and Bank Holiday Mon;
also July and Aug, Wed; 2–5
£3.25, children £1.50

The series of wooded valleys that run off the western edges of the Cotswolds hide some of the area's most sleepy, romantic houses and Owlpen Manor is no exception. Ancient in origin, the combination of gabled grey stone manor and equally old yew-hedged garden prompted Vita Sackville-West to write in 1941, 'Owlpen, that tiny grey manor-house, cowering amongst its enormous yews, that make rooms in the garden with walls taller than any rooms in the house; dark, secret rooms of yew hiding in the slope of the valley.'

The house evolved from a medieval building of which remnants survive in the L-shaped plan. Most of the house was built by the Daunt family, the block that includes the hall during the sixteenth century, and the west range with the parlour is dated 1616. Early-eighteenth-century alterations were made by Thomas Daunt (the 5th), who also replanned the garden into the form that survives today. From c. 1770 first the Daunts and subsequently the Stoughton family (to whom Owlpen passed by marriage to a Daunt daughter) effectively abandoned the manor and it slumbered until the early-twentieth century when it was visited by various Arts and Crafts enthusiasts and Gertrude Jekyll included a description and plan of the garden in *Gardens for Small Country Houses*, published in 1914.

In 1925 it was bought by Norman Jewson, a young architect fired with enthusiasm for vernacular architecture and the ideals of simple craftsmanship that inspired the Cotswolds Arts and Crafts group. Jewson worked with the leading member of the group, Ernest Gimson, and in his restoration of Owlpen he was able to put into practice many of the ideas and principles he had come to admire. In November 1926 Jewson sold the house as it was impractical for him to live in alone, but he had secured its survival and reputation as a place that embodied the ideal of 'old England' so dear to the Arts and Crafts movement – and captured in F.L. Griggs's etching of the house in its setting of towering clipped yews.

Mr and Mrs Mander bought Owlpen in 1974 and came with a distinguished Arts and Crafts background as he is a descendant of the Manders of Wightwick Manor, Staffordshire. Owlpen today presents an atmosphere of random accumulation well-suited to its medieval origins and there is no fixed division between private, family rooms and those open to the public. Centuries-old original features of timber and stone work, or curiosities such as the painted cloths (widely used in interior decoration before the advent of wallpaper), mix happily with a rich assortment of Arts and Crafts additions.

These include furniture by Sidney Barnsley (whose niece Mary, daughter of Ernest Barnsley, married Jewson) and by Ernest Gimson, and delicate decorative plasterwork by him and Jewson, and an assortment of other pieces including a Wedgwood stem pot of 1928 with a painted illustration of Owlpen by Alfred Powell. Together with the garden, the church and other associated buildings, Owlpen appears to have evolved out of its landscape.

STANWAY HOUSE, *Broadway*

The Lord Neidpath
Tel: 01386 584469

On B4077, 8 km (5 miles) south-west of Broadway via B4632

Open: June to Sept, Tues and Thur, 2–5
£3, children £1, concessions
Tea room in village

Tucked beneath the steep wooded edge of the Cotswolds, where the road runs down towards Tewkesbury, Stanway and its village that clusters around has an undisturbed romanticism that few visitors forget. In addition to its long continuity – only one change of ownership in over 1,280 years, its atmosphere is enhanced by the halcyon period at the end of the nineteenth century when, under its chatelaine, Lady Elcho, Stanway was a favourite haunt of the 'Souls' group. Elcho is a subsidiary title of the Wemyss earldom, the family name being Charteris.

The Wemyss ownership of Stanway dates from the eighteenth century with marriage to the heiress of the Tracy family. They had been established at Stanway since its medieval ownership by Tewkesbury Abbey and during the seventeenth century built the present Jacobean house and the superb gatehouse, decorated with the shells of the Tracy coat-of-arms, that adds so much to the collection of buildings. Another highlight is the medieval tithe barn that dates from the abbey ownership.

The Wemyss connection brought many outstanding works of art to Stanway during the eighteenth century, notably the portrait of Lord Elcho by Raeburn, the two Charteris children by Romney, and two 'Chinese' Chippendale day beds with pagoda tops. During the late-nineteenth and early-twentieth century the Souls connection brought to the house wallpapers by William Morris, and paintings and drawings by Burne-Jones, Poynter and Sargent.

SUDELEY CASTLE, *Winchcombe*

The Lord and Lady Ashcombe
Tel: 01242 602357

On B4632, 11 km (7 miles) north-east of Cheltenham
Open: Apr to end Oct, daily, 11–5
£5.40, children £3, concessions
Restaurant

The riches of Sudeley's history, in particular its royal ownership from the reign of Edward IV through to Tudor times when it was granted to successive royal favourites, are very evident in its atmosphere. Jane Seymour's brother was created Lord Sudeley and lived here; he married another of Henry VIII's wives, Katherine Parr, but his ambitions led him to the scaffold. Katherine died at Sudeley only a year after their marriage and is buried in the chapel. Thereafter Mary Tudor granted Sudeley to Thomas Brydges, 1st Lord Chandos, whose family remained until the nineteenth century. In 1837 it was purchased by two brothers, John and William Dent.

Much of Sudeley had originally been built during the fifteenth century by Ralph Botelar, including St Mary's chapel where Katherine Parr is buried, and Portmare Tower by the gatehouse, named after a French admiral who was imprisoned by Botelar and whose ransom was part of the fortune he acquired during the wars against France. But the castle suffered extensive destruction by Parliamentary forces during the Civil War, followed by nearly two centuries of neglect when it was little more than a ruined heap.

The Dents commissioned Sir Gilbert Scott to carry out restoration work that was continued by other architects and by the 1850s much of the castle was again habitable, a fine restoration of its original medieval and Tudor period character. After inheritance by John Coucher Dent, his wife, Emma Brocklehurst, continued to build up the contents of the castle with many important items. One notable source was the sale in 1842 of Horace Walpole's home Strawberry Hill, including the most important picture, Lucas de Heere's 'The Tudor Succession', and Turner's delightful view of Pope's villa at Twickenham.

The Victorian Dents re-established Sudeley to a remarkably high degree, their restoration of the castle matched by new gardens they laid out and the works of art they carefully gathered together. Other outstanding paintings include Van Dyck's portrait of Charles I, 'The Four Evangelists' by Rubens, distinguished Dutch Old Masters, and works by Lely, Poussin and Claude. Needlework and tapestries are other highlights, in particular the sixteenth-century Sheldon Tapestry.

Lady Ashcombe was previously married to Mark Dent-Brocklehurst who died in 1972 aged only forty. Sudeley today celebrates its long, distinguished history and the combination of the venerable castle walls, its encircling gardens which have been considerably redeveloped, and the treasures inside, provide enjoyment for all visitors.

WHITTINGTON COURT, *Andoversford*

Mrs Jenny Stringer
Tel: 01242 820218

On A40, 6.5 km (4 miles) south-east of Cheltenham

Open: 1st half of April and 2nd half of Aug, daily, 2–5
£2.00, children £1, concessions

Whittington's history is that of manor houses up and down the country; ancient origins followed by construction, continuous occupation and alteration during the sixteenth and seventeenth centuries; subsidiary status and irregular occupation during the eighteenth and nineteenth centuries; welcome return and restoration during the twentieth. Now the gabled house that so typifies Cotswold manors contains accumulated evidence of its often-changing history.

It must have been a substantial house when built by John Cotton during the sixteenth century, for Elizabeth I lunched there on her progress through Gloucestershire in 1592. His son, Ralph, extended the house around 1600 and internal alterations were made later in the century, notably the replacement of the existing staircase with the present Jacobean one. With the demise of the Cottons during the 1660s Whittington became a secondary house. It passed through successive hands – and via an acrimonious court case in 1823 – to the Lawrence family, a member of which took up residence in 1910 after decades of tenancy.

Little visual evidence of the Cottons survives, but there is ample testimony to the quality of their house, not least the early-classical stone chimney-piece in the library. Most of the portraits are of Lawrences and the furniture came from their main homes at Sevenhampton and Sandywell – especially the latter, which provided Whittington's finest possession, the set of three bookcases in the library almost certainly made by Gillow of Lancaster.

BURTON COURT, *Leominster*

Lt-Cmdr and Mrs R. M. Simpson
Tel: 01544 388231

Off A44, 8 km (5 miles) west of Leominster

Open: end-May to end-Sept, Wed, Thur, Sat, Sun and Bank Holidays, 2.30–6
£2.50, children £2
Home-made teas

Burton Court's hilltop position is adjacent to an ancient British camp and in 1402 the dashing Henry, Prince of Wales camped here before moving on to deal with Owen Glendower. Such historical mists are today concealed by the house's Victorian and Edwardian appearance. The building was carried out in two periods for the Clowes family who bought Burton in 1865 from the Brewster family who had occupied since the seventeenth century. The Hereford architect, Frederick Kempson carried out the earlier work which replaced the old half-timbered house. Then, encouraged by the fortune of a shipping heiress from Liverpool, in 1912 Colonel Peter Clowes commissioned the young and rising Clough Williams-Ellis to remodel the entrance front to its present appearance.

Williams-Ellis was responsible for the billiard-room that every fashionable Edwardian house required. Kempson's period is retained in the dining-room with its ornate set of High-Victorian furniture. The style of the cantilevered stone staircase with an open lantern would suggest that it was inserted into the old house, but all this disguises the main feature and surprise of Burton Court, the survival of a substantial fourteenth-century hall which retains its original five-bay sweet chestnut roof. The elaborately carved oak overmantel is later, dated 1654, but exactly suits the hall's scale. Here – and in other rooms of the house – is the extensive costume collection which is Burton's main attraction. The oldest item is a pair of Charles II gauntlets; possibly even rarer is the nineteenth-century uniform of an officer of the Chinese Imperial Guard. Mrs Simpson, whose husband bought Burton Court in 1960, is engagingly knowledgeable and enthusiastic about the collection.

CROFT CASTLE, *Leominster*

The National Trust / The Lord Croft
Tel: 01568 780246

Off B4362, 8 km (5 miles) north-west of Leominster

**Open: Apr and Oct, Sat, Sun and Bank Holiday Mon, 1.30–4.30; May to end
Sept, Wed to Sun and Bank Hol Mon, 1.30–5.30
(last admission ½ hour before closing)
£3.20, children £1.60, concessions**

The surroundings of Croft Castle exemplify the spectacular, undisturbed countryside of the English–Welsh borders, or Marches. Camden's *Britannia*, published at the end of the seventeenth century, describes the Croft family as the 'very ancient Family of the Crofts Knights who have flourished there in great and good esteem'. They were actively involved in the constant struggles along the border from Norman times on and rose to positions of importance in successive medieval and Tudor royal households.

A sense of long establishment is immediate as you approach from the gateway along an avenue of ancient oak and beech trees. Beyond a curtain wall, eighteenth-century in date but realistically creating an impression of medieval defences, the castle stands four-square, built around a courtyard and with a tower at each corner. The walls are fourteenth or fifteenth century but almost certainly replaced an older building. During the eighteenth century, when the Croft family fell on hard times, the mortgaged castle was bought by Richard Knight in 1746 whose nephews were Richard Payne Knight, the well-known enthusiast for the 'Picturesque' and who lived nearby at Downton Castle, and Thomas Andrew Knight, the horticulturalist. Richard Knight's daughter married Thomas Johnes and he commissioned the Shrewsbury architect, Thomas Farnolls Pritchard (who built the Iron Bridge at Coalbrookdale), to carry out extensive alterations to the house. Croft was sold by Johnes's son to Somerset Davies, whose descendants remained owners until 1923 when it was bought back by the trustees of the child Sir James Croft, 11th Bt. In 1957 it passed to the National Trust with the family continuing as occupants.

Pritchard's alterations included the staircase decorated with Gothic patterns of plasterwork, as well as delightful chimney-pieces, ceilings and Gothic windows. There was a further phase of change in 1913 when alterations to the exterior included the addition of the present battlemented porch between the earlier bays with Gothic windows, and the removal of battlements and gables from the roof. Inside, some of Pritchard's rococo decoration was taken down and chimney-pieces moved.

The main rooms, from the entrance hall to the group along the south front, contain a variety of fine eighteenth-century Gothic and 'Chinese' Chippendale chairs. Croft family portraits begin with Elizabethan figures, progress in date to the seventeenth-century

Bishop Croft, who defied Cromwellian soldiers from his pulpit in Hereford Cathedral in 1645, and include works by Gainsborough and Beechey. There are also some important drawings by Sir Thomas Lawrence and distinguished Old Masters.

EASTNOR CASTLE, *Ledbury*

Mr James and the Hon Mrs Hervey-Bathurst
Tel: 01531 633160

On A438, 3 km (2 miles) east of Ledbury

Open: Easter to end Sept, Sun and Bank Holiday Mon; also July and Aug, Sun to Fri; 11.30–4.30
£3.50, children £1.75, concessions
Home-made teas

Few buildings in England are as uncompromisingly massive as Eastnor Castle, which the visitor discovers brooding in the gentle foothills of the Malverns. A member of the family, Lady Henry Somerset, wrote blithely in 1889, 'It is castellated in the style of a Norman baronial castle at the time of Edward I, combining the comfort and convenience of a modern home with the stately grandeur of a feudal fortress.' Visitors entering the enormous great hall which towers through four floors to a height of 18 m (60 ft), would question its qualification as a typically convenient modern home.

Lady Henry was the granddaughter of Eastnor's builder, the aggressive 1st Earl Somers, who commissioned Robert Smirke to replace his existing family home with something more substantial. Inside, the baronial character continues – most obviously in the great hall – in the staircase hall and dining-room which retains Smirke's original furniture. The fan-vaulted plaster ceiling of the drawing-room is theatrically Gothic but the decoration was changed for the 2nd Earl by Pugin and the set of Brussels tapestries (which were a wedding present to his wife) were introduced.

The 3rd Earl built up an outstanding collection of armour – notably half of the famous Meyrick collection – confessing to an infection of what he called 'armouritis'. He also commissioned George Fox to redecorate the great hall in Venetian Romanesque style, and his Italian enthusiasms account for the library which contains tapestries collected in Mantua and originally woven for Catherine de Medici and two Ischian marble chimney-pieces.

Other rooms contain impressive Italian furniture and paintings — among which Bassano's 'Last Supper' is a highlight — which add to good family portraits, mostly hung in the dining-room. The 3rd Earl is reputed to have fallen in love with his wife when he saw her full-length portrait by G.F. Watts which he purchased; her friendship with Watts accounts for the quantity of pictures by the artist. Recently many items of the 3rd Earl's collection of Italian furniture and works of art have been retrieved from store and their display in various rooms has coincided with enlivening redecoration.

The 3rd Earl built up one of the best arboretums in the country. The quantity of rare conifers is fascinating to the enthusiast and their towering forms complement the architecture in a manner more conventional gardens would struggle to achieve. Plants of more modest proportions can be bought at Eastnor's thriving new garden centre.

HELLEN'S, *Much Marcle*

The Pennington-Mellor-Munthe Trust
Tel: 01531 660668

In Much Marcle on A449, 8 km (5 miles) south-west of Ledbury

Open: Good Fri to Oct, Wed, Sat, Sun and Bank Holidays, 2–6
(last admission 5)
£3, children (must be accompanied) £1

Hellen's, part medieval, part Tudor and part Stuart, internally rearranged at different times with somewhat haphazard results, has an atmosphere of long slumber that disguises much of interest. The house's story is dotted with names familiar to schoolboys: wicked Roger Mortimer, who arranged the murder of Edward II in Berkeley Castle and whose sister Yseult lived at Hellen's; the more popular Black Prince, friend of James Audley of Hellen's who supposedly built the chimney-piece in the hall or court room and decorated it with the Prince's feathers in honour of a visit; and Mary Tudor who is reputed to have stayed and slept in the room whose overmantel bears her initials and the Tudor portcullis. The house's descent was made tortuous by constant inheritance by females and actually takes its name from the son of a steward, Sir John Helyon, who went on pilgrimage to the Holy Land and was so revered by the local people that they named the house Hellyon's Home.

The complicated descent eventually simplifies with the inheritance of Hellen's by Hilda Pennington-Mellor who married the Swedish doctor and philanthropist, Axel Munthe. They were the parents of Major Malcolm Munthe, who established the trust that now owns the house. For visitors, in addition to the charmingly undisturbed atmosphere, the major interest is the distinguished collection of pictures, in particular fine portraits of many generations of inhabitants of Hellen's, their relations and other connected personages.

The collection includes works attributed to Mytens, Cornelius Johnson, Van Dyck, Lely and Raeburn, and there are many surprises: one of three editions of Reynolds's delightful work 'The Laughing Girl'; the eighteenth-century courtesan Kitty Markham by Hogarth; and a splendid full-length portrait of another of Hellen's blackguards, Philip, Duke of Wharton (whose aunt lived at Hellen's), a Jacobite plotter who dabbled in black magic with the Hell-Fire Club and died an outlaw aged thirty-two. His presence at Hellen's well illustrates the surprises that the ramshackle house disguises.

MOCCAS COURT, *Hay-on-Wye*

Trustees of the Baunton Trust
Tel: 01981 500381

Off B4352 on River Wye, 8 km (5 miles) north-west of Hay-on-Wye

Open: Apr to Sept, Sun, 2–6
£1.95

In 1771 Sir George Amyand, Bt, a successful banker, married Catherine Cornewell, the heiress of Moccas. As well as assuming her name, he wished to impress his bride by rebuilding the home where her family had lived for a hundred years. No doubt they were planning the change when painted together in front of the scar on the far side of the Wye valley looking back to the old house, a delightful watercolour preserved at Moccas. The result was the present house, austerely elegant outside, full of surprises within,  set in parkland laid out by 'Capability' Brown and later altered by Humphry Repton. The architect was Anthony Keck, but the most important contribution was made by Robert Adam, who supplied the plans from which Keck worked, and himself designed and decorated the outstanding series of rooms.

The music room celebrates the Cornewell's musical interests (his father was a friend and trustee of Handel) and Adam's decoration carries a theme of instruments in the frieze and marble chimney-piece. In the library the frieze, doorcases and mahogany doors, and rich scagliola chimney-piece are of similar quality, but the decorative climax comes in Adam's glorious circular drawing-room with an elaborate plaster ceiling and curved doors and chimney-piece. Adam's 'Pompeian' decoration of the walls was carried out, but not in paint as he suggested, instead with an intricate pattern of paper panels from Paris. One moves from decorative to architectural quality in the oval inner hall rising through three storeys, where a curving cantilevered stone staircase ascends to the first-floor landing.

The notable contents of Moccas – including the 3,000 books from the library – were sold in 1946 and the house has been refurnished by the Chester-Master family who inherited on the death of Sir William Cornewell in 1962. Their contributions are entirely fitting with the house: fine Japanese and Chinese porcelain, English and French furniture and paintings including an accomplished eighteenth-century portrait of Mrs Richard Master and Mme Saladin by their sister, Ariana Egerton, and van Meulen's painting of Louis XIV travelling with his entourage.

SUFTON COURT, *Mordiford*

Major and Mrs J. N. Hereford
Tel: 01432 870268

In Mordiford on B4224, 5 km (3 miles) south-east of Hereford
Open: 14–27 May and 13–26 Aug (telephone for further details)
£1.50, children 50p

John Martin Robinson, the authority on the Wyatt family of architects, wrote of Sufton: 'I have no doubt at all that the house is by James Wyatt.' It has an air of quality and many details suggest a fastidiously skilful hand such as Wyatt, working here in his early years of neo-Greek enthusiasm before the castles and Gothic houses that later clients demanded. At Sufton he was working for a squire, not an extravagant grandee, and the house is especially interesting when considered in this light. Wyatt quite clearly made the best of a limited budget and gave his client a gentleman's residence with a handful of features of real quality.

The exterior is typically late-Georgian, a neat formal box built of traditional Hereford brick faced in stone – an economic but distinctive combination in an area where brick predominates. It rises through four storeys, but Wyatt appreciated that to make all four show would look cumbersome so he skilfully disguised the top floor within the roof and lit it from central wells. The sparseness of external decoration heightens its effect, especially the central Venetian windows between Ionic columns.

Inside, features of Wyatt's decoration are typical of his high standards, but again with a clear order of priority. The most important room was the music room, now the drawing-room and its decoration is more extensive and elegant than in the others. The mahogany doors with inlaid panels are set in doorcases with fine plasterwork which continues in the frieze and chimney-piece; all bearing delightful arrangements of musical instruments set in floral cartouches. In the dining-room across the central hall the level of decoration is slightly reduced; the doors have no inlaid panels or plasterwork on their cases; here the frieze contains a pattern of goblets with grapes flowing out of them. The staircase at the end of the hall continues the theme of unostentatious quality.

No doubt it greatly appealed to Humphry Repton who was called in in 1795 to advise on the grounds. His contribution is the second of Sufton's strings of distinction. His *Red Book* with suggested designs is preserved in the house and has the mix of salesmanship and light artistry which made the technique such a success. He made the most of the house's enviable position on an eminence overlooking the Wye valley and his planting survives today.

The Hereford family have lived in Mordiford since 1140 and have occupied Sufton since it was built. Sadly a large proportion of the house's contents was sold during the 1950s to pay death duties, and it is an enjoyable feature of the house that its most charming pictures – a series of watercolours – were painted by a member of the family, Edward Hereford, a naval officer and a talented, prolific artist, who died in 1921.

MOAT HOUSE, *Longnor, Nr Shrewsbury*

Mr and Mrs C.P. Richards
Tel: 01743 718434

In Longnor, off A49, 13 km (8 miles) south of Shrewsbury
Open: Apr to end Sept, Thur, Spring and Summer Bank Holidays, 2.30–5
£2

A fifteenth-century moated, timbered manor house deep in the Shropshire countryside, Moat House is rare and distinguished – and a lucky survivor. Converted into two cottages during the nineteenth century, it was condemned as unfit for human habitation in 1962. It was purchased by H.K. Rouse who returned it to a single home and carried out initial restoration. This has been continued by the present owners who bought the property in 1970, especially since 1988 when an ambitious programme of work began.

The restoration work removed a number of partitions that had been inserted during the nineteenth century, returning the downstairs parlour and great chamber above to their original proportions. The original timberwork was revealed, and repaired where necessary. Roof timbers in the hall have decorative carving and, as well as massive corbels, there are intriguing original details such as two carved wooden human heads on the bases of two corbels. The old service and screens passage runs along the north end of the house. With its backdrop of the Lawley Hills the house today combines an air of tranquillity with its great antiquity.

SHIPTON HALL, *Much Wenlock*

J.N.R.N. Bishop
Tel: 01743 636225

On B4378, 10 km (6 miles) south-west of Much Wenlock
Open: Easter to end Sept, Thur, Bank Holiday Sun and Mon, 2.30–5.30
£2.50, children £1.50

Set in the Corve Dale, positioned enticingly above a walled garden with stone steps ascending, with Saxon church on one side, Georgian stables on the other and its medieval dovecote perched above and encircled by lawn and flower garden, Elizabethan Shipton Hall idealizes an English manor house in its community. The dovecote was probably built by monks from Wenlock Abbey who owned Shipton. The first – timber-framed – house was destroyed by fire and replaced in 1587 by Richard Lutwyche. He built the Elizabethan part of Shipton as a dowry for his daughter, Elizabeth, when she married a Thomas Mytton from the Worcester area.

The stable block hints at what the gabled Elizabethan façade conceals, a series of distinguished eighteenth-century interiors executed by Thomas Pritchard, best known for building the Iron Bridge that became the symbol of the Industrial Revolution. As well as building the stable block, Pritchard added two new wings to the house, doubling its size. The one to the rear presents an almost Georgian façade that contrasts interestingly with the Elizabethan front. The most impressive addition to the 'modernization' of the house was interior plasterwork. The Italian craftsman, Francesco Vassalli executed the ceiling in the hall. Pritchard himself was responsible for the staircase hall with its tall Gothic window and plaster ceiling, and for the upstairs library's outstanding plaster overmantel.

Part of Shipton's charm derives from the fact that these additions blended with, rather than replaced, the old Tudor features. Thus from Georgian plasterwork and pedimented doors one goes to oak panelling and diamond window panes. One window records the sorry imprisonment of eighteen-year-old Harriott Mytton to prevent her romancing with a local squire. She scratched in the glass: 'By dint of time this argument Ann learned, who'd be happy must be unconcerned, must all her secrets in her bosom wear, and seek for peace and comfort only these; hope travels thro' nor quits now.' Her fortitude was rewarded; in 1795 she married the squire, Thomas More of Larden.

A hundred years since they bought Shipton Hall the Bishop family successfully perpetuate its appealing informality and the sense that it has evolved from generation to generation rather than been designed as a show-piece at one time.

WESTON PARK, *Shifnal*

Weston Park Foundation
Tel: 01952 850207

On A5 at Weston-under-Lizard, 10 km (6 miles) west of M6 exit 12

Open: Apr to Sept, selected days, (Aug, daily), 1–5
£5, children £3, concessions
Tea room

Weston Park was designed in 1671 by its owner, Lady Wilbraham, a formidable character and the Mytton heiress through whom Weston passed. The house was in the vanguard of Palladio-inspired classicism in England as her copy of his architectural work in the archives confirms. The symmetrical broad façades, the unusual semi-circular pediments on the park front and the warm brick with stone quoins and window dressing are immensely satisfying.

The park is one of a series by 'Capability' Brown in the West Midlands including Chillington, Coombe Abbey and Tong Castle, which together represent some of his most distinguished work. Brown was commissioned by Sir Henry Bridgeman who built the farms and was a renowned improver. James Paine designed the Roman bridge at one end of the lake and the Temple of Diana, a garden building of rare distinction.

Lady Wilbraham's house was altered internally during the eighteenth century, again in the late-nineteenth century and finally during the 1960s when the present Earl of Bradford's mother carried out extensive redecoration — the standard of which is demonstrated in the enchanting dining-room — and reversed a number of the Victorian alterations. The tapestry room is hung with one of the six sets of ravishing Boucher-Neilson tapestries woven at the Gobelins factory for English customers.

Weston's descent has often been plagued by a lack of male heirs. Lady Wilbraham and her husband had no sons. Their daughter married Richard Newport, 2nd Earl of Bradford; that title died out with the next generation (despite there being six sons) and Weston passed on to the Bridgemans. Sir Henry Bridgeman married Lady Ann Newport who inherited Weston in 1762. He was made Lord Bridgeman and his son Earl of Bradford in a new creation.

The changes and different characters make for a house full of interest. Paintings, furniture and porcelain in particular are outstanding. Van Dycks, Lelys and Reynolds set the standard among the family portraits, but the rarest likeness is that of Sir George Carew by Holbein. As well as the Gobelins there are Beauvais tapestries, eighteenth-century French furniture, and Bow, Derby and Chelsea porcelain. Most intriguing is the correspondence between Disraeli and his confidante, Selina, Countess of Bradford.

WHITMORE HALL, *Nr Newcastle-under-Lyme*

Rafe Cavenagh-Mainwaring
Tel: 01782 680478

On A53, 6.5 km (4 miles) south-west of Newcastle-under-Lyme
Open: May to end Aug, Tues and Wed, 2–5.30
£2

Whitmore is an unexpected rural haven within a few miles of the sprawling conurbation of Newcastle-under-Lyme and the Potteries. The property has survived undisturbed through eight centuries, changing hands only by descent or marriage, never sale. The setting is enviable, the warm brick Carolean entrance front looks down an avenue of limes to the parish church, to one side the eighteenth-century park (so Brown-like that, given his quantity of commissions in the area, it is hard to believe he did not have a hand in it although there is no evidence), stretching along a gentle valley and up the slope beyond, and on the far side of the house, gardens stretching down to an expansive lake.

Edward Mainwaring (the fourth of eight successive Edwards) added the Carolean front to join the wings of the existing Tudor house and closed in the small courtyard to form an entrance hall. The striking stonework around the door is contemporary but the porch was added by Admiral Rowland Mainwaring who lived at Whitmore from 1837 until his death in 1862. His arrival is recorded in his diary. He and his family were met at the station by 'about 120 tenantry and friends on horseback, the children of the national schools and the band playing "See the Conquering Hero Comes"'. His presence is very evident today. He was painted in uniform by John Phillip and collected the fine marine pictures by Luny, including a superb view of the Battle of the Nile where he had served as a midshipman.

After his death the furniture and other contents of Whitmore were sold, but fortunately not the fine collection of portraits. These include works attributed to Mark Gheeraerts and Cornelius Johnson and a splendid double portrait by Michael Dahl of Edward Mainwaring VII and his wife. Throughout the seventeenth century the Mainwarings were staunch parliamentarians in a royalist area; Edward continued the tradition by leading his tenantry against the advancing Jacobite army during the 1745. He made important alterations to the house, including the screen of Corinthian columns in the hall and curving staircase behind, as well as creating the park and lake.

Whitmore's main distinction is, however, neither house nor park, but one of the most important stables in the country. The modest sandstone building dates from the turn of the seventeenth century and inside are nine bays with turned columns, carved arches and carved hay racks. Their unique age is made the more fascinating by the knowledge that the family also built a similar, slightly later and more elaborate set at their other home, Peover Hall in Cheshire (see page 213), which also survives.

ARBURY HALL, *Nuneaton*

The Viscount Daventry
Tel: 01203 382804

Off B4102, 3 km (2 miles) south-west of Nuneaton

Open: Easter Sun to Sept, Sun and Bank Holiday Mon, 2–5.30
(last admission 5)
£3.50, children £2
Tea room

Sir Roger Newdigate was among the foremost scholar-connoisseurs of the eighteenth century. His twin legacies were the prize named after him for verse at Oxford University, and his home, Arbury Hall, England's finest eighteenth-century Gothic house. Newdigate was a pioneer of the Gothic revival; work at Arbury (contemporary

with Horace Walpole's Strawberry Hill) began in 1750 and went on for half a century until the year before Sir Roger died in 1806.

The long gallery survives as evidence of the Elizabethan house that Sir Roger transformed. Externally Arbury's Gothic character is announced on all sides but especially on the south looking out over park and lake. The interiors were executed room by room with Sir Roger employing a succession of architects: the gifted amateur Sanderson Miller (another leading gentleman enthusiast for the Gothic), then Henry Keene and finally Henry Couchman of Warwick. Although copied from noble medieval originals in stone (in particular Henry VII's chapel in Westminster Abbey), the scheme at Arbury – like most eighteenth-century

Gothic – was decorative not structural and executed in plaster. The three most elaborate rooms are the dining-room, drawing-room and saloon with different but equally striking detail. The dining-room was made out of the old great hall and its height allowed for fan vaulting that recalls church interiors; the drawing room has a vaulted ceiling with groining; while in the saloon ceiling the decoration reaches its climax. In all three rooms the vaulting and decoration extends into window-cases, niches and enormous chimney-pieces.

While these are the show-pieces, Sir Roger's changes extended throughout most of the house and the sense of continuity is emphasized by the vaulted corridor or cloisters which extends around two sides of the Elizabethan courtyard. He was painted by Arthur Devis in his Gothicized library, the gallery was given a delicate ribbed ceiling and lesser rooms such as the small sitting-room and school-room were given fan vaulting and Gothic chimney-pieces. The chapel was untouched, preserving its fine plaster ceiling executed for Sir Roger's grandfather, Sir Richard, who also commissioned from Sir Christopher Wren the design of the classical doorway to his new stable block.

Sir Roger's portraits show him as the gentle scholar described in *Scenes of Clerical Life* by George Eliot who was brought up on the Arbury estate. They hang with numerous other Newdigates dating from the early-Tudor period and other fine paintings including Elizabeth I by John Bettes, and distinguished Old Masters. The Gothic theme extends to some of the chairs but the most important piece of furniture is Archbishop Laud's cabinet.

BADDESLEY CLINTON, *Lapworth, Knowle*

The National Trust / T. W. Ferrers Walker
Tel: 01564 783294

Off A41, 12 km (7½ miles) north-west of Warwick
Open: March to end Sept, Wed to Sun and Bank Holiday Mon (closed Good Fri), 2–6; Oct, Wed to Sun, 2–5
£4.50, children £2.25, concessions
Restaurant

The moat, dug in the thirteenth century, confirms the medieval origins of this deeply atmospheric house, for centuries home of the Roman Catholic Ferrers family who had accompanied William the Conqueror to England. In 1980, after a decade of complex negotiations, and when two local donors provided a £300,000 endowment, the government bought Baddesley Clinton from Mr Thomas Ferrers-Walker, and passed it to the National Trust.

The present house was originally built during the fifteenth century by the Ferrers's predecessors, the Brome family. But successive alterations were made by the Ferrers so that each of the house's three ranges around a courtyard is full of architectural variety which add to the picturesque vision of grey stone or brick walls, gables, tiled roofs and tall brick chimneys, seen across the surrounding moat. The only access across the moat is the eighteenth century stone bridge which leads to the crenellated gatehouse.

The Elizabethan Henry Ferrers, known as the Antiquary, made many alterations to the house and added splendid heraldic stained glass and carved oak to the interiors. The rooms contain fine oak panelling, and in the great hall the splendidly carved stone chimney-piece, decorated with family coats of arms, matches the richness of the carved oak here and elsewhere. Victorian Baddesley Clinton and its occupants are illustrated in a series of portraits and paintings by Rebecca Dulcibella Orpen, who married Marmion

Edward Ferrers. Suffering from the financial constraints that plagued successive members of the family, they were assisted by her aunt, Lady Chatterton and her husband, Edward Heneage Dering, who came to live with them in the house. When Ferrers and Lady Chatterton died, Rebecca married Dering – an intriguing series of events which typifies the absorbing, often complicated, family history in which Baddesley Clinton remains steeped.

COUGHTON COURT, *Alcester*

The National Trust / Mrs Clare Throckmorton
Tel: 01789 400777 / 762435 (visitor information)

On A435, 3 km (2 miles) north of Alcester

**Open: mid-Mar to end Apr and Oct, Sat and Sun (Easter, Sat to Wed);
May to Sept, daily (except Thur and Fri); 12–5 (last admission 4.30)
£4.95, children £2.50 (under-5 free)
Restaurant**

The name Throckmorton conjures up scenes of Tudor and medieval knights, and later intrigue in the Throckmorton and Gunpowder Plots, and it is no surprise that the family have owned Coughton for nearly six hundred years – owned, but not always occupied. From the eighteenth century grander homes provided alternative family seats, but by the beginning of this century, Coughton became once again the family's primary base. Sir Robert Throckmorton, 11th Bt, died in 1989 and the title passed to a cousin living in America, who has since died without an heir. During the Second World War Sir Robert's mother had arranged for the transfer of Coughton Court to the National Trust, with a three-hundred-year lease for the family and Sir Robert's niece, Clare Throckmorton, has inherited the lease and taken over management of the house from the National Trust. Now the evidence of the family's long history is gathered together at

Coughton and the house, with its neighbouring stable block and rare distinction of both Anglican and Roman Catholic churches, present an absorbing ensemble.

Coughton's architectural glory is the Tudor gatehouse, built by Sir George Throckmorton who inherited in 1519 and died in 1553. Today the gatehouse rises dramatically between the symmetrical façades of the west front which were refaced in Gothic style during alterations at the end of the eighteenth century. This combined ensemble, that greets the visitor makes for a surprise discovery through the gatehouse, where Sir George's vernacular gabled wings in brick and timber flank a central courtyard.

Fiercely devout Roman Catholics, the Throckmortons regularly suffered for their religion. Coughton also suffered, on two occasions, first during the Civil War when Royalist troops sacked part of the building and later following the Glorious Revolution in 1688 when a Protestant mob set fire to the east wing, which was later demolished.

Eighteenth-century alterations to the Tudor original appear at intervals through the house, for instance the fan vaulting added to the ceiling of the gatehouse's ground floor room when it was made into an entrance hall. The most significant addition was the cantilevered stone staircase that climbs beside the gatehouse and provides the link to what might otherwise be a random arrangement of rooms. The walls of the staircase provide the first introduction to the house's array of portraits, a collection with a number of notable highlights, not least the two portraits by Nicolas de Largillière which hang in the drawing-room. The largest is a flamboyant study of Sir Robert Throckmorton, 4th Bt, complete with a richly carved French rococo frame, and to one side the arguably more arresting study of Sir Robert's aunt, Ann Throckmorton, one of successive Throckmorton girls who became nuns.

The drawing-room also contains Batoni's suave study of Robert Throckmorton, who was heir to his grandfather, the 4th Bt, but died aged forty-nine while the old man lived on to the age of eighty-nine. Perhaps the house's most charming portrait, of Mary, daughter of the 1st Marquess of Powys, by Francois du Troy, hangs in the little drawing-room where fine early Worcester and Coalport porcelain is also displayed.

A late-seventeenth-century Anglo-Dutch veneered Mass cabinet is among the most important pieces of furniture at Coughton, but in almost every room the quality of works of art is matched by items which tell of the family's progress, such as the Throckmorton coat in the saloon, made in a day in 1811 for a wager of one thousand guineas. The courtyard and lawn beyond now contains an outstanding new formal garden designed by Mrs Throckmorton's daughter, Christina, who is carrying out a further series of ambitious new designs in the old walled gardens.

HONINGTON HALL, *Shipston-on-Stour*

Benjamin Wiggin
Tel: 01608 663717

Off A34, 2.5 km (1½ miles) north of Shipston-on-Stour
Open: June to end Aug, Wed and Bank Holiday Mon, 2.30–5
£2.75, children £1

Honington is one of a select group of Carolean houses, which for many visitors provide an ideal of country-house architecture and interior decoration. Built for Sir Henry Parker during the 1680s, it has the satisfying proportions and detail that exemplify Carolean architecture: a block of seven by six bays, with the end two bays on the main fronts projecting slightly; two storeys with a hipped roof and dormer windows above; brick with stone dressing; and niches with marble busts of the twelve Roman Caesars between the sash windows of the ground and first floors.

In 1737 the house was sold to Joseph Townsend for whom the interiors were remodelled to their present memorable appearance. Honington contains some of the most delightful decorative plasterwork in any English country house, and it is typical of

the eighteenth century that a relatively modest country home should conceal such riches.

The hall provides the introduction with its plaster bas-relief panels and swirling overmantel. Its plaster ceiling is matched by those in the oak room and boudoir, but the *tour de force* is the octagonal saloon, created slightly later between 1751 and 1752, and replacing the staircase hall. Whereas the earlier plasterwork is attributed to the Anglo-Danish craftsman, Charles Stanley, the saloon was designed by a gentleman architect, John Freeman, and executed by a professional one, William Jones. The dome with its octagonal coffers, the doorcases and overmantels with broken pediments are clearly Palladian, but perhaps Jones's influence accounts for the exotically rococo patterns in the plaster decoration, notably the mirror frames.

During the 1970s drastic restoration had to be carried out after the discovery of extensive dry rot and it is a tribute to the determination of Sir John Wiggin (father of the present owner, whose father had bought Honington in 1924), that the work was successfully executed. Around the house interesting remnants survive of the romantic landscape containing a variety of buildings and ornaments, which Joseph Townsend created with the advice of another gentleman architect-gardener, Sanderson Miller, who lived nearby.

RAGLEY HALL, *Alcester*

The Earl and Countess of Yarmouth
Tel: 01789 762090

Off A435, 3 km (2 miles) south-west of Alcester
Open: Apr to end Sept daily, except Mon and Fri
(open Bank Holidays), 11–5
£4.50, children £3, concessions

Wyatt's monumental portico disguises Ragley's age, and not many country houses can have been so long in the making. In 1677 Sir Edward Seymour wrote to a friend: 'Here you will find me playing the fool in laying out money upon building . . .' He commissioned Robert Hooke (the little-known contemporary of Wren) to carry out his most important commission. Over half a century later decoration was still going on.

The delay was fortuitous, for it enabled Ragley to acquire what Robin Fedden calls 'the finest late Baroque interior in England'. This is the great hall by James Gibbs, a memorable assembly of plasterwork, pilasters and pink-painted walls. Gibbs executed the room in 1750 and the furniture was specially made in 1756. The Prince Regent was a friend of the 2nd Marquess of Hertford and, more particularly, of his wife. There are portraits of the Prince by Lawrence and Hoppner and the bed specially built for his first visit, surmounted with gilded Prince of Wales's ostrich feathers. His bust by Nollekens in the hall was a gift to Lady Hertford.

The urge to compete with the Prince Regent led their son, the 3rd Marquess, to assemble the art collection which in turn his son further increased to form what is now the Wallace Collection in London. Both collectors neglected Ragley – living in London and Paris respectively. Only when the 5th Marquess, a cousin, inherited, did the house and estate's fortunes become rosier.

Today the healthy condition of the house is thanks to the spirited efforts of the Lord and Lady Hertford. They moved into Ragley after their marriage in 1956, opened it to the public and carried out extensive redecoration over many years. Successful continuity has been established and they have now been succeeded in the house by their son, Lord Yarmouth and his family. Lord and Lady Hertford's most significant addition was to commission Graham Rust to decorate one of the two matching staircases with an ascending series of sparkling murals.

In all the main rooms the fruits of successive generations of connoisseurship are clearly evident. Important furniture and mirrors by Chippendale and later Regency pieces are complemented by Louis XV commodes, a suite of Louis XVI chairs and Sèvres porcelain. One drawing-room contains a series of Seymour portraits by Reynolds; other highlights among the paintings include Vernet's 'Salt Mines near Rome', 'The Raising of Lazarus' by Cornelius van Haarlem and 'The Holy Family' by Cornelius Schut.

WARWICK CASTLE, *Warwick*

Warwick Castle Ltd
Tel: 01926 408000

In Warwick

**Open: Apr to end Oct, daily, 10–6; Nov to end Mar, daily
(except Christmas), 10–5
£8.25, children (4–16) £4.95, concessions
Two restaurants/tea room**

Since 1978, when the Earl of Warwick sold his eponymous castle, it has become a tourist attraction on an impressive scale and is the most visited member of the HHA. Its high exposure and a strongly theatrical note notwithstanding, it remains an indelibly impressive medieval castle, its position on the banks of the Avon greatly enhanced by 'Capability' Brown's park. Inside are magnificent seventeenth- and eighteenth-century state rooms and quantities of evidence of its illustrious occupants, Earls of Warwick from 1068, medieval lords and leading figures in the Hundred Years War and Wars of the Roses, and from 1604 the Greville family, who became Barons Brooke and, in 1759, Earls of Warwick.

The series of state rooms are all lavishly decorated and furnished. One drawing-room has red lacquer panelling, another the same in carved cedarwood and throughout are sets of rich English, French and Italian furniture – gilded tables and gilded tapestry chairs. One room contains Queen Anne's imposing state bed and its attendant gilded furniture from Windsor Castle, given to the Earl of Warwick by George III, but probably the most monumental piece of furniture is in the great hall: the Kenilworth cabinet made by Cookes and Sons of Warwick for the 1851 Great Exhibition. Its carving depicts Elizabeth I's visit to Kenilworth and it was given to Lord Brooke (later the 4th Earl) as a wedding present.

Portraits from the studios of Van Dyck and Lely abound; other paintings include a powerful likeness of Henry VIII after Holbein and a pair of lions by Frans Snyders which could have been a study for the lions in Rubens's 'The Chariot of Victory' in the Louvre. As one might expect, there is a formidable collection of armour – up to a thousand pieces, much of it rare and important, including the suit worn by the daredevil Scottish royalist general, James Graham, Marquess of Montrose, whose portrait by Dobson hangs in the red drawing-room. A miscellany of such distinguished but unrelated figures greatly adds to Warwick's rich historical tapestry.

CHILLINGTON HALL, *Wolverhampton*

Mr and Mrs Peter Giffard
Tel: 01902 850236

Via A449 north through Coven to Gailey, then 6.5 km (4 miles) south-west of A5, following signs to Codsall

Open: Easter Sun and Suns before May Bank Holidays; June to mid-Sept, Thur; Aug, Sun; 2.30–5.30
£2.50, children £1.25

The arrival at Chillington is a surprise. Sprawling Wolverhampton leads to winding country lanes to the north, at different points along which you glimpse an estate   park walls, belts of woodland and entrance gates.

At the Brewood lodge the visitor suddenly comes upon the vista down a great avenue looking like a seventeenth-century bird's eye view by Kip. In the far distance the red brick house, standing four-square on an eminence, presents an arresting eye-catcher.

Long establishment adds to the sense of the estate's dominance of this rural enclave; the Giffards have lived at Chillington since 1178 and inasmuch can claim to be one of the oldest resident families in Britain. The house and estate are imbued with the ebbs and flows of the family's fortunes. The medieval structure still lies beneath the present building redesigned in the eighteenth century by Smith of Warwick, then John Soane. Inside are wonderful early-eighteenth-century Baroque rooms with plaster work thought to be by Altieri, or maybe Vassalli, alongside the more monumental interiors created by Soane later in the century. His magnificent central saloon was made on the site of the Tudor hall. The outstanding works of art date from the Soane period, notably a bust by Hewetson and – unusually – portraits of two generations by Batoni, Giffard father and son, who successively commissioned Brown and Soane. Other treats are the early-nineteenth-century paintings and the charming depictions of the pool, with the Giffard yacht.

The pool is the major feature of the eighteenth-century landscape which lies beyond the park surrounding the house; the two together are one of 'Capability' Brown's most skilful works. The park provides the imposing house with a setting of suitable scale, while the landscape beyond contains an ideal mix of trees and architecture around the enormous lake or pool which he created with a dam. Soane's classical temple is the outstanding garden building, but the most delightful is James Paine's arched bridge at one end of the pool – matched by a false bridge by Brown over his dam at the far end. Peter Giffard has carried out superb maintenance of this landscape, in spite of the horror of a motorway carving through the park so that you have to cross it before reaching the lodge gates.

It was to nearby Boscobel, then a Giffard property, that Charles II escaped after the Battle of Worcester and hid in his oak tree. Chillington's qualities of antiquity and beauty are somewhat more accessible today.

HAGLEY HALL, *Stourbridge*

The Viscount Cobham
Tel: 01562 882408

Off A456, 11 km (7 miles) north-west of Kidderminster
Open: April, May, July and Aug, selected days, 2–5 (telephone for details)
£3.50, children £1.50, concessions

Hagley Hall and its Lyttelton occupants are often overlooked in discussions of eighteenth-century taste. Sir Thomas Lyttelton married Christian, the sister of Viscount Cobham of Stowe (whose title the family later acquired). Their son, George, 1st Lord Lyttelton, was Secretary to Frederick, Prince of Wales, and was acquainted with most of the leading artistic figures of the day, many of whom made contributions to his new house at Hagley, designed by Lyttelton's friend, Sanderson Miller, in 1753. It was the last of England's great eighteenth-century Palladian houses; much of the decoration, notably the plasterwork, is reminiscent of the earlier part of the century in its light, rococo character.

Before beginning his new house George Lyttelton set about transforming the park. When complete with a variety of buildings, of which many survive including Miller's ruined castle and James 'Athenian' Stuart's Grecian temple, it was among the most influential picturesque landscapes in the country.

As befitted a Palladian plan, the arrangement of rooms is symmetrical around a central hall and saloon with staircases on both sides. In 1925 a disastrous fire destroyed the rooms on one side. Meticulous restoration was carried out by the 9th Viscount Cobham and his wife and in recent years most of the main rooms have been redecorated.

The hall gives an introduction to the plasterwork that follows in other rooms, notably with its medallions and the overmantel of Pan by Vassalli. Beyond, the saloon contains Vassalli's most exuberant plasterwork with winged *putti*, festoons and trophies hanging from ribbon bows. The tapestry drawing-room was designed for its set of Arabesque Soho tapestries and the rococo theme is continued in the outstanding pair of pier glasses with legendary Ho-ho birds, above matching console tables.

Although the library was one of the main losses of the 1925 fire, the present collection extends to some 3,500 volumes, most of them in the classical bookcases of the present library. Here also hangs the portrait of Alexander Pope by Jonathan Richardson. In the broken pediments of the bookcases stand four busts by Scheemakers of Shakespeare, Milton, Dryden and Spenser, that originally belonged to Pope. He gave them to Prince Frederick who in turn bequeathed them to his Secretary, Lyttelton.

The gallery running the length of the east front has a plaster ceiling and is given classical character by bold fluted Corinthian columns. It contains a second fine pair of pier glasses, attributed to Thomas Johnson, and was originally planned by Lord Lyttelton to display sculpture and paintings, in particular the collection of seventeenth-century portraits bequeathed to Sir Charles Lyttelton (his grandfather) by Lord Brouckner. The paintings are still *in situ*, having survived occasional direct hits during the nineteenth century when the precocious eight sons of the 4th Lord Lyttelton used the room for cricket practice.

Other portraits include a rare venture away from landscape work by Richard Wilson, who painted the full-length portrait of Admiral Thomas Smith that hangs in the saloon with Baroni's portrait of Sir Thomas Lyttelton. For most visitors, however, the vibrant combination of decoration and furnishings leaves the most lasting impression, along with Hagley's memorable setting – only a few miles from the centre of Birmingham.

BODRHYDDAN HALL, *Rhuddlan*

Col the Lord Langford
Tel: 01745 590414

On B5151, south of Rhyl, 3 km (2 miles) east of Rhuddlan
Open: June to Sept, Tues and Thur, 2–5.30
£2, children £1
Tea room

Bodryhyddan is a seventeenth-century house although traces of an earlier building exist; it has been in the hands of the Conwy family since the first house was built five hundred years ago, and is still lived in as a family home.

The main part of the present house dates from 1695 but in 1875 Conwy Grenville Hercules Rowley-Conwy, the grandfather of Lord Langford, the present owner, arranged extensive alterations with the result that Bodrhyddan is now one of the best surviving examples of the work of William Eden Nesfield, an eminent Victorian architect and the son of William Andrews Nesfield, the most fashionable garden designer of the High Victorian period. Nesfield junior gave Bodrhyddan its distinctive Dutch Queen Anne style entrance front that greets the visitor, while his father planned the formal parterre which centres on the old front door on the south side and replaced the carriage circle at the end of the approach avenue, the former front drive.

Gates at the end of this avenue bear the Conwy crest of a Moor's head, given in recognition of their service in the Crusades. In the entrance hall the fine collection of armour came from Rhuddlan Castle, of which the Conwys were hereditary constables from 1399. Their earlier establishment in the town is confirmed by the original Charter from Edward I dated 1284, which is also displayed in this room. The great hall was the central room of the original house, while the big dining-room was added towards the end of the eighteenth century by William Shipley who married into the family and was Dean of St Asaph while his father was Bishop. The Dean's portrait by Beechey hangs in the room, as does Reynolds's portrait of the Bishop, among other members of the Beechey family painted by Hudson, Vanderbank, Dahl and Ramsay.

Bodrhyddan must be the only house in Britain to boast an original body inside a mummy case. It is one of two brought back from Egypt by Richard and Charlotte

Rowley in 1836. Another peculiarity is the Cantonese altar set looted by the French during the Peninsular War and subsequently captured from the French Army baggage trains after Waterloo.

PENHOW CASTLE, *Newport*

Stephen Weeks
Tel: 01633 400800

On A485, 10 km (6 miles) east of Newport
Open: Good Fri to end Sept, Wed to Sun and Bank Holidays (Aug, daily),
10–5.15 (last admission); winter, Wed, 10–4, Sun, 1–4
£3.15, children £1.85, concessions
Tea room and bar

Penhow has been saved by the spirited restoration that Mr Weeks has carried out since buying the virtually ruined castle in 1973. Now visitors can enjoy its history that stretches back to the establishment of the Norman foothold in Wales, at Chepstow, shortly after the Conquest.

One of a ring of castles that defended Chepstow from marauding Welshmen, early in the twelfth century Penhow was granted to Sir Roger de St Maur, whose ancestor had travelled from the Touraine village of St Maur to accompany William the Conqueror to England, and whose descendants would adapt the name St Maur to Seymour, provide Henry VIII's favourite queen, Jane Seymour, and establish the titles, Duke of Somerset and Marquess of Hertford. Sixteen years after the sadly premature death of Jane's son Edward VI, the Seymour connection with Penhow was severed by its sale in 1569 and the castle embarked on four centuries of repeatedly changing ownership. The Lewis family made an important contribution during the late-seventeenth century, but by the early-eighteenth Penhow was tenanted as a farmhouse and its decline began.

The gradual extension of the castle from its Norman tower to include gatehouse, hall and later north wing, give Penhow an amorphous look, but its clustered appearance retains the air of defence that it was originally built for. Where possible the restoration has highlighted original features, notably the panels with inset paintings in the old parlour, the oak staircase and the surprisingly sophisticated dining-room with Restoration plasterwork and broken pediments over the doorcases, all dating from the Lewis occupation. In the older parts of the castle the medieval and Tudor history is strongly evoked, the effect enhanced by the stereo audio-tours that Mr Weeks pioneered and which enables visitors to tour in imaginative seclusion.

183

TREDEGAR HOUSE, *Newport*

Newport Borough Council
Tel: 01633 815880

At junction of A48 and B4239, 3 km (2 miles) south-west of Newport (M4 exit 28)

Open: Good Fri to end Sept, daily except Mon and Tues (open Mon and Tues in Aug); Oct, weekends; 11.30–4
£3.80, children £3, concessions
Tea room

Tredegar is the most architecturally distinguished country house in South Wales, and was for some five hundred years home of the Morgan family who in the nineteenth century became Lords and later Viscounts Tredegar. A rare Caroline Restoration house built between 1664 and 1672 it is on an unusually grand scale and remodelled around the Morgan old medieval home. Successive generations of Morgans enjoyed the splendours of Tredegar but after extravagance and crippling death duties during the twentieth century, the estate was sold in 1951, two years after the death of Ewan Morgan, last of the family to inhabit the house. A photograph of Ewan Morgan, whose second wife was Princess Olga Dolgorouky, at a garden party at Tredegar in 1936, wearing morning dress but standing with his pet parrot on his shoulder, illustrates the raffish eccentricity that he combined with extravagant entertainment.

Tredegar was bought by the Sisters of St Joseph to become a Roman Catholic girls' boarding school. It remained independent until 1967 when it was absorbed into the state education system and the inevitable wear and tear of all the main rooms becoming classrooms inevitably took its toll. In the early-1970s Tredegar was vacated by the school and a disastrous question-mark hung over its future. In advanced disrepair (of which the collapse in 1951, of the splendid original plaster ceiling in the main hall, was but one example), riddled with dry rot, and devoid of the paintings, furniture and other works of art that had adorned the rooms for the Morgan family, it was a potential white elephant.

In 1974, however, Newport Borough Council took the spirited decision to buy the property and, with grants and donations from various sources, carried out impressive restoration – which has included buying back much of the original contents, while others have returned on loan. The widow of the last Lord Tredegar sold back a large proportion of the family portraits and these are added to by a selection of loans from Dulwich Picture Gallery.

The wonderfully vigorous doorway on the main entrance front with spiral columns with twisted laurel leaves and the lion and griffin supporters of the Morgan arms above the broken pediment in which the armorial shield is positioned, is a Baroque feature of great rarity and offsets the impressive expansiveness of the two-storey brick walls with the roof and dormer windows above. Many of the main rooms are panelled, notably the brown room with lavishly carved oak panelling with pilasters, acanthus and *putti*, while the glittering gilt room retains the only original seventeenth-century stucco and painted ceiling.

Morgan family portraits extend from the sixteenth century to an elegant study of Katherine, Viscountess Tredegar, mother of Ewan, which hangs in one of the group of bedrooms that have been redecorated in the style of the early-twentieth-century Indian summer at Tredegar. Visitors should not miss the intriguing cedar closet on the first floor, but as enjoyable as the main 'state' rooms are the series of restored and recreated 'below stairs' rooms that illustrate country-house life at the turn of this century. Probably the most distinguished feature outside the house (other than the contemporary stable block in the same architectural style as the house) is the superbly worked set of wrought iron Edney gates, made between 1714 and 1718 for John Morgan, by the Edney brothers, William and Simon.

BRYN BRAS CASTLE, *Llanrug*

Mr and Mrs N.E. Gray-Parry
Tel: 01286 870210

Off A4086, 6.5 km (4 miles) east of Caernarfon

Open: details available on request
£4, children £2, concessions
Home-made teas

Wales is rich with eighteenth- and nineteenth-century castles that revive the romance of the country's medieval examples, and Bryn Bras is one of the most typical. Positioned between Snowdon and the Menai Straits, the castle and surrounding gardens nestle harmoniously into the foothills of the Llanberis valley which had attracted enthusiasts for picturesque landscape long before Bryn Bras was built during the 1830s. With its turrets and battlements it has the air of a toy fort, but the broad circular towers and the symmetrical central arches on the garden front add considerable substance.

Bryn Bras was possibly built by Thomas Hopper (who built the larger Penryn Castle a few miles away) for Thomas Williams, a prosperous Bangor lawyer. Following Williams's death in 1874, it was sold in 1897 and changed hands a number of times until the present owners acquired it in 1964 and carried out welcome restoration. The library with richly carved panels and chimney-piece and the staircase hall are especially striking rooms, while the rejuvenation of the gardens has been an outstanding success. In front of the castle the two statues are impressive copies of Canova's pugilists 'Creugante and Damosseno' in the Vatican Museum, while the romantic woodland and water gardens, knot garden and borders – largely dating from when the castle was built – have all been carefully restored.

MARGAM PARK, *Port Talbot*

West Glamorgan County Council
Tel: 01639 881635

Off A48 (M4 exit 38), 5 km (3 miles) south-east of Port Talbot
Open: daily all year, 10.30–5
Prices available on request

Margam is not a conventional country house but a park where adventurous commercialism mixes happily with fascinating history. Margam was the home of the Mansel Talbot family, who built Port Talbot to increase their fortune built on the shipping industry, coal and steel. Architecturally, the park is dominated by Margam Castle, completed in 1840 for Christopher Rice Mansel Talbot, the richest commoner in Britain. A fire in 1977 completely gutted the brooding, fantastical Tudor-Gothic stone building but extensive restoration has been carried out and some of the castle interiors are open to the public.

For quality, however, Margam's supreme building is the Orangery, designed by Anthony Keck for Thomas Mansel Talbot and built between 1786 and 1790. This building also underwent extensive restoration and was reopened by the Queen during her Silver Jubilee in 1977. Talbot had employed Keck to build his elegant country house at Penrice, but the Margam orangery was probably the architect's most distinguished work. It has the longest façade of any orangery in Britain, stretching for 99.6 m (327 ft) and is a study in symmetrical classical elegance. A succession of twenty-seven windows lights the main length of the building, their rusticated stonework providing the perfect contrast to the smooth grey ashlar of the upper walls (and, more particularly, the pedimented pavilions on cither end). The ashlar came from Talbot's own quarry at Pyle. Each pavilion has a triple-light venetian window with Ionic columns.

Later in date than most other surviving orangeries in Britain, Margam's demonstrated the classical idea of repeat symmetry in a manner that practically suited the type of building required to enable Talbots' orange trees to live through the winter.

NORTHERN ENGLAND

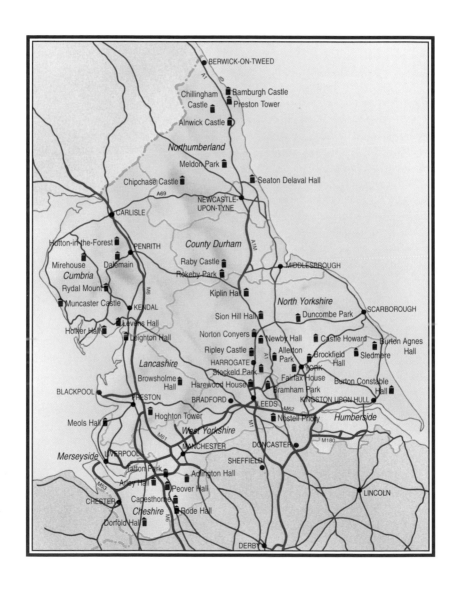

DALEMAIN, *Penrith*

Robert Hasell-McCosh
Tel: 01768 486450

On A592, 5 km (3 miles) south-west of Penrith
Open: Apr to Oct, daily except Fri and Sat, 11.15–5
£4, children £3
Home-made teas

The passing road leading from Penrith to the Lake District's heartland presents an irresistible view of Dalemain, a balustraded house of the utmost restraint, built of wonderfully pink sandstone quarried a mile away, facing down to where Dacre Beck joins the River Eamont before running into Ullswater. Behind the well-mannered early eighteenth-century façade of Dalemain exists a fascinating mixture of domesticity and surprises. The elegant staircase hall, hung largely with family portraits, leads through to one of the best eighteenth-century Chinese rooms in England. The dining-room, which has a mellow, clubbable quality, abuts on the medieval stone-vaulted hall now used as a restaurant. An ancient stone spiral staircase leads to charming small panelled rooms characterizing early-eighteenth-century domesticity.

The estate was purchased in 1679 by Mr Hasell, agent to Lady Anne Clifford, and has remained in the family ever since. They established themselves as the largest landowners on the northern shores of Ullswater. Hasell's house was built around the existing Pele-tower and stone staircase which dated from Dalemain's fortification to repel Border raiders. Hugh de Morville took refuge in the tower with his brother after he had taken part in Becket's murder in Canterbury. Hasell added his house around a courtyard and during the 1730s another Edward added the two Georgian fronts to the block's grander apartments for entertaining. The cantilevered staircase is of the same period.

The main rooms contain the family portraits by Lely, Beale and Richardson, to Devis and Zoffany and a succession of later works to the present day. Here too is furniture by Gillow of Lancaster, porcelain and other works of art. Elsewhere there is a good collection of glass and silver. The rooms have a nicely judged mixture of the expected and unexpected: of the latter the hall contains a massive view of Venice, one of the small upstairs rooms a splendid pair of globes. There is a nursery exhibition, a Yeomanry Museum and a recently established museum devoted to local agriculture and crafts.

The present owner's mother created the garden which is full of quality and greatly enhances the setting; her work brought the family history full circle as the walled garden and buttressed terrace that she has made such features were originally built by Sir Edward Hasell.

HOLKER HALL, *Cark-in-Cartmel*

The Lord and Lady Cavendish
Tel: 01539 558328

On B5278, 1.6 km (1 mile) north of Cark-in-Cartmel, 6.5 km (4 miles) west of
Grange-over-Sands (M6 exit 36)
Open: Apr to end Oct, daily except Sat, 10.30–4.30
Prices/concessions available from Administrator
Restaurant

Where the foothills of the Lake District drop away into Morecambe Bay, a large Tudor-revival Victorian house is a surprising discovery. Holker's inaccessibility tells much about its history. It enjoyed a lengthy period as a subsidiary home of the Cavendish

family, Dukes of Devonshire, until the nineteenth century when William Cavendish, who had been brought up at Holker, married one cousin, inherited the titles to become the 7th Duke from another, but retained his love of his childhood home in preference to the treasures on offer at his other main seats, Chatsworth and Hardwick Hall.

Parts of the house are much older, some dating from the 1604 reconstruction, others from alterations during the 1720s. But its immediate and abiding impression is Victorian, vividly portraying the home of a patrician, politically active family. Both the 7th Duke's sons became cabinet ministers and the younger, Lord Frederick, was the target of a political assassination that stunned Victorian society. His wife, Lucy, was a niece of the Liberal Prime Minister Gladstone who, in 1882, appointed Lord Frederick Secretary of State for Ireland. On the day he arrived in Dublin to take up the appointment, he was murdered in Phoenix Park.

The 7th Duke made substantial alterations to the house between 1838 and 1842 and later built the stable block. But most of his work met a tragic end; in 1871 fire gutted the west wing – the largest block. Undeterred the Duke set about rebuilding and it is his second effort which visitors to Holker admire today. Paley and Austin of Lancaster carried out the work which enlarged the house and, from the outside, the warm red sandstone provides unity to the varied detail whose scale might otherwise be confusing.

The rooms continue the theme of confident quality. The detail of craftsmanship, in linenfold panelling, rich plaster ceilings and sombre marble fireplaces, is unfailingly excellent. Even when electricity was installed, in 1911, great care was taken so that modern comfort did not intrude; in the library the light-switches are concealed behind dummy books. As befits a ducal home, the four monumental twisted oak columns that flank the dining-room fireplace were carved from trees felled on the estate. The cantilever oak staircase was built with similarly local timber, and the limestone for the monolithic archway which divides the hall from the staircase was quarried at nearby Allerston.

Victorian families were renowned for their love of busily cluttered rooms and mixing furniture, pictures and works of art from different styles and periods. But few families had the combination of quality and quantity that has survived seemingly unchanged at Holker, whether it is the 3,500 books with which the 7th Duke filled his library, or the mixture of French and English furniture and Old Master paintings in the drawing-room. The family played carpet bowls with heavy granite balls along the broad upstairs gallery.

Holker's present owners, Lord and Lady Cavendish have ensured that visitors are able to enjoy the inside of the house apparently unaltered from the end of the last century. Outside their efforts are immediately visible in the restoration and replanting of the old woodland gardens, and creation of new formal areas near the house, which together brought deserved recognition in 1991 with the award of the HHA/Christie's Garden of the Year prize.

HUTTON-IN-THE-FOREST, *Penrith*

The Lord and Lady Inglewood
Tel: 01768 484449

On B5305, 10 km (6 miles), north-west of Penrith 4 km (2½ miles) from M6 exit 41

Open: Easter Sun to following Fri; May to end Sept, Thur, Fri, Sun and Bank Holidays (also Aug, Wed); 1–4
£3.50, children £1.50

Both house and garden at Hutton-in-the-Forest are well worth discovering, folded into the understated country north of Penrith. Distinguished for the successive waves of architectural improvement wrought in every century since 1600 when Hutton was developed around a defensive Pele-tower, the house continued to throw out shoots. The 1630 long gallery is an unusual survivor in the county; having fallen into disrepair in the eighteenth century it was restored by Webster around 1830. It is now hung with family portraits and contains good examples of early-seventeenth-century furniture.

In the late-seventeenth century Edward Addison, William Talman's master-mason at nearby Lowther Castle, added the exuberant Baroque façade. This encloses an enfilade of rooms, confirming the pattern of the first floor overlooking the gardens. The staircase, richly carved with *putti* and foliage, leads to the library, ante-room and drawing-room. The Fletchers, as can be seen in the fine sequence of portraits, were a cosmopolitan family; the inlaid seventeenth-century furniture supports blue and white oriental porcelain, the height of fashion at the time. Mainly Chinese, there is also a rare Japanese piece as well as Dutch and English Delft. The period decoration continues with fine Mortlake tapestries on the stairs, and the elaborate gardens also date from this period, laid out in the formal Dutch style.

The eighteenth century saw the house pass to the Vane family and the series of elegant 1740s rooms – recently superbly restored – are their work. The Cupid room has a delicate plaster ceiling and set against the panelling is good period furniture. One of the house's highlights, the early Hogarth portrait of Walter Vane and his family, hangs in this room.

The house was the subject of almost constant work during the nineteenth century, first by Webster, subsequently by Salvin in a surprisingly sympathetic mood. The collections were also enriched by Sir Henry Vane and his wife, Margaret Gladstone, cousin of the Liberal Prime Minister. She introduced the William Morris decorative schemes and the William de Morgan studio pottery. With its successive changes, Hutton is an excellent example of how 'contemporary fashionable improvements' were introduced harmoniously to the advantage of the old house.

LEVENS HALL, *Kendal*

C.H. Bagot
Tel: 01539 560321

On A6, 8 km (5 miles) south of Kendal
Open: Apr to end Sept, daily except Fri and Sat, 11–5
£4.80, children £2.50, concessions
Tea room

House, interiors and garden at Levens present an unusually integrated whole, together celebrating the Elizabethan and late-seventeenth-century periods when the major developments took place. Even the uncomfortable proximity of passing main roads cannot disturb the place's air of establishment, which dates back to the thirteenth century and the construction of the Pele-tower which forms part of the present house.

In 1562 Levens was bought by Alan Bellingham and at the hands of his son, James, the defensive tower became a comfortable home. James Bellingham, later knighted by James I, rebuilt Levens and the irregular but well-assembled exterior has changed little since. His interior work was more spectacular: panelling with local oak, plaster wall decoration and moulded plaster ceilings. Most vigorous of all are the carved oak overmantels, especially the one in the drawing-room which has ascending pilasters in the three classical orders, dividing and flanking heraldic panels with the arms of Bellingham and Elizabeth I. Bellingham was obviously a loyal subject; the Queen's arms in brilliantly painted plaster also surmount the great hall fireplace.

James Bellingham's great-grandson, Alan, gambled Levens away and in 1688 it was bought by his kinsman, Colonel James Grahme, Keeper of the Privy Purse to James II. Lely's fine portraits of the colonel and his wife hang in the drawing-room along with his daughter by Hudson. He was responsible for much of the important late-Stuart and William and Mary furniture which is so well-suited to the panelled rooms. Carved oak and walnut chairs abound, with pride of place going to the Charles II walnut set in the dining-room.

Grahme also commissioned Levens' best-known feature, the now wonderfully mature topiary garden laid out by the Frenchman, Guillaume Beaumont who lived in a small house at Levens. The assembly of clipped yew trees that fill the garden to the east of the house are a feature of national importance and Beaumont's work extended to the very early ha-ha and avenue in the parkland beyond. Both the present owners and Mr Bagot's parents have carried out important work in the garden, which deservedly won the HHA / Christie's Garden of the Year Award in 1995.

MIREHOUSE, *Keswick*

Mr and Mrs Spedding
Tel: 01768 772287

On A591, 6.5 km (4 miles) north-west of Keswick

Open: Apr to Oct, Sun and Wed; also Aug, Fri; 2–4.30
£3, children £1.50, concessions
Tea room

Of Cumbrian houses open to the public, Mirehouse most closely reflects the Lake District. Set on the shore of Bassenthwaite with the ground rising dramatically behind, it has long been the home of the Spedding family, whose friends, including Wordsworth, Tennyson and Carlyle, have left an indelible mark on the place. The contents accurately tell of the family's activities: a portrait of the Mayor of Newcastle; rare whaling paintings; portraits by the local George Romney; and a clock by Jonas Barber of Winster. They also confirm the family's involvement in literature, history and

philosophy through the nineteenth century.

The library is impressively full of books and documents relating to Thomas Carlyle and Tennyson, while the smoking-room contains manuscripts by Francis Bacon whose works were edited by James Spedding during this period. The walls are hung with important portraits by Samuel Laurence and photography by Julia Margaret Cameron. Not only the library, but most of the house presents history in a most digestible and enjoyable fashion. Each room from the dining-room to the school-room contains interesting artefacts clearly shown and waiting to be explored. There are coins 'hidden' for children to find, a Queen Anne cabinet with sweets hidden in secret drawers for the enquiring to discover, and a gong for the outgoing to bang.

Outside the walks by the lake incorporate the spot where Tennyson composed 'Morte d'Arthur', and the adventure playground in the woods provides further enjoyment for children.

MUNCASTER CASTLE, *Ravenglass*

Mrs P. Gordon-Duff-Pennington
Tel: 01229 717614

On A595, 1.6 km (1 mile) south-east of Ravenglass

Open: end Mar to end Oct, Tues to Sun and Bank Holidays, 1–4; gardens and Owl Centre, daily all year,11–5
£4.90, children £2.80, concessions (1995 prices)
Restaurant

Ruskin called the view from Muncaster over Eskdale to the peaks of the Lake District 'the gateway to paradise', and the castle's position is among the most spectacular in the country, enhanced by its remoteness. Defensive potential accounted for the fourteenth-century pele-tower built by the Penningtons from which their castle originally developed, but today Muncaster is as transformed by Anthony Salvin from 1862.

Externally, his design in warm pink granite is in the style of noble restraint that he employed at Peckforton, rather than one of his more fantastical efforts such as Harlaxton. Inside, the variety of the hall, dining-room, octagonal library and drawing-room pay tribute to his skilful versatility. In the library a high brass-railed gallery surmounts the bookcases that are broken by doorcases, panels and niches, and the ceiling is imaginatively ribbed and vaulted. Equally enjoyable is the barrel ceiling of the drawing-room with plasterwork by Italian craftsmen.

Salvin was commissioned by the 4th Lord Muncaster (the title acquired by the Penningtons in 1783), but on the death of his brother in 1917 the castle passed to his mother's family, the Ramsdens, and it is their first incumbent, Sir John Ramsden, whose hand is most evident inside and out. He brought Ramsden portraits of considerable quality, including four by Reynolds, which hang together in the drawing-room. The Penningtons decorate the walls of the dining-room. Sir John was a discerning collector and among the items that he acquired are the alabaster nude by John of Bologna, the painting 'Boy with a Falcon', by an Italian master and the Italian bronzes. They add variety to fine seventeenth-century furniture, glittering silver, and important porcelain such as the Derby service in the dining-room. For family history, however, the most prized possession is the 'Luck of Muncaster': a drinking bowl presented by Henry VI to Sir John Pennington who took in the King at Muncaster after his defeat at the battle of Hexham. So long as the cup remains intact, it will ensure that the family continue to thrive at Muncaster.

Sir John Ramsden's other major contribution was the gardens. He financed a number of plant-collecting expeditions to the Himalayas during the 1920s and from the seeds brought back by Ludlow, Sheriff and Kingdon Ward, established the superb collection of rhododendrons and azaleas ideally suited to their woodland setting. They provide a fitting addition to Muncaster's other garden feature: the long grass terrace made in the eighteenth century which provides unforgettable views over the landscape beyond.

RYDAL MOUNT, *Ambleside*

The Trustees of Rydal Mount
Tel: 01539 433002

Off A591, between Ambleside and Grasmere

Open: March to end Oct, daily, 9.30–5; Nov to end Feb, daily except Tues, 10–4

£2.50, children £1

Rydal Mount is a shrine to William Wordsworth who lived here from 1813 until his death in 1850, bought by his great great-granddaughter, Mary Henderson, and now preserved by her family. The typically Lakeland house, extended from a sixteenth-century cottage during the eighteenth century, with views out to Windermere in one direction, Rydal Water in another and fells all around, encapsulates the area's appeal to the poet. He designed the garden to consist of, in his own words, 'lawn and trees carefully planted so as not to obscure the view'.

The warm, homely rooms recreate the life of the group who lived harmoniously together: William, his wife Mary and their three surviving children, John, Dora and William, the poet's sister Dorothy and his sister-in-law, Sara Hutchinson. Work and relaxation were obviously carefully separated; a visitor was apparently told by a member of the staff, 'This is my master's library where he keeps his books: his study is out of doors.' Sadly the library does not survive intact but the happy domesticity is brought to life in the various pictures: a number of Wordsworth himself, including the drawing by B.R. Haydon whose original hangs in the National Portrait Gallery, and a softer likeness by the American, Henry Inman. Originally the latter was painting a portrait to mark Wordsworth's appointment as Poet Laureate and Mary Wordsworth was so taken with the result that she commissioned another for herself.

Contrastingly unsettled is the portrait of Dorothy by S. Crosthwaite, painted three years before her mental collapse. It is her only known portrait. Although Wordsworth and Coleridge had fallen out before he came to Rydal Mount, the friendship is perpetuated in Coleridge's portrait by Northcote in the library.

RABY CASTLE, *Staindrop*

The Lord Barnard
Tel: 01833 660202

On A688, 1.6 km (1 mile) north of Staindrop

**Open: Good Fri to following Wed; May to end June, Wed and Sun; July to
end Sept, daily except Sat; Bank Holidays (Sat to following Wed incl); 1–5
£3.50, children £1.50, concessions
Tea room**

Massive Raby Castle is testament to how far south Anglo-Scottish border struggles
stretched; the Nevills who built and steadily extended the castle were Wardens of the
Scottish Marches and a family of considerable power – one married Joan, daughter of
John of Gaunt, and the castle's Joan's Tower is named after her. They became Earls of
Westmorland but fell from grace in 1569 when the 6th Earl led the Rising of the North.
Raby was confiscated by the Crown and acquired in 1626 by Sir Henry Vane whose
descendants have lived here since.

The gateway survives from the old curtain wall which provided protection from the
bleak surroundings, a far cry from today's parkland with large lake and sloping walled
gardens. Many of the nine towers date from different periods of the castle's original
construction – mainly during the fourteenth century, and the walls retain sections of
monumental medieval masonry, 9 m (30 ft) high and in places 3.6m (12 ft) thick.

The great kitchen was built in 1360 and in use until 1954. Otherwise the interiors
were remodelled during the eighteenth and nineteenth centuries. The 1st Lord Barnard,
furious at his son's marriage, determined to disinherit the miscreant and sold the
contents, took off the castle roof and cut down most of the trees in the park. His son
took his case to Chancery and won. Restoration was carried out by a number of
architects, principally Daniel Garrett and James Paine, and the park was planted at the
same time.

In 1754 the Earldom of Darlington was added to the Barnard barony, and during the
1780s more alterations were carried out for the 2nd Earl of Darlington by Carr of York,
in particular the creation of the present entrance hall. Carr raised the ceiling and made a
new entrance large enough to accommodate a carriage (solving the problem of carriages
turning in the inner court). The room became a striking example of Gothic revival on a
huge scale, its high vaulted ceiling supported on deep red scagliola pillars.

The most extensive changes came during the 1840s when Darlington's son, who was
made the 1st Duke of Cleveland, employed William Burn whose 'baronial' reputation
was well suited to working at Raby. He transformed the old medieval hall into the
enormous Barons' Hall extended to a length of 40 m (130 ft) with a new timber roof.
The portraits here give an indication of the array of works of art to be found at Raby.

In the hall there are family portraits by the leading artists of successive sixteenth-, seventeenth-, eighteenth- and nineteenth-century generations. There are Old Masters in the ante-library, and, in the small drawing-room, outstanding English sporting paintings. It is a source of amusement that the family ancestor, Barbara, Duchess of Cleveland, does not hang at Raby while her rival Nell Gwyn, painted by Lely, does. The huge Kandler Meissen birds in the Barons' Hall are a splendid adornment, while the marble statue by the American Hiram Powers in the entrance hall, of a manacled, nude Greek slave girl caused a sensation at the 1851 Great Exhibition.

The collection of sporting pictures was begun by the 1st Duke and has continued, the latest addition being a portrait by Munnings of the present Lord Barnard's grandfather, Mr Montagu Cradock, left to Lord Barnard by his mother in 1993. The 1st Duke's love of hunting left its mark throughout the Raby estate. He had all his farmhouses and cottages whitewashed so he could identify them if in need of assistance when out with the hounds. Today they remain a landmark stretching from the A68 to the Cumbrian border in Teesdale.

ROKEBY PARK, *Barnard Castle*

Sir Andrew Morritt
Tel: 01833 637334

Off A66, north of Greta Bridge
Open: 6 May, then end May to early Sept, Mon and Tue, 2–5
(last admission 4.30)
Prices available on request

Rokeby is an important and little-known Palladian villa, built between 1725 and 1730 by the distinguished amateur architect, Sir Thomas Robinson. Robinson was rebuilding his own family home (which had been acquired by an ancestor *c.*1610), and he corresponded about his work with the leading exponents of Palladianism: his father-in-law, Lord Carlisle at Castle Howard, Lord Burlington, and the architect, William Wakefield. The delightful, chaste exterior introduces the series of fine interiors with many distinctive Palladian features including impressive doorcases with columns and pediments and fine carved marble chimney-pieces.

Robinson had no heir and in 1769 sold Rokeby to J.S. Morritt whose family have lived in the house ever since. Morritt's portrait by Benjamin West hangs in the saloon, the house's most impressive room and originally Robinson's hall, with, among other Morritt paintings and Reynolds's 'Hope Nursing Love'. Above are a series of historical portraits that were some of the works of art included in Robinson's sale. Morritt's sister, Anne, was an artist of great talent and worked in needlework the copies of famous pictures which still hang in the house. The most important contribution to the collections, however, was made by Morritt's connoisseur son, John, who collected during a grand tour of Europe and in 1813 purchased Velasquez's 'Rokeby Venus'. (The picture was sold in 1906 and hangs in the National Gallery.)

Victorian alterations to the house were sensitively in keeping with its Palladian character and appearance, at the same time as bringing enjoyable period introductions such as the gasoliers in the saloon and dining-room. But today Rokeby retains the mood and elegance of its eighteenth-century origins and, with its fine pictures and other works of art, is a surprising treat among the windswept Durham moors.

ALNWICK CASTLE, *Alnwick*

The Duke of Northumberland
Tel: 01665 510777

In Alnwick, on north side of town centre

Open: Easter to mid-Oct, daily except Fri, 11–5, (last admission 4.30)
£4.50, children, £2.50, concessions
Home-made teas

The first view of Alnwick immediately conjures up images of the border struggles in which for centuries the castle was constantly embroiled. Some battlements and gatehouse turrets still bear the eerie stone figures put up to fool the Scots into thinking there were more soldiers defending than in reality. Percys succeeded de Vescys as hereditary Wardens of the Scottish Marches in 1309 and have been at Alnwick ever since. From undisputed masters of the region they progressed through more peaceful centuries to become cultivated, collecting grandees as befitted their dukedom, to which the ancient earldom was elevated in 1766.

The rugged, strategic fortress, with its undulating levels of battlemented stone walls, became superbly picturesque during the eighteenth century with the landscaping of the surrounding park by 'Capability' Brown. Around the same time the interiors were transformed by Robert Adam who created a series of Gothic interiors. Adam's work was swept away during the 1850s by the 4th Duke, and it is his decorative work, consciously evoking the Italian Renaissance, that survives today, an abundance of richly carved and gilded ceilings, brilliant gold and scarlet damask walls, and monumental Carrara white marble chimney-pieces.

Paintings, furniture and works of art throughout illustrate the combination of distinguished family history and connoisseurship. There is no other English family whose three main houses (Alnwick, Northumberland House in London, and Syon House on the Thames) were specially painted by Canaletto. All three paintings hang at Alnwick. Portraits of successive Percys and their connections are matched by important Italian Old Masters, collected by the 4th Duke for his newly decorated home. When Northumberland House was demolished in 1874, its superb English furniture – pieces by William Kent, Robert Adam and John Linnell – went to either Alnwick or Syon; but none rivals the castle's most outstanding pieces, a pair of cabinets with Florentine *pietra dura* made for Louis XIV by Domenico Cucci at the Gobelins factory, removed from the Tuileries during the French Revolution and bought by the 3rd Duke in 1822.

The mixture of medieval history with later cultivation and establishment is constantly evident to the visitor and illustrates with rare quality the progression of one of England's most senior families through successive centuries.

BAMBURGH CASTLE, *Bamburgh*

The Lady Armstrong
Tel: 01668 214215

On B1340, 26 km (16 miles) north of Alnwick
Open: Easter to end Oct, daily, 11–variable closing
£2.50, children £1.10
Tea room

High on a cliff dramatically overlooking its village to the west and the North Sea in the opposite direction, Bamburgh Castle conforms to every picturesque notion of an ancient impregnable stronghold. Vast and intimidating from the outside, it is therefore surprising to enter a comfortable Victorian country house. The castle was restored by the 1st Lord Armstrong who purchased it in 1894 (after his even more ambitious work on the house and garden at Cragside, also in Northumberland.) At Cragside he transformed nearly 404 ha (1,000 acres) of rough hillside into ornamental woods and gardens, and built a house which he eventually extended by over a hundred rooms. He is estimated to have spent £1.5 million on the restoration of Bamburgh; the two projects together represent one of the great Victorian millionaire's follies.

While the interiors perpetuate the atmosphere of Lord Armstrong's period, strong echoes of Northumbrian wars and saints are also heard at Bamburgh. Lindisfarne is just across the water and it is impossible not to feel something of the Dark Ages when visiting the castle. Indeed the greatest period in its history was the seventh century when it was conquered by Edwin of Northumbria and became the seat of the kings of Northumbria. Under King (Saint) Oswald the monastery on Holy Island or Lindisfarne was founded, before the castle was sacked by the Vikings.

For the tourist there are ghostly tales and, of course, dungeons (with gruesome tableau vivant), There are fine contents, including the series of portraits, but they have to take second place to the grandeur and quality of Lord Armstrong's restoration work.

CHILLINGHAM CASTLE, *Wooler*

Sir Humphrey Wakefield, Bt
Tel: 01668 5359

Off A697, 19 km (12 miles) north-west of Alnwick
Open: Easter and May to end Sept, daily except Tues, 1.30–5
£3.30, children £2.50, concessions
Tea room

The recent restoration of Chillingham has been an heroic and serious undertaking by Sir Humphrey Wakefield. A grand and very handsome medieval border fortress, with 'the true rust of the Barons' Wars', Chillingham has been saved with great panache. Famous for its wild cattle, a unique kind of safari, everything about a visit to Chillingham is out of the ordinary. Internally, it is full of touches that leave one wondering how much Sir Humphrey is indulging his sense of humour. An enormous and highly erotic nude (Susannah and the Elders) forms a backdrop in the chapel. The arched stone altar had emerged from behind the rotten nineteenth-century plasterwork in a study. Here 'Put out more Flags' seems to have done the trick with many a cherished battle banner given a last flourish.

The experience is akin to a visit to an eccentric Irish country house with a touch of 'Carry on Castle'. The theme of fun continues (with dire warning to the faint-hearted) in the Dungeon which has a connoisseurs' collection of instruments of torture any Inquisitor would be proud of. The gardens and grounds have been superbly restored and are immaculately maintained in intriguing counterpoint to the surrounding Cheviot Hills.

CHIPCHASE CASTLE, *Wark-on-Tyne*

Mrs P. Torday
Tel: 01434 230203

Off B6320, 16 km (10 miles) north-west of Hexham
Open: June, daily (to 28th), 2–5
£3

Occupying a key strategic position in the North Tyne valley, Chipchase was for centuries involved in the roaming struggles and skirmishes of the the Scottish borders. The great Pele-tower with corner turrets perched against the skyline dates from the fourteenth century and must have provided wide observation over the surrounding country as well as secure defence. Now it abuts the south-east corner of the more comfortable house

203

built of similar stone in the 1620s and then altered during the mid-eighteenth century.

At that time the south front overlooking parkland and the Tyne valley beyond was made symmetrical with an arrangement of sash windows, the geometry completed with dummy ones in the tower, string courses and a Doric doorway. The 1620 Jacobean entrance front retains its E-shape. The two side bays, with battlemented two-storey window bays, flank the central arrangement over the protruding arched doorway, which comprises semi-hexagonal windows on two floors and the upper flourish of an armorial shield charger of the Heron family who built the Jacobean house. Today the arrangement of bays, battlements and generous fenestration presents an impressive picture on both main fronts.

Inside, the central hall is flanked by dining- and drawing-rooms which extend into the two west-facing bays. James Paine is credited with designing the delicate plaster ceiling in the drawing-room, but the most striking decorative feature is in the upstairs billiard-room, the ornately carved oak overmantel supported on triple clusters of pillars, and incorporating the five senses, Time's winged chariot and the seven graces on armorial shields. The billiard-room's lofty ceiling with plaster decoration contrasts with the cosy lower ones of the ground-floor rooms. The dining-room contains a fine set of mid-nineteenth-century furniture by James Mein of Kelso. Interesting paintings include Richardson's 'Wreckers off the Mouth of the Tyne' in the entrance hall.

At a short distance from the entrance stands a small chapel of medieval origins, but rebuilt at the same time as the mid-eighteenth-century work on the house and of considerable note for the box-pews and choir stalls with Ionic pilasters and other furnishings which have no rival for the period in Northumberland.

MELDON PARK, *Morpeth*

Michael Cookson
Tel: 01670 72 661

On B6343, 11 km (7 miles) west of Morpeth
Open: late May to late June, daily; also Aug Bank Holiday; 2–5

Meldon is an important Greek Revival house by one of the leading figures in the early-nineteenth-century movement, John Dobson. The impact of the chaste stone exterior is heightened by the house's position overlooking the Wansbeck valley. Dobson spent a month inspecting the Meldon estate before choosing this particular spot for its picturesque qualities that would best offset his planned house. The lack of decoration to the main south, west and east façades is severe and extends to the style of the Ionic entrance portico on the west side arranged like a Greek propylarum, but the proportions are so exact that the overall effect is one of satisfying quality.

Inside, Dobson arranged the main rooms around a large two-storey staircase hall. The south front contains the library, central ante-room with a bow, and drawing-room, interlinking through sets of double mahogany doors so arranged that the first doorcase exactly frames the second and the second frames the windows on the east side. Internal decoration is restrained in the utmost: marble chimney-pieces – black in the library, austere white in the drawing-room – and ceilings with subdued cornices and simple geometric patterns. The dining-room ceiling is coffered with slightly more vigour, but the only room with any hint of theatre is the staircase hall, its single lower flight dividing into two return flights. Ornament was limited to the ceiling and a delicate wrought iron handrail, but between the wars the composition was upset, albeit by a distinguished hand, Sir Edwin Lutyens. He left his mark on a number of Northumbrian houses after his daughter had married Viscount Ridley of Blagdon and after a Cookson had married a Ridley girl, he made alterations to the Meldon staircase hall, replacing the handrails with the more robust mahogany ones, extending the plaster decoration to wall panels, and setting four columns in the upper landing.

Dobson's charming watercolours of the house survive at Meldon and his fastidious taste would have approved the other paintings and furniture that the main rooms contain. Successive generations of Cooksons hang in the dining-room, their hunting attire suggesting an hereditary enthusiasm for the chase confirmed by the outstanding stables a short distance from the house. Horses are not the only animals to have been faithful friends; Isaac Cookson lost his dog while travelling in Maryland, USA, and it reappeared at Meldon some time after his return to England. The house is open to the public at the time when the woodland garden with its rhododendrons are at their best and the walled kitchen garden beyond should not be missed.

PRESTON TOWER, *Chathill*

Major T.H. Baker-Cresswell
Tel: 01665 589227

Off B1340, 1.6 km (1 mile) from A1, 11 km (7 miles) north of Alnwick
Open: all year, daily during daylight
£1, concessions

Tall gaunt Preston Tower is evidence of the gruelling, violent life in medieval Northumberland. It was built by Robert Harbottle around 1392 after he had been promoted by Henry IV for good support in the border clashes. Contemporary with the dashing Harry Hotspur, Harbottle fought at the battles of Otterburn and Halidon Hill and his cousin, Sir Guiscard, was slain at Flodden.

The battlemented stone turrets have only small arrow slits to give light, although

there is the surprising decoration of a large clock near the top of the centre block. The few rooms are deliberately stark and provide a vivid suggestion of life for those under the endless threat of 'Border Raids': guard room and prison on the ground floor, primitive quarters above. In an upper room there are details of the Battle of Flodden. A far cry from later, more civilized country houses, it re-creates history as enjoyed by generations of schoolchildren.

SEATON DELAVAL HALL, *Whitley Bay*

The Lord Hastings
Tel: 0191 237 3040/237 1493

Off A190, between Blyth and Whitley Bay
Open: May to end Sept, Wed, Sun and Bank Holidays, 2–6
£2.50, children 50p
Tea room

It is a tribute to the genius of Sir John Vanbrugh that the burnt-out shell of Seaton Delaval presents one of the most impressive visions among English country houses. The splendours of his other two masterpieces, Blenheim and Castle Howard, provide scant preparation although the scale is similarly monumental. The warm Oxfordshire countryside and rolling Howardian Hills are replaced by bleak, windswept Northumbrian coast. Deprived of decoration by a catastrophic fire in 1822, its stone blackened by industrial pollution, the central block of the house stands stripped to the architectural skeleton that Vanbrugh conceived. The combination of the setting and the reputation of his patrons, the 'gay Delavals', who careered through life sometimes talented and worthy, more often reckless and dissipated, urged Vanbrugh to a design to match.

The purse of Admiral George Delaval – who commissioned the house in 1718, but who died in 1723 as a result of a riding accident before the building was complete – was not as large as those of Vanbrugh's patrons at Blenheim and Castle Howard. But any reduction in size is more than compensated for by the gargantuan scale of the detail and the extremes of the component parts. Certainly the vast courtyard facing north towards the sea 1.6 km (1 mile) away and the port of Blyth beyond, makes no concessions.

On either side are the east and west wings, reminiscent of Castle Howard, their long two-storey façades with central pediments, and elegant arcades which continue in curves to join the north-facing central block. The transfer from the horizontal proportions of the wings to the vigorous verticality of the central block is abrupt. Great ringed Doric columns – grouped in threes – stand on either side of the central door at the top of broad steps. Octagonal towers on the corners, of which there are a matching pair on the south front, are balanced by taller square towers that contain staircases, while across the centre extends the bizarrely tall attic storey topped by its pediment and chimney-cases. The overall impression is one of architectural metamorphosis, as though the house has thrust its way up out of the ground.

The restless movement is exaggerated by the rusticated stonework and other details and is equally evident on the south front dominated by an Ionic portico. Inside the heroic scale continues in two rooms that fill most of the space: the entrance hall – originally two-storey and open to the roof but retaining its symmetry in the arched recesses on two levels – and the saloon beyond, which stretches the length of the south front. On either side the staircases wind giddily up their towers.

After the fire in 1822 the central block was abandoned for nearly one hundred and forty years and was open to the elements for much of that time. Only enlightened restoration by Lord Hastings, whose family inherited Seaton Delaval in 1814, having married the Delaval heiress, saved the house from total dereliction after requisition during the Second World War. Neither wing was damaged in the fire and the west wing which once housed cavernous kitchens, is now the family home, its elegantly furnished rooms providing a stark contrast to the adjacent shell. In the east wing Vanbrugh's stables survive as he built them; fit for horses that drew Apollo's chariot. Vanbrugh did not live to see Seaton Delaval completed in 1828, but the house strongly evokes the mood of a requiem and its idiosyncrasies present a suitable monument.

ADLINGTON HALL, *Macclesfield*

Mrs C.J.C. Legh
Tel: 01625 829206

On A523, 8 km (5 miles) north of Macclesfield

Open: all year by prior arrangement
£4, children £1.50
Tea room

Cheshire is famous for its black-and-white timbered houses but Adlington presents a startling contrast of the old house in this style, fronted with an eighteenth-century red-brick wing with a central portico of bizarre size. The stables to one side are the same period, and equally imposing. These Georgian additions were carried out by Charles Legh who considerably altered and extended the old courtyard house where his ancestors had lived since the thirteenth century, although his work was reduced to a more practical scale in 1928. His staircase, drawing-room and dining-room survive, the

last two with warm classical panelling and there is an overmantel of carved fruit and foliage in the drawing-room. Both rooms and the staircase hall contain good Legh portraits by Cornelius Johnson, Hudson, Van Reyschoot and Opie among others.

But none of Charles Legh's work compares with Adlington's oldest and most important room, the great hall; indeed it is one of the most astonishing interiors to be found in any English country house. It was built by Thomas Legh between 1480 and 1505, with a lofty hammerbeam roof and towering spere trusses hewn − so it is said − out of live oak trees. Between the oaks is the house's chief glory, the great Baroque organ built during the seventeenth century by 'Father' Bernard Smith, the master of his trade. It rises with increasing bravado through the delicately balustraded gallery to clusters of pipes and up to the family arms with their unicorn crest between trumpeting angels. Handel played on it when he visited Adlington in 1741; he composed a hunting song with words by Charles Legh. The organ was silent for over a century until restored in 1959 by Noel Mander.

At the opposite end of the hall is a coved canopy that dates from the original building, with sixty later heraldic panels, continuing the heraldry of the angels on the roof hammers who carry shields. There are only windows along the south side. The other three walls bear enormous murals depicting scenes from the Trojan legends, whose date is uncertain but which were plastered over for a long time until accidentally uncovered in 1859 during a game of shuttlecock.

Mrs Legh inherited Adlington from her father in 1991 and is restoring the important eighteenth-century picturesque garden with a Palladian tea house, shell house and an arched Chinese bridge.

ARLEY HALL, *Northwich*

The Hon Michael and Mrs Flower
Tel: 01565 777353

Off A50 at High Legh, 11 km (7 miles) south-east of Warrington (M6 exits 19 and 20, M56 exits 9 and 10)

Open: Apr to Oct, Tues to Sun and Bank Holidays, 12−5
Gardens £2.80, house £1.60 (children half-price)

Cheshire abounds in Victorian country houses built on mercantile or industrial fortunes. Arley, one of the county's most imposing, was contrastingly the product of a long-established landed estate and built by the personification of a serious-minded patrician Victorian landowner, Rowland Egerton-Warburton. In 1813 he inherited the estate from his great-uncle, Sir Peter Warburton, and during a long tenure from 1831 until his death in 1891 he rebuilt the house. With the help of his wife Mary he created the gardens which have been immaculately maintained and improved by future generations.

Arley was a close collaboration between Egerton-Warburton and the Cheshire architect, George Latham. The former decided that the house would be 'Elizabethan' and to guarantee authenticity the pair toured sixteenth-century houses noting architectural and decorative details. These were incorporated: swirling chimney stacks, pointed gables and Tudor heraldic beasts on the roofline (some now removed to the garden), stone-mullioned windows, decorative stonework and diapered brickwork. The main flourish was a room with an oriel window over the entrance porch surmounted by an octagonal tower and cupola.

Inside, some panelling from the old house was reused but Latham's new work predominated. The main rooms were all given elaborate ceilings, some barrel-vaulted. The library and gallery had tall 'Elizabethan' chimney-pieces. Latham's *tour de force* was the oak staircase, its strapwork and panelled plasterwork powerfully authentic. Rowland and Mary's portraits hang in the drawing-room which contains the set of Louis XV-style furniture they purchased for the room. Rowland's enthusiastic support of the Oxford Movement led him to commission Salvin to build the imposing chapel adjacent to the house.

The major features of the Arley garden all survive as important testimony to its original quality; the double herbaceous border laid out in 1846 is probably the oldest in England and was painted by George Elgood in 1889 and the series of individual gardens are as planned by Rowland and his wife. Their son, Piers was a highly accomplished watercolourist and his charming scenes of the house and garden at Arley – as well as other picturesque Cheshire seats – hang in the house. Michael Flower and his wife, and his mother, Lady Ashbrook (who had inherited Arley) before him, have all been devoted custodians of the garden and made important new contributions of their own.

CAPESTHORNE, *Macclesfield*

Mr and Mrs William Bromley-Davenport
Tel: 01625 861221

On A34, 11 km (7 miles) south of Wilmslow

Open: Apr, Sun; May, Aug and Sept, Wed and Sun; June and July, Tues,
Wed, Thur and Sun; Bank Holidays; 1.30–3.30
£4, children £1.50, concessions
Tea room

The Bromley-Davenport family's unusual crest, of a felon's head encircled by gold noose, tells of powerful positions held by ancestors during medieval times, from when they steadily acquired and consolidated their landed estates. The consolidation involved an unusual number of marriages within the family, so that when William Davenport, wanted to marry his cousin, Ellen Davenport, in 1529 the Archbishop of York had to give special dispensation because they were 'third and fourth degree of kindred'. This sense of accumulation is reflected in their home, Capesthorne, which surprises many visitors by its size and is the combination of three different architectural efforts.

Between 1719 and 1731 William Smith of Warwick, elder brother of the better-known Francis, built a rectangular brick house with flanking wings for John Ward whose daughter and heiress married Davies Davenport. In 1837 their great-grandson, Edward Davenport, decided to 'update' the house and commissioned the fashionable architect, Edward Blore, to carry out rebuilding and extension. It is Blore's style and broad expanse that survives today. In 1861 a fire broke out and gutted all the central block, but when Anthony Salvin was commissioned to rebuild, he was asked to keep to the style of Blore's original, although he did lower the central block between the great turreted towers from three storeys to two with an attic.

Inside, Salvin's hand is more obvious as he planned the set of main rooms and their decoration. The prosperity and wide connections of the family through both the eighteenth and nineteenth centuries are well demonstrated in the paintings and other works of art, while there are also interesting special features. The sculpture gallery contains the pieces collected in Italy by Edward Davenport while the American room contains a fine collection of eighteenth- and nineteenth-century furniture from the present owner's mother's home, Villanova Pa in the United States. Among quantities of family portraits, a Lowry is a surprise discovery. He painted Capesthorne in 1954.

DORFOLD HALL, *Nantwich*

R.C. Roundell
Tel: 01270 625245

On A534, 1.6 km (1 mile) west of Nantwich

Open: Apr to Oct, Tues and Bank Holiday Mon, 2–5
£3, children £1.50

Dorfold is a fine, original Jacobean house in a county where there are a greater preponderance of Victorian replicas. Nonetheless, it was given a strong Victorian flavour by the garden designer, William Nesfield. The two periods meet in the balustraded, cobbled forecourt which greets visitors, where the low gabled buildings are part Jacobean, part dated 1824, while Nesfield added the gates, and a dog sculpture that he purchased at the Paris Exhibition of 1855.

In front is the handsome block of the main house, built of diapered brick with stone-mullioned windows, gables and octagonal chimneys. The house was built in 1616 for Ralph Wilbraham whose portrait by Cornelius Johnson hangs in the dining-room, but because of the Wilbrahams' Parliamentarian loyalty, the house suffered badly at the hands of Royalists during the Civil War. In 1754 it was bought by James Tomkinson (whose family, like the Wilbrahams, were lawyers), who began the garden and park that survive today and commissioned Samuel Wyatt to remodel the downstairs rooms. Carved marble chimney-pieces were introduced, but Wyatt's most enjoyable addition was the plaster ceiling in the library, done to commemorate a Tomkinson wedding in 1772 with a pair of doves in the centre and panels of the four seasons in the corners.

The finest room, the upstairs drawing-room, is part of the Jacobean original. The barrel-vaulted ceiling is decorated with complex strapwork incorporating heraldic emblems and the high fireplace flanked by Doric columns also carries armorials. The panelling and frieze are also original and the decorative mood is complemented by portraits of Sir Francis Bacon and Lord Burghley.

Mr Roundell's family inherited Dorfold from the Tollemaches (who had married a Tomkinson and were descended from the Wilbrahams). Among Roundell family portraits the most striking are the most recent, of the present owners by Howard Morgan, which hang adventurously among the Jacobean splendours of the drawing-room. The more intricate, labour-intensive parts of Nesfield's garden design have been simplified, but it remains full of interest, the impressive lime avenue approach contrasting with the woodland and water gardens.

PEOVER HALL, *Knutsford*

Randle Brooks
Tel: 01565 722404/722135

Off A50, 6.5 km (4 miles) south of Knutsford

Open: May to end Sept, except Bank Holidays (telephone for further details)
£2.50, children £1.50
Teas (Mon only)

The flat Cheshire countryside lends itself to improvement with parkland and William Emes gave Peover Hall an expansive setting during the eighteenth century shortly after its owners, the Mainwaring family, had added a new wing to their originally Tudor house. The Mainwarings lived at Peover from shortly after the Conquest until 1919, when the property was sold. Mr Brooks's parents bought Peover in 1941.

The austerity of the dark brick house's entrance front is enhanced by its abrupt end on one side, following the demolition of a Georgian wing during the 1960s, when the house returned to its original proportions. The panelling and timberwork in some rooms – in particular the beamed roof of the great hall – is original; in others it has been introduced, saved from country houses less fortunate than Peover. The panelling and Corinthian columns in the dining-room and the carved cornice in the morning-room are good examples. The most spectacular introductions are the three splendid Victorian bookcases, two in the upstairs drawing-room and one in the morning-room, which came from Oteley near Ellesmere, another Mainwaring seat.

Mr Brooks has introduced a fine collection of furniture including four-poster beds, bobbin and other unusual chairs and an immense sideboard, elaborately carved with King John signing the Magna Carta, made for the 1851 Great Exhibition. The compact integration of rooms on three floors – the top floor gallery has a fine ceiling of arched trusses – combines with the oak furniture and panelling to give an atmosphere of warmth. Among many fine paintings, a distinguished double portrait, after Van Dyck, of the ill-fated Earl of Strafford and his secretary, Sir Philip Mainwaring, hangs over the drawing-room fireplace.

It is remarkable that the two most important Jacobean stable blocks to survive in England were both built by the Mainwaring family. Those at Peover, dating from 1654, are later than the ones at Whitmore Hall described on page 171, but they are considerably grander, their merit reflected in their Grade I status as opposed to the house's Grade II. The thirteen bays have wooden Tuscan columns and carved strapwork and a decorated plaster ceiling. The adjoining coach house is from the same period as the 1764 addition to the house. These, the park and the garden which Mr Brooks has greatly improved, make Peover's surroundings as enjoyable as its interiors.

RODE HALL, *Nr Congleton*

Sir Richard Baker Wilbraham, Bt.
Tel: 01270 883237

Off A50 and A34 south of Congleton, 14.5 km (9 miles) north of Stoke-on-Trent
Open: Apr to end Sept, Wed and Bank Holidays, 2–5
£3.50

On the map Rode Hall looks uncomfortably close to Stoke-on-Trent and its satellites. In reality, encircled by park bounded by a long lake on one side, it is remarkably secluded. The original house was built in 1708 by Randle Wilbraham. His son, also Randle, whom Horace Walpole described as 'a very able lawyer' built a new block immediately adjacent in 1752. As finished, his house had its entrance on the north side – now facing the garden. In 1799 his grandson, another Randle, commissioned John Hope to make alterations.

Inside, the house illustrates these changes and the contributions of succeeding generations. The entrance hall is part of Hope's Regency work – as are most of the interiors. But beyond, the fine staircase hall with delicate plaster decoration survives from the mid-eighteenth century. Hope redecorated the three main rooms of the 1752 house: a central octagonal hall with the library (originally the dining-room) on one side and the drawing-room on the other, which make an agreeable ensemble.

The library bookcases – like those in the hall – are some of the fine Gillow furniture bought for the house during the Regency work. At the same time, the present dining-room was added, the work of Lewis Wyatt who took over after Hope's death in 1808. Wyatt extended the room into an apse at one end and gave it a vaulted ceiling whose two ribs stretch between pairs of green scagliola columns. With a black marble chimney-piece, green walls and Gillow furniture it is Rode's most impressive room.

Hudson's portrait of Randle Wilbraham, the lawyer, hangs over the dining-room chimney-piece and among many other Wilbrahams, the delightful Beechey of Letitia Rudd, whose husband commissioned Hope and Wyatt, hangs in the drawing-room. Many other pictures date from the marriage in 1872 of Katharine Wilbraham, heiress of Rode, and Sir George Baker, 5th Bt, of Loventor in Devon. Sir George Baker, 1st Bt, was a physician of great distinction. He was George III's doctor and a friend of Reynolds whose portrait of his wife, and a self-portrait, hang in the drawing-room.

Sir Richard Baker Wilbraham has made a notable collection of early English porcelain. His wife has carried out extensive restoration in the garden which is historically interesting. Humphry Repton supplied designs for the park, which account for the delightful approach, and he moved the main road to accommodate the boundary lake. This work was added to during the 1850s by William Nesfield whose design for the rose garden survives in the house, along with Repton's *Red Book*.

TATTON PARK, *Knutsford*

The National Trust / Cheshire County Council
Tel: 01565 750250

Off A50, 5.5 km (3½ miles) north of Knutsford (M6 exit 19)

Open: Apr to end Oct, Tues to Sun and Bank Holiday Mon, 12–5
£2.50, children £1.50, concessions

Like a number of families, the Egertons abandoned the original house at Tatton, built during the sixteenth century by their predecessors, the Breretons, and built themselves a new house a mile away. Both now stand in Tatton's enormous 404-ha (1000-acre) park and the old hall is open to the public. But it is the 'new' house, originally seventeenth-century and then enlarged in two stages from 1780 and again from 1807, that is the main attraction and deservedly so. The combination of its architecture and interiors by two generations of the Wyatt dynasty of architects, Samuel and then his nephew, Lewis, as well as the Egerton picture collection and furniture made for the house by Gillow of Lancaster, is a rich experience.

Samuel Wyatt was commissioned by William Egerton and he built the south front with its unforgettably massive Corinthian portico. Inside, the succession of ground floor rooms are mainly as designed and decorated by Lewis Wyatt, but make a progression around his uncle's central neo-classical staircase hall. The younger Wyatt's decorative style was flamboyant Regency and the red porphyry Ionic columns in the entrance hall set the tone that follows. His most architecturally accomplished interior was the domed rotunda. The Gillow furniture was commissioned by Wilbraham Egerton and Tatton's collection is one of the most important groups that survive from the Lancaster cabinet makers.

It was Wilbraham Egerton and his grandson, the 2nd Lord Egerton, who between them collected the majority of the pictures. They include Van Dyck's 'Martydom of St Stephen' in the drawing-room and Guernico's 'Absalom and Tamar' in the music-room, and Chardin's 'La Gouvernante' in the card-room. But the two most widely admired paintings in the house, a pair of Canaletto views of Venice, belonged to Samuel Egerton (William's uncle) who had worked in Venice for the legendary British Consul, Joseph Smith. Samuel Egerton's elegant portrait by Bartolomeo Nazzari shows him in Venice, and in the early 1760s he commissioned Thomas Shrewsbury to decorate the rococo dining-room which adds to the variety of styles that visitors can enjoy.

Wilbraham Egerton's Regency house was given the perfect setting when he commissioned Humphry Repton to redesign the park (although fortunately he ignored Repton's suggestion that the beech avenue from the old formal park be divided into clumps). Repton's park was the first stage in the changes of Tatton's surroundings that gave it one of the most distinguished nineteenth- and early-twentieth century gardens in

England. In 1818 Lewis Wyatt built the delightful orangery and in 1850 Joseph Paxton built the Fernery and laid out the terraces of the Italian garden to the south of the house, with grandiose flights of steps and central fountain basin. In 1910 Japanese gardeners were brought from Japan to make what is the outstanding Japanese garden in England, its Shinto temple overlooking the lake.

In 1958 the 4th Lord Egerton gave Tatton Park to the National Trust, for whom it is managed by Cheshire County Council.

BROWSHOLME HALL, *Clitheroe*

Mr and Mrs Robert Parker
Tel: 01254 826719

Off B6243, 8 km (5 miles) north-west of Clitheroe

Open: Easter, Spring and Aug Bank Holiday Sun and Mon; July, Sat; Aug, Sat and Sun; 2–5
£3, children £1.50, concessions

The Forest of Bowland is among the most unspoilt and undiscovered pieces of countryside in Britain; among the wooded hills around the valleys of the Ribble tributaries one gets the impression that human habitation has scarcely increased over the centuries. Into this romantic landscape Browsholme, pronounced Brusom, with its long pink-grey stone façade, fits with disarming ease; successive generations of Parkers have been involved in the forest and they held the medieval position of Bowbearer of the Forest of Bowland.

The Hall was built in 1507, with later additions such as the arrangement of the three classical orders rising up from the front door, a piece of early-seventeenth-century bravado by a local craftsman. The eighteenth century saw the additions of modest wings before the most important changes were wrought by Thomas Lister Parker, an intriguing connoisseur. He wished to return his home to its Elizabethan origins and commissioned Jeffry Wyatt (later Sir Jeffry Wyatville).

Wyatt's two main designs, for which his drawings remain at Browsholme, were the drawing-room with its Elizabethan-revival decoration, and the new dining-room to display Parker's considerable collection of pictures. Among fourteen by Northcote, the most distinguished are the large groups 'Grouse-shooting in the Forest of Bowland' and 'Scene in the Forest of Bowland'.

With his commissions of paintings, purchases of Regency furniture and lavishing of

217

gifts on a young actor called William Betty, Thomas Lister Parker overreached himself and had to sell Browsholme and its contents to his cousin and heir. Important contents date from other generations. In the library there are two fine Devis portraits of Robert Parker and his cousin Edward (Thomas Lister's grandfather). Batoni's likeness of Daniel Wilson was a gift from the sitter to his friend, Edward. Robert Parker, who married his cousin Elizabeth, Edward's sister, was a supporter of Prince Charles Edward, and gave the house its collection of rare Jacobite relics.

In recent years the most welcome addition has been the watercolour of Browsholme by Turner. More crucial has been the demanding post-war restoration carried out by Christopher Parker and his son Robert, the present owner. Visitors are greeted by intriguing variety in the hall which carries echoes of the antiquarian Thomas Lister Parker.

HOGHTON TOWER, *Preston*

Sir Bernard de Hoghton, Bt,
Tel: 01254 852986

On A675, 8 km (5 miles) south-east of Preston

Open: Easter, then Sun to end Oct, 1–5; also July and Aug,
Tues to Thur, 11–4
£3.50, concessions
Tea room

The de Hoghtons of Hoghton Tower boast descent from an illustrious companion of William the Conqueror and the notorious Lady Godiva of Coventry; the hill-top house is best known as the place where James I knighted the [sir] loin of beef during his visit of 1617. Such ancient and varied history whets the appetite of the visitor as he climbs towards the powerful castellated building that looks as though it dates from early in the family occupation (unbroken male succession since the early-twelfth century), but is in fact Tudor, the third home on the site of which the earliest was built *c*.1100. Built around two courtyards, its originally brown millstone walls blackened by past industrial pollution, the house is forbidding rather than welcoming, but nonetheless impressive. During the Civil War the twelfth-century Keep was blown up and now only the inner arch remains.

It was the pure medievalism which appealed to Sir Henry de Hoghton, 9th Bt who, during the 1860s, returned to the house after over 150 years' absence by the family and began extensive restoration. He employed the architects, Paley and Austin, and the work was completed by his younger brother, Sir James, 11th Bt, in 1901. The work was of high standard; Gillow supplied furnishings such as the new panelling for the ballroom, and the house was successfully rejuvenated. Today it consciously evokes the period of its construction and the heyday of the generations who followed until the death of Sir Gilbert de Hoghton, 2nd Bt. The great 'Banqueting' hall still contains the oak table on which James I is reputed to have dubbed the privileged joint and a magnificent oak bed emphasizes the seventeenth-century atmosphere. Most of all, however, it is the survival of the secluded courtyard character, in contrast to the austere exterior, which is the most evocative part of Hoghton's appeal.

LEIGHTON HALL, *Carnforth*

Mr and Mrs R.G. Reynolds
Tel: 01524 734474

Off A6 (M6 exit 35), 16 km (10 miles) north of Lancaster

Open: May to end Sept, daily except Sat and Mon (open Bank Holidays), 2–5 (Aug, 11.30–5)
£3.40, children £2.20, concessions
Tea room

It is heartening that Leighton's setting has not changed since William Linton's views were painted in 1825. Gates lead into the park at its highest point and the pale stone house appears at the foot of the bowl-shaped park, its roofscape silhouetted against a background of Lakeland peaks. Linton's views were intended to record the Gothicization of the house, since when the only alteration has been the addition of the large west (left) wing and tower during the 1870s.

The architect's drawing of 1763, showing the sober Georgian house that was so enlivened half a century later, survives at Leighton. The work was carried out from 1822, when the house was bought by Richard Gillow, grandson of Robert who founded the family furniture-making business. (He went to Lancaster because his father was a prisoner in the castle.) Richard Gillow and his family moved in in 1825 when his alterations were complete.

The Gillow furniture is Leighton's highlight, much of it mid-eighteenth-century, considerably earlier than the period of the firm's greatest renown. The rarest item is the 1750 altarpiece in the family chapel (the household have always been Roman Catholic), but all the main rooms have pieces emphasizing the firm's unfussy, elegant quality. The Gothic character of the interiors is limited to fine windows, doorcases and occasional features such as the hall screen, beyond which the cantilevered stone staircase curves gracefully upwards. The dining-room's warm panelling incorporates a series of eighteenth-century romantic landscapes and the furniture is almost exclusively Gillow's. In the drawing-room notable Gillow pieces are the late-eighteenth-century games table, the satinwood writing table, and a rare lady's work-box, their interest heightened by comparison with French furniture in the room.

Three generations of Gillows spanned from 1822, when Richard bought Leighton, to 1966 when his great-grandson's widow died aged 96. Her daughter had previously married James Reynolds and their son and family are the present owners. Through the nineteenth century the family enriched their home with the paintings, French clocks and many other works of art that remain today. The most striking Reynolds' contribution is the portrait of Lady Reynolds and her daughter by Luke Fildes which dominates the music-room on the ground floor of Paley and Austin's Victorian wing. Among the other pictures, some Gillow pastels reveal that they were not only furniture-makers; Monseigneur Gillow was the finest sporting shot of any priest of any denomination in England and his sister Josephine became the all-England ladies' billiards champion.

MEOLS HALL, *Southport*

Mr and Mrs R. Hesketh
Tel: 01704 29826

Off A5267, 5 km (3 miles) north of Southport
Open: Aug, daily, 2–5
£3, children £1 (under 10 accompanied, free)

Meols is among the most distinguished post-war country houses. Although a surviving seventeenth-century entrance block and wing provided the nucleus, the most substantial parts are post-1950, designed and executed by the present owner's father, Colonel Roger Hesketh and his brother. There had been a house on the site of Meols since the early thirteenth century, but during the eighteenth century the resident Hesketh married a Fleetwood heiress and they moved to her family home, Rossall Hall, Meols assuming a subsidiary position. Roger Hesketh inherited in 1938 but shortly afterwards the Second World War and subsequently restrictive building regulations delayed work until around 1950.

At a time when more country houses were being destroyed than rebuilt, Meols benefited from the outstanding old materials that were available. The bricks for the east front – the most substantial exterior – came from Tulketh Hall near Preston after its demolition in 1960. The fine doorcase, whose rusticated style is perfect for the house's early-eighteenth-century appearance, is the work of Giacomo Leoni, part of his designs for Lathom House, Lancashire's premier Palladian house, whose prolonged demolition ended in 1960.

Other materials were re-used inside, including marble chimney-pieces and a new balustrade for the stairs, but the major influence – and impetus for the rebuilding project – was the collection of Fleetwood-Hesketh furniture, paintings and works of art that Roger Hesketh had from a cousin in 1938. Thus, for instance, the height between cornice and dado in the new library was dictated by the size of the early-nineteenth-century painting of Sir Peter Fleetwood-Hesketh's Arab stallion by James Ward.

BURTON AGNES HALL, *Great Driffield*

Burton Agnes Hall Preservation Trust Ltd
Tel: 01262 490324

In Burton Agnes on A166, 10 km (6 miles) south-west of Bridlington

Open: Apr to end Oct, daily, 11–5
£3.50, children £2, concessions
Tea room

Burton Agnes is well suited to its exposed position and like other distinguished houses in the area defies the often inhospitable nature of the surrounding wolds which extend the few miles to Flamborough Head and the North Sea. The delightful gatehouse provides the ideal welcome to what lies beyond, an approach which Celia Fiennes called 'a pretty ascent'. Rows of squat yews lead across a courtyard to the house's vigorous entrance front. It would be hard to imagine major alterations to such a composition, and the family, who have eight hundred years of continuity at Burton Agnes from Griffiths by marriage in 1654 to Boynton, has resisted the temptation.

Built between 1601 and 1610, Burton Agnes was one of the last major houses by Sir Robert Smythson and is similar – not least in the gatehouse-house arrangement – to Doddington in Lincolnshire (see page 138) that he had just completed. As with all his houses, there is plenty of originality: the combination of five-sided, semi-circular and square bays surmounted with

battlements, balustrades and carved stone cartouches; the entrance concealed in the side of one of the square projections which also contain ascending statues in niches; gables with over-sharp finials; and the symmetry of windows, brick and stone quoining. The generous fenestration is exaggerated by the later sashes and white painting but greatly adds to the house's friendliness.

The interior decoration is dominated by the quantities of carved plaster and wood – chimney-pieces, screens, panelling and the oak staircase which survive incorporated into extensive eighteenth-century alterations. Robin Fedden commented that there were so many 'figures of Virtues and Vices and other sententious motifs' that the house was 'like a perpetual sermon'. The hall chimney-piece and screen provide a dramatic moral introduction; only the size of the elegant full-length portraits by Francis Cotes, of Sir Griffith Boynton, 6th Bt, and his wife, allows them to compete with the Bunyan-like compositions. The smaller scale of the main bedrooms, the king's and queen's bedrooms make the combination of warm carved panelling and plaster ceilings more readily accessible.

Sir Griffith, his father and grandfather (four generations in a row bore the same name) were between them responsible for the eighteenth-century alterations, including the coromandel screens in the Chinese room, ceilings, the decoration and furnishing of the upper drawing-room and the Venetian window in the long gallery. An interesting eighteenth-century feature are the portraits and other paintings by Philip Mercier, a Frenchman born in Berlin who spent a number of years working in York.

A more recent and unusual addition to Burton Agnes is the array of late-nineteenth- and twentieth-century paintings collected by Mr Wickham-Boynton including works by Corot, Courbet, Boudin, Augustus John and a number of Impressionists. It was thanks to Mr Wickham-Boynton that the long gallery was restored after the ceiling had collapsed in 1987 and the room was divided into bedrooms. The work was carried out by Francis Johnson and included the reconstruction of the original barrel ceiling; similar restoration was carried out in the library and with the upper drawing-room these rooms contain much of the important modern collection.

BURTON CONSTABLE HALL, *Sproatley*

Burton Constable Foundation
Tel: 01964 562400

In Burton Constable off B1238, 11 km (7 miles) north-east of Hull, 1.6 km (1 mile) north of Sproatley

Open: Easter to end Sept, Sun to Thur; also July and Aug, Sat, 1–4.15 (last admission)
£3.50, children £1.50, concessions
Tea room

Burton Constable is an Elizabethan house that has the appearance of a great ship marooned on the flats of Humberside. Always the home of the Constable family, it combines a mellow Elizabethan exterior, rich eighteenth-century interiors and eclectic collecting by the family from all periods.

The presiding genius of the house is William Constable, collector, patron, antiquary and scientist (he was a patron of Priestley and friend of Banks). His Museum or Cabinet of Curiosities with shells, minerals, scientific instruments, coins and medals and so on, has survived intact, one of the few of its kind to do so from the eighteenth century.

William Constable brought in a series of distinguished eighteenth-century architects – Timothy and Thomas Lightholer, James Wyatt, and Thomas Atkinson among others – to modernize and improve the interiors with magnificent results. Chippendale made the set of gilded furniture for Wyatt's superb ballroom and an impressive array of other craftsman supplied different work for the house. The picture collection has an extensive group of portraits of the families – mainly Catholic – whom the Constables married.

SLEDMERE, *Great Driffield*

Sir Tatton Sykes, Bt
Tel: 01377 236637

At junction of B1251 and B1253, 13 km (8 miles) north-west of Great Driffield

Open: Easter to end Sept, 5 days a week (telephone for further details)
£3.50, children £2, concessions
Restaurant

House and estate at Sledmere have steadily matured since their inception in the mid-eighteenth century. Then a small manor house and a tract of desolate land was transformed by the ingenuity of Richard Sykes, his brother Parsons Sykes (the agricultural improver), and Richard's son, Sir Christopher Sykes. The latter remodelled his father's modest house. The new neo-classical block, echoing both Carr of York and Samuel Wyatt, dominates the landscape and yet sits contentedly among the model stables, other outbuildings, cottages and farms.

Internally, the house was decorated with refined plasterwork by Joseph Rose. A series of gracious rooms on the ground floor act as a foil to the dramatically placed staircase leading to Sir Christopher's library, the outstanding interior which majestically spans the whole length of the first floor. Its windows look out over 'Capability' Brown's park where great roundels of trees seem to float like ships. The form and decoration of the library re-creates Piranesi's evocations of the bath houses of ancient Rome. Here was housed Sir Christopher's superlative collection of books. Romney's marvellous double portrait of him with his wife, which hangs in the dining-room, confirms the charm and intelligence of this squire whose personality remains instilled in both house and estate.

The large number of rooms contain a rich diversity of paintings, furniture and works of art. During the nineteenth century the famous Sledmere Stud was developed, and the horse-room affords a fascinating summary of British sporting pictures with works by Herring, Chalon and Ferneley. Elsewhere are portraits by Lely, Lawrence, Mengs and Grant, good Italian and Flemish paintings and furniture of comparable quality. The bedrooms contain a collection of lace work; other highlights include rare works of art ranging from Italian bronzes to a needlework of Columbus and Queen Isabella.

It is a shock to discover that Sledmere was largely gutted by fire in 1911, mercifully most of the art collection was saved. The house was rebuilt with improvements and additions, such as a unique Turkish room based on the Sultans' apartments in Istanbul. The ability to improve and extend the house, its collections and surrounding estate continues unabated; the present owner, Sir Tatton Sykes, has conserved at the same time as adding both furniture and works of art and new plasterwork in the main hall.

ALLERTON PARK, *Nr Knaresborough*

Gerald Arthur Rolph Foundation for Historic Preservation and Education
Tel: 01423 330927

On A59, 7 km (4½ miles) west of Knaresborough
Open: Easter to end Sept, Sun and Bank Holidays, 1–5
£4, children £3, concessions
Tea room

The clustered turrets and gables of Allerton Park are easily visible from the A1 which passes less than a mile away, and only closer inspection reveals the true size of the largest Gothic Revival house to survive from the nineteenth century. Shortly before 1850 the 19th Lord Stourton commissioned George Martin to rebuild the existing Georgian house, previously owned by Prince Frederick, the Duke of York, brother of George IV. Martin's work doubled the size and transformed the house into an assembled union of gables, mullions, oriels and pointed turrets of constant variety. His most spectacular work was the interior of the great hall, a heroic space often credited with being the largest room in England, rising almost 24 m (80 ft) to the top of a hammerbeam roof. A gallery runs around the first floor and at ground level the staircase leads up through a Tudor arch in a panelled oak screen.

Allerton Park had been empty for some years in 1983 when it was bought from the Stourton family by an American, Dr Gerald Arthur Rolph. He has carried out extensive restoration. Many of the original decorative fittings survive or have been repurchased. There is a fine collection of carved furniture and panelling, including furniture by the Victorian makers, Holland & Son.

BROCKFIELD HALL, *Warthill*

The Lord and Lady Martin Fitzalan Howard
Tel: 01904 489298

Off A166 and A64, 8 km (5 miles) east of York
Open: Aug, daily except Mon, 1–4
£2.50, children £1

'Built the Farm Yard and cottage at Brockfield in 1800 and at Christmas 1800 I left Stockton and in June 1801 came [ ] the cottage at Brockfield. [Co]mmenced the building of my mansion house [at] Brockfield in 1804 and on August 12th 1807 [cam]e to live in it.' Benjamin Agar's description of the building of his new home and the carefully detailed account book which begins with this passage, suggests him to have been a man of prudence – if justifiably proud of his new home. And Brockfield is the house one might expect in such circumstances, elegant and well-proportioned, but without excessive frills or decoration.

Agar's architect was Peter Atkinson, whose father Thomas was assistant to John Carr of York, the county's most distinguished eighteenth-century architect. The younger Atkinson produced an initial set of plans for Agar in 1799, showing a typical design for the period, a house of three storeys with a pediment above. Perhaps it was too expensive for his client. Atkinson was asked to produce an alternative plan, showing a two-storey house with 3.6 m (12 ft) taken off the width of the front. Reduced in external scale, the new plan included one flourish by Atkinson which reveals his fine architectural skill, the circular entrance hall with a stone cantilevered staircase curving up past an impressive Venetian window. With the oval room to which the hall leads, Atkinson's design enabled Agar to have a house of quality that did not exceed his budget.

The Agar family sold Brockfield in 1923 and the house was bought by Lord and Lady Martin Fitzalan Howard in 1951. He is a son of Lord Howard of Glossop and a younger brother of the present 17th Duke of Norfolk, and formerly lived at Carlton Towers near Selby, ancestral home of his mother, Baroness Beaumont. The atmosphere of a family home is happily evident throughout Brockfield and family mementoes mix happily with fine furniture and paintings, including a conversation piece by Simon Elwes of Lord and Lady Martin and their five children. Among enjoyable, unusual discoveries to be made is Lord Martin's collection of glass walking sticks in the oval drawing room, and a number of items confirming his family's long, distinguished Roman Catholic history.

CASTLE HOWARD, Nr York

The Hon Simon Howard
Tel: 01653 648333

Off A64, 24 km (15 miles) north-east of York

Open: mid-March to end Oct, daily (telephone for further details)
£7, children £3.50

Castle Howard never fails to excite the visitor. However you approach it, the extraordinary originality of Vanbrugh's buildings, and the powerful interplay of lakes, avenues, vistas and gardens have an overpowering effect. This is not just a house but a massive estate which builds up to a crescendo around the Baroque palace at its centre. Here is a domestic building approached by columns, arches, pyramids and temples: a house surmounted by a dome, only previously seen in England on St Paul's cathedral.

The Howards of Castle Howard have always been great builders and collectors. The

house and park were created for Charles Howard, 3rd Earl of Carlisle, whose works of art form the bedrock of the collection, among which the paintings by Marco Ricci are a forte. His son acquired in Italy the famous collection of antiquities. These are still displayed, as intended, in the passages and central hall and are complementary to the Baroque exuberance of the architecture. The 5th Earl completed the building. He also commissioned contemporary British paintings from Reynolds, Gainsborough and Zoffany, as well as purchasing a portion of the Orleans Collection of Old Masters. These include the Gentileschi and Guercino hanging in the Long Gallery. Further additions to the collection came during the life of the 9th Earl, himself an artist. There is a room devoted to his achievements and those of his friends, and a beautiful Italianate chapel has stained glass windows designed by Edward Burne-Jones.

The collections of English and European porcelain, works of art and furniture are equally strong. Much of the furniture of the 3rd Earl's time has survived, added to by eighteenth-century French pieces and crisp neo-classical furniture by Linnell and Tatham. In one of the recently decorated bedrooms is Linnell's newly restored domed bed.

All of this might hve been lost had the Howard energy failed after the disastrous fire in 1940, which gutted the south-east wing. But George Howard, Lord Howard of Henderskelfe, and his successors have made a brilliant job of restoring and opening the house. The treasures are well displayed and augmented by Vanbrugh's heroic grounds and the new rose gardens. The visitor can enjoy Castle Howard in many ways: delightful walks in the grounds, rewarding study of works of art, a family day out, or an absorbing glimpse of one of the greatest eighteenth-century estates.

DUNCOMBE PARK, *Helmsley*

The Lord and Lady Feversham
Tel: 01439 770213

On south-western edge of Helmsley town

Open: April, May and Oct, Sat to Wed; June to end Sept;
daily; 11–5
£4.95
Restaurant

The return of Lord Feversham to his family seat after it had been a girls' school for sixty years was considered admirably brave by some, foolhardy by others. A few years later, after restoration of an uncompromisingly high standard, and with a clutch of awards, he would appear to have silenced the doubters.

At the end of the seventeenth century Charles Duncombe was possibly the richest man in the city of London. People were staggered and jealous when in 1689 he paid £90,000 for the profligate Duke of Buckingham's estates in Yorkshire, sold by the Duke's trustees to pay debts after his death. Charles's portrait as an effete, bewigged young man disguises his financial acumen. Helmsley was inherited by his nephew who assumed the Duncombe name and, in 1713, commissioned the gentleman Yorkshire architect, William Wakefield, to design a suitably impressive house. Wakefield was almost certainly advised by Vanbrugh who was finishing off his work at nearby Castle Howard. The result was vigorous and authoritative Baroque. During the 1840s Barry replaced the original wings with the present ones and enclosed the giant forecourt; the result was even more impressive than the original, if slightly ponderous.

Disaster struck in 1879 when the main house was gutted by fire. Restoration was not begun until 1895 and was carried out by William Young following the original eighteenth-century plan, but in classical Edwardian style which produced an occasional flourish. The quality of the work could not be faulted: the window frames were all made of teak. They give the house a sombre look but have never needed to be replaced. The long oak-panelled saloon was gilded; mahogany doors were faced in oak. The family's departure from Duncombe was caused by the death of the young 2nd Earl on the Somme in 1916, following which the contents were sold and the house let.

Much of the joinery and other decorative work for Lord Feversham's restoration was done on the estate or by local firms. The 12-m (40-ft) cube hall has giant Corinthian pilasters and stretches up to a circular roof panel; the ceiling has been repainted and the angels, *putti* and other details adorning doorway arches or walls have been restored. Central doors lead straight through to the saloon which stretches along the garden front for over 30 m (100 ft) between end walls with niches for statues and pairs of Corinthian columns. The drawing-room is decorated in rich yellow silk and, like the saloon, its plaster ceiling was originally done by George Jackson, the Adam brothers' craftsman.

Family portraits include a lovely group of three daughters of the 1st Earl as children, who became famous beauties (portraits of two as married ladies hang in the dining-room), and a conversation piece by Soldi of Thomas Duncombe and his family. In the drawing-room there are landscapes by Desiderio and in all rooms the furniture introduced by the Fevershams continues the theme of quality as well as being of adventurous variety.

Duncombe's most important feature lies outside the house, beyond the huge expanse of lawn that stretches away from the garden front between flanking blocks of woodland. Thomas Duncombe made a crucial contribution to the English landscape movement when he laid out the broad grass terrace that stretches between classical temples along the edge of the wooded Rye valley below. Later in the eighteenth century his grandson laid out a similar terrace – its deliberate picturesqueness showing the changes in taste – a short distance away on the estate, overlooking the ruined Rievaulx Abbey. The two together have been called the 'supreme masterpiece of the English landscape gardener' and should not be missed.

FAIRFAX HOUSE, *Castlegate, York*

York Civic Trust
Tel: 01904 655543
In city centre of York
Open: end Feb to end Dec, Mon to Thur and Sat (also Fri, Aug), 11–5, Sun, 1.30–5
(last admission 4.30)
£3, children £1.50, concessions

The history of Fairfax House passes from ambitious origins to constant changing of ownership and then miraculous escape from insensitive conversion and almost certain demolition, to its present reputation as one of the most distinguished town houses in Britain. Built for Charles, 9th and last Viscount Fairfax of Gilling Castle in Yorkshire, by the county's outstanding architect, John Carr, it overstretched Fairfax's insecure finances and his only daughter, Anne, for whom it was always intended, sold the house in 1772, within a year of her father's death and only eleven years after it had been built.

Regular change of ownership followed until 1865 when it ceased to be a family home. Occupied by Friendly Societies and Clubs, in 1919 the house was sold to St George's Hall Entertainments Company with a license for conversion to a cinema and dance hall. It became and remained a place of entertainment until the 1960s when the cinema was closed and Fairfax House sold to York City Council. Little, other than steady deterioration, occurred until 1981. Then the council accepted an offer from York Civic Trust, to buy the house and carry out comprehensive restoration, which was completed after £750,000 had been raised for the work, and the house opened in 1984. Equally significant, the agreement with the city council and the raising of the necessary money had been carried out in the knowledge that one of York's most distinguished patrons of the arts, Noel Terry (of the York-based chocolate family), had recently died, and that his trustees were honouring his wish for his superlative furniture collection to remain in York, by offering the collection to the York Civic Trust to display at Fairfax House.

The combined result for today's visitor is a house restored to the highest standard under the guidance of the Yorkshire architect, Francis Johnson, and one brimming with decorative flourishes and

artistic treasures. The compact arrangement of rooms serves to emphasize the richness of the plaster ceilings and carved doorcases, some with broken pediments and the decorative forte of the staircase hall. Here the Venetian window, the cantilevered staircase with exquisite wrought iron balusters by Maurice Tobin, and the decorative plaster and woodwork make for a flourish that typifies the best eighteenth-century town-house architecture.

The quality is complemented throughout the rooms by the contents, not least Noel Terry's furniture. This includes a collection of mid-eighteenth century carved mahogany furniture with very few equals, and there are also earlier walnut and marquetry pieces and outstanding early English clocks.

The paintings, including a number of loans, range from Dutch Old Masters to eighteenth-century portraits, two of which perpetuate the Fairfax family connection in charming style: Anne Fairfax dressed as a shepherdess, attributed to Philip Mercier, and another elegant portrait by Mercier, almost certainly of Anne's mother, Lady Mary Fairfax. Throughout Fairfax House, the blend of connoisseurship and conservation triumph is something to be savoured by any enthusiast for our heritage.

KIPLIN HALL, *Scorton*

Kiplin Hall Trust
Tel: 01748 818178

**On B6271, 24 km (15 miles) north-west of Northallerton, 6.5 km (4 miles) east
of A1 at Catterick**

**Open: late May to end Aug, Wed, Sun and Bank Holiday Mon, 2–5
£2, children £1
Teas on Sun**

Kiplin Hall is a unique gem of Jacobean architecture, its quality enhanced by its
delightfully small scale. At first sight its combination of steep gables and towers topped
with octagonal ogival domes seems typical of the period and reminiscent of, for
instance, Hatfield. But Kiplin's plan of a rectangle with a tower in the centre of each
side – rather than at the corners as would be more usual – is unique. The similarity of
certain features to Hatfield is not surprising. George Calvert, who built Kiplin during
the 1620s, was secretary to Robert Cecil, Earl of Salisbury, before following his master
as secretary to James I. Calvert was a pioneer of the new colonies in America. He
founded the colony of Avalon in Newfoundland and later the state of Maryland whose
capital took its name from his peerage, Lord Baltimore.

During the early eighteenth century the interiors of Kiplin were extensively
remodelled by Christopher Crowe, who bought the house from his stepson, Lord
Baltimore. From 1705 to 1716 Crowe was British consul in Leghorn where he was a
leading figure in the city's thriving mercantile and artistic community. Some of the fine
Italian pictures that he collected still hang at Kiplin and when he returned to England, he
transformed most of the rooms with early-eighteenth-century decoration. Around 1820
a Gothic wing was added for Lord Tyrconnel, who married a Crowe heiress, and from
his family Kiplin passed to the Talbots.

Miss Bridget Talbot established a charitable trust in 1968. This important step was
followed by urgently required restoration work. The Gothic wing was removed with
the exception of the nineteenth-century library which was retained; otherwise the house
returned to its original proportions. The balance of stone dressing and brickwork is
particularly fine and Calvert absorbed the quality of his Cecil master's houses at Hatfield
and Cranborne. Many details, such as the front door flanked by twin pillars, are
extremely similar. The safeguarding of a house of such importance is a considerable
achievement and it is to be hoped that the Trust is able to establish long-term security
and continuing improvements at Kiplin.

NEWBY HALL, *Ripon*

R.E.J. Compton
Tel: 01423 322583

Off B6265, 6.5 km (4 miles) south-east of Ripon

Open: Apr to end Sept, daily except Mon (open Bank Holidays), from 12
Prices available on request
Restaurant

Newby Hall fits effortlessly into the gentle valley of the River Ure, and successive generations have left their mark to treat the visitor with a veritable feast. The house dates from the late-seventeenth century, when Celia Fiennes thought it 'the finest I saw in Yorkshire', with eighteenth- and nineteenth-century alterations. The park contains William Burges's splendid church commissioned by Lady Mary Vyner, while the gardens, stretching from house to distant river, were originally designed by Major Edward Compton. Now the house, gardens and surroundings have been totally renovated and restored by his son, Robin Compton and his wife Jane, with substantial attractions for visitors

recognized by awards in 1979 and 1983 from the BTA for their outstanding contribution to tourism and, in 1986, the HHA/Christie's 'Garden of the Year' award.

Newby was built by the Blackett family and sold in 1748 to Richard Weddell who bought it for his son, William, a leading member of the Dilettanti Club. One hesitates to refer to Weddell's work at Newby as 'alterations'; it marked a highpoint of eighteenth-century taste. The fashionable portrait-painter, Pompeo Batoni was adept at giving the English gentleman who sat in his Rome studio an air of cultivated elegance, in few cases was it more justified or better executed than Weddell's. Batoni painted him twice, and both the small oval and grand full-length pictures show an instantly appealing, kindly connoisseur. Weddell's grand tour produced two major trophies, his collection of antique classical sculpture and one of the six sets of Gobelins tapestries woven for English houses.

The Weddell family commissioned Carr of York to remodel the house, adding the wings that flank the entrance east front. When William Weddell returned from his grand tour, Robert Adam was commissioned to design the interiors. Joseph Rose executed the plasterwork, Angelica Kauffmann and Antonio Zucchi the painted panels.

233

The cool hall celebrates antique Rome, the Gobelins tapestry drawing-room remains uniquely intact complete with Chippendale furniture covered in the same material, but Adam's consummate design was the sculpture gallery which fills one of Carr's wings: three sections centre on a rotunda that recalls the Pantheon. Weddell's collection remains as he arranged it, with the recent addition of his own bust by Nollekens surveying his trophies.

Weddell had no children and left Newby to the son of his cousin and close friend, Lord Grantham. After inheriting his father's title Weddell's heir subsequently became Earl de Grey. He changed Adam's original dining-room into the library and added a new dining-room. His daughter Mary married Henry Vyner and inherited Newby which passed to their son Robert, then to his daughter, Mr Compton's grandmother. The Vyners added the Victorian wing and later panelled billiard-room, which are startlingly different to Weddell's rooms, but richly period. The billiard-room contains a portrait of Frederick Vyner, murdered by Greek Brigands, whose death caused his mother to commission Burges's church.

Among the furniture commissioned by Weddell, there are outstanding pieces by Chippendale, as well as a pair of card tables by Vile, while Lord Grantham added the French furniture and was drawn by Ingres. The portraits illustrate the different families connected with Newby; after Weddell come Granthams, de Greys, Vyners and Comptons. Other connections constantly appear: the Vyners' friend Sir Jospeh Banks, trophies from the family's nineteenth-century racing successes and the delightful curiosity of the rare collection of chamber pots collected by Robert de Grey Vyner and arranged by Mrs Compton. The view from the house down the 275-m (300-yd) double herbaceous borders is one of England's finest garden vistas, in a garden now filled with rare and interesting plants, including the National Collection of Dogwoods.

NORTON CONYERS, *Ripon*

Sir James and Lady Graham
Tel: 01765 640333

Near Wath, 5 km (3 miles) west from A1, 6.5 km (4 miles) north-west of Ripon

**Open: Bank Holiday Sun and Mon; end June to Sept, Sun; July,
Mon and daily 23–27; 2–5
£2.95, children (10–16) £2.50, concessions
Teas by arrangement**

Charlotte Bronte visited Norton Conyers in 1839 and the house remains the most convincing model for Thornfield Hall in *Jane Eyre*. The direct link is the Graham family legend of a mad woman confined in the attics during the eighteenth century, but the whole mood of the roughcast house, its Dutch gabling a peculiarity in Yorkshire, is suitable. The Conyers were a powerful Norman family who owned the land by the time of Domesday. It was bought by the Nortons at the end of the fourteenth century, who remained there until rashly taking part in the Catholic uprising of 1569; their estates were confiscated.

The earliest parts of the house date from the Conyers occupation. It was substantially rebuilt around 1500 in red brick with arrow-slits, one of which remains. The Grahams bought Norton Conyers in 1624; some time later they covered the brick in roughcast, added the gables and made internal changes such as the broad oak staircase – which is, as Charlotte Bronte wrote, 'spacious and slippery'. The fine walled garden is early-eighteenth-century and the slightly later park provides an expansive setting. The 5th baronet commissioned William Belwood (a York architect who worked under Adam at Harewood and Newby) to build the stables, add the south-facing bow windows, and install chimney-pieces and ceilings which remain today.

The Victorian Grahams were sporting squires and the hall, which survives from the fifteenth-century house, is dominated by the Ferneley painting of the Quorn hunt when Sir Bellingham Graham, 7th Bt, was master. He won the picture from the other sitters on the throw of a dice. His swaggering portrait by Beechey more than hints at the recklessness which proved ruinous and in 1862, shortly before his death, the house and estate were sold. Fortunately his son was able to buy back the estate in 1882 and continuity was preserved. Though many of the house's contents had been irretrievably dispersed during the interval, an abundance of portraits has survived: two Romneys, a group of the 5th Baronet and his family by Zoffany's pupil, Henry Walton, and a Batoni of Sir Humphrey Morice, who remains a mystery at Norton Conyers as he had no connections with the Grahams.

RIPLEY CASTLE, *Harrogate*

Sir Thomas Ingilby, Bt
Tel: 01423 770152

In Ripley off A61, 5 km (3 miles) north of Harrogate

**Open: Apr, May and Oct, Sat and Sun (also Good Fri and Bank Holidays);
June and Sept, Thur to Sun; July and Aug, daily; 11.30–4.30
£4, children £2, concessions
Tea room**

The Ingilbys, who came to England with William the Conqueror, have been at Ripley for nearly seven hundred years and this long establishment is confirmed in the satisfying unity of the castle with its neighbouring model village and expansive landscape park. The gatehouse is medieval and Sir William Ingilby built the tower in 1555. Otherwise the castle dates from substantial rebuilding during the 1780s by Sir John Ingilby. Unfortunately the work was due to be largely financed by the fortune of his wife's father, Sir Wharton Amcotts. When he refused to part with any money, Sir John and his wife were forced to leave Ripley and live in exile in Europe for some years.

Despite such tribulations Ripley today presents a fine balance between its impressive battlemented stone exterior, and elegant well-proportioned interiors exemplified by the curving cantilevered staircase in part of the entrance hall. William Belwood was Sir John Ingilby's architect and the Gothic flavour of the exteriors is well balanced by the classical interiors, which offset the few surviving older chambers such as the Knight's Chamber and the Tower Room. Ingilby portraits and a priest's hiding hole tell of the family's progress through unsettled Tudor times to the Civil War when the then Sir William Ingilby was among the King's defeated forces at the nearby battle of Marston Moor. The Knight's Chamber also contains a fine collection of Royal Greenwich Armour and Weaponry, displayed against a background of original 1555 panelling and wagon roof.

Fine chairs in the round drawing-room tell of the connection between Ripley and Thomas Chippendale, whose family had lived in the village for generations and whose father was an estate carpenter. The 1.6-ha (4-acre) walled gardens contain the National Hyacinth collection, impressive herbaceous borders and the kitchen garden. Visitors can now enjoy the recently opened parkland walk through the deer park, giving access around the 6.9-ha (17-acre) lake and fine views of the castle.

SION HILL HALL, *Kirby Wiske*

H.W. Mawer Trust
Tel: 01845 587206

In Kirby Wiske, off A167 and 8 km (5 miles) south of Northallerton
Open: mid-Mar to Oct, Wed to Sun, 12.30–4.30
£3.75, children £2, concessions
Restaurant

The present house at Sion Hill was built in 1912 by the York architect, Walter Brierley. He was commissioned by Percy Stancliffe and his wife who had bought Sion Hill that year but were persuaded to rebuild by the surveyor's report which – as well as saying there was no drinking water in the house – concluded, 'The outside appearance and internal construction, with the exception of a few rooms, are so faulty that it would be necessary to pull down the house and rebuild.'

The style of Brierley's house characterized the unfussy neo-Georgian popular during the decade before the First World War and the house was an impressive size for the period. In 1949 it was sold following the death of Percy Stancliffe and, after two further changes of ownership, was bought in 1962 by Herbert Mawer. Mawer had worked in catering and his baker's shop in Stokesley was called 'Our Herbert's'. But he was the happy beneficiary of his wealthy aunt Matilda's will and his new-found prosperity enabled him to retire from trade and spend the rest of his life indulging his love of antiques and collecting. Married but childless, before his death in 1982 Mawer passed ownership of his collection to a charitable trust.

The collection includes a rich quantity of eighteenth- and nineteenth-century furniture and a series of impressive English and Continental porcelain services and decorative figures, vases and urns. In fact the sheer quantity of Mawer's collection, which gives an intriguing completeness to the displays in each room, is one of Sion Hill's most absorbing features. The house is certainly a fitting monument to a passionate collector, and Mawer's acquisitions are there to enthuse others to seek out and collect.

BRAMHAM PARK, *Wetherby*

Mr and Mrs George Lane Fox
Tel: 01937 844265

On A1, 8 km (5 miles) south of Wetherby
Open: mid-June to Sept, Tues, Wed, Thur, Sun and Bank Holidays,
1.15–5.30
Prices/concessions available on request

'Bramham is a grand and unusual house, but its gardens are grander and even more unusual.' Pevsner's opinion is entirely accurate. The early-eighteenth-century house has many qualities but its gardens are the largest and best preserved French-inspired formal landscape in England. The whole ensemble was the creation of Robert Benson who inherited a fortune and the Bramham estate from his lawyer father and prospered as a politician, Lord Treasurer to Queen Anne (who elevated him to being Lord Bingley), and as George II's Ambassador to Spain. Contemporaries considered him socially inferior but aspersions cast on his origins could not be extended to his taste. The design of the house and garden were almost certainly his, based on what he had seen and enjoyed on a grand tour of France and Italy during the 1690s.

Bingley's work was consolidated by his daughter Harriet who married George Lane Fox. Thereafter Bramham's progress was less smooth. Disorder after their deaths in 1773 was followed by disaster during the Regency thanks to George Lane Fox 'the gambler' and his witty, pretty but notoriously extravagant wife, Georgina. As the debts mounted, in 1828 fire broke out and gutted the house. Their son, 'the squire', eventually paid off his father's gambling debts of some £175,000 but could never contemplate rebuilding the house. The work did not start until 1906 when his grandson, another George, commissioned Detmar Blow and together they planned a reconstruction of Bingley's original.

Bingley envisaged Bramham in the style of an Italian villa or casino, a house primarily of architectural quality rather than size. The quality is evident in the first view through splendid Baroque gate-piers, and even more so on the house's garden front. Here, Blow's new doorway and curving double staircase was a good replacement for a nineteenth-century bow window. The doorway is positioned centrally in the saloon that Blow created out of three smaller rooms. The new room's impressive proportions are emphasized by full-length family portraits reflected in tall pier glasses between the windows, and by a flamboyant Lely portrait of Popham Conway at one end. Double doors open from the saloon to the entrance hall – an exact 9.14-m (30-ft) cube. The hall's stone walls make for an austere greeting, but the room is enlivened by Reynolds's full-length portrait of 'Butcher' Cumberland, as well as Kneller's fine portrait of Queen Anne.

The other main rooms are – while not small – warm and intimate. More good portraits, such as 'the gambler' looking dashing but slightly raddled by Hayter, mix with notable sporting pictures (Bramham is home to the Bramham Moor hounds), especially the Walker in the library and the Wootton in the sitting-room, Dutch and Italian still lifes and landscapes. Upstairs a charming set of watercolours by Ziegler depict Bramham before the fire.

The sunken parterre below the south front gives little idea of the true character of Bramham's gardens, but heading towards the fine temple by James Paine (who also built the splendid Tuscan stables flanking the forecourt), the visitor is soon led into the series of grassy *allées* through woodland that cover two large areas. The formal canals, temples and other architectural ornaments, and the constant revelation of spectacular vistas, allow for hours of absorbing exploration. The Gothic temple in particular has few peers among garden buildings and the damage wrought by a catastrophic gale in the 1960s has been made good by replanting.

HAREWOOD HOUSE, *Leeds*

The Earl of Harewood
Tel: 0113 288 6331

At junction of A61 and A659, 13 km (8 miles) north of Leeds
Open: Mar to end Oct, daily, 11
Prices available on request

Eighteenth-century Harewood extolled the composition of landscape, architecture and decoration which defined the acme of English country houses. It has long contained great treasures. Now, recent imaginative reorganization and rediscovery of long-hidden masterpieces have made it one of the country's great show houses. Charles Barry remodelled the exterior but his interference inside was mercifully limited. The arrangement and decoration of rooms – in particular the suite along the south front – remain one of Robert Adam's greatest achievements, on a par with Kedleston and Syon.

Edwin Lascelles, whose family fortune came from Barbadian sugar plantations, was a man of taste, but cautious and forthright. He only commissioned Carr of York to build his new house in 1759, when Carr had executed the stable block first and his plan was almost certainly preferred to one by William Chambers because of its lower cost. Lascelles next consulted young Robert Adam, ambitious and in the ascendant. He was given control of the interiors, with the proviso from Lascelles, 'Let us do everything properly and well, *mais pas trop.*'

The result gives little impression of any constraint. The sense of progression from room to room, the variety and quality of design throughout, are masterful. Adam was

239

also able, no doubt with advice and preferences from Lascelles, to commission the leading craftsmen: Joseph Rose and William Collins for decorative plasterwork; Angelica Kauffmann, Antonio Zucchi and Biagio Rebecca to paint decorative panels; and Thomas Chippendale to supply the furniture. In Robin Fedden's opinion, 'Here is not only the best of Thomas Chippendale's work, but possibly the finest furniture ever to be made in England.' Lascelles was painted by Reynolds — as were the other members of his family. By the mid-1770s, when 'Capability' Brown had completed the park falling away from the house to the vast lake he created, Harewood was not so much a house as an expression of taste — this accounting for its regular illustration by Turner, Girtin and other contemporaries whose superb watercolours provide brilliant evidence.

The 3rd Earl of Harewood — or more precisely his wife, Louisa, a Thynne from Longleat — commissioned Charles Barry to enlarge the house. Carr's elegant roofline was replaced with an extra storey, his portico removed from the south front and the eighteenth-century lightness sunk in the impressively grand but lifeless classicism with which Barry encased the house. Along the south front he placed the broad Italianate terrace.

Inside he remodelled the Dining-Room, whence he removed Adam's chimney-piece from the Gallery, and turned the Saloon into the main Library (of which the house boasts three). The twentieth century brought two distinguished new arrivals to Harewood. In 1922 the present Lord Harewood's father married the Princess Royal, daughter of George V, and, having inherited the fortune of his great-uncle, the last Marquess of Clanricarde, collected the Old Masters that are almost exclusively Italian, but include El Greco's 'Allegory'.

The rooms occupied by the 6th Earl and the Princess Royal are among the first seen by visitors and retain an evocatively period atmosphere. Beyond, the full success of the present Lord and Lady Harewood's reorganization — greatly helped by Alec Cobbe's advice on redecoration and hanging of pictures — becomes apparent. The cabinets in the China Room show off part of Harewood's incomparable Sèvres collection. The yellow Drawing-Room has been redecorated to Adam's original colour, but the two climaxes are the Cinnamon Drawing-Room and the Gallery. In the former, Cobbe grouped together the Reynolds portraits including the ravishing Lady Worsley (one of Edwin Lascelles' step-daughters), renowned for her love affairs, and looking the part in a red hunting habit. The Gallery, long hung with family portraits, has had its chimney-piece and other features returned, and contains the Old Masters. Two of the Chippendale mirrors were recently discovered dismantled in store.

What Edwin Lascelles would think of Epstein's great alabaster figure of Adam that stands alone in the centre of the hall, is hard to say but there is little doubt that both he and Adam would approve of the manner in which Lord and Lady Harewood have reassembled and rejuvenated so much of their distinguished home. The most recent projects have been the accurate restoration of the formal parterre on Barry's south terrace and the creation of two dedicated Watercolour Rooms to display, in the style of a nineteenth-century 'Connoisseur's Cabinet' the fine collections of watercolours and sketches.

NOSTELL PRIORY, *Wakefield*

The National Trust / The Lord St Oswald
Tel: 01924 863892

Off A638, 10 km (6 miles) south-east of Wakefield
Open: Apr to end Oct, Sat and Sun; Aug, daily except Fri; 12–5 (Sun 11–5),
last admission 4
£3.50, children £1.80, concessions

Nostell Priory and its park survive as an oasis encircled by urban sprawl and the legacy of intensive coal-mining – the latter now healed by skilful landscaping. But it was not long ago that those who lived at Nostell remember the rooms and their contents being constantly coated with coal dust and the blackened stone of the Palladian exterior remains a reminder of this industrial past.

The medieval priory that stood close to the present house was dedicated to St Oswald, from whom the Winn family took their title when elevated to the peerage in 1885. In 1953 the house was given to the National Trust, but the family continue as occupants and organizing the opening to visitors. In 1729 Sir Rowland Winn returned to Nostell from his grand tour of the continent (which lasted for five years) and set about building a new house. He employed James Paine as his architect who appears to have adapted an existing design by the Yorkshire gentleman-architect, Colonel James Moyser. The design was dominated by the main central block with an Ionic portico on the east (entrance) front. Paine also designed a number of the interiors, including the two staircases and other rooms notable for their rococo plasterwork. But in 1765 the 5th Baronet, succeeded after his father had died following an accident in his carriage. The 5th Baronet, who also made an extensive grand tour, replaced Paine with Robert Adam who added the family wing to the north-east, and the raised perron with curving flights of steps below the portico, but, most importantly, designed the enfilade of rooms from

the central top hall on the east front, around the north end of the house to the saloon which is central on the west front.

Paine's superb rococo designs remain evident in the plasterwork of the two staircases, the dining-room and the state bedroom. The contrast between this and the later work carried out to Adam's designs is one of the many intriguing discoveries to be made at Nostell. Adam's rooms have decorative painting by Antonio Zucchi, plasterwork by Joseph Rose the younger (whose father may have executed some of Paine's earlier designs) and, most important, furniture by Thomas Chippendale.

Chippendale was born nearby at Otley and Nostell contains an ensemble of his furniture (an estimated total of a hundred pieces), only rivalled for quality by that at nearby Harewood. Sets of chairs, pairs of side tables and pier tables, commodes, bookcases and mirrors, and many other pieces all meticulously documented with dates and prices, provide a rare feast, with a number of highlights, not least the mahogany library table in the library, which cost £72. 10s. 0d. and was the most expensive piece of furniture that he supplied for the house. Quite different is the remarkable suite of green and gold lacquer chinoiserie furniture that he supplied for the state bedroom (where he was also responsible for the decoration with sheets of Chinese paper).

The 4th baronet's full-length portrait hangs at one end of the dining-room and his son's (with his wife) stands on an easel in his library, showing them in the room soon after it was completed. Throughout the house the impeccable taste of these two men and the consummate skill of their architects and craftsmen is evident in every single detail, and it was nothing short of a miracle that a potentially disastrous fire that broke out in 1980 was contained. The fire gutted the breakfast-room and damaged the amber room, south staircase and top hall. The most serious loss was all the contents of the breakfast-room. All four rooms have been redecorated. Thick walls and mahogany doors combined with admirably swift action by estate staff and the fire brigade to ensure that one of England's richest series of eighteenth-century interiors has survived.

STOCKELD PARK, *Wetherby*

Mr and Mrs P.G.F. Grant
Tel: 01937 586101

On A661, 3 km (2 miles) north-west of Wetherby

Open: Apr to early Oct, Thur, 2–5
£2, children £1

Stockeld is a good example of the depth of quality displayed by Yorkshire country houses. Far smaller than its grand neighbours such as Harewood, it is nonetheless a house of considerable distinction and one of James Paine's foremost designs. The Roman Catholic Middleton family commissioned Paine in 1756 and Stockeld was complete in 1763. During the nineteenth century the house was bought by Robert John Foster whose family had founded the Black Dyke Mills, famous for its brass bands. In the twentieth century Stockeld passed to the Grants by marriage to a Foster.

Paine's original house of three deep, pedimented blocks, was characteristically Palladian and yet full of ingenuity, designed to afford the maximum effect from a limited ground-plan. Inside, his most spectacular achievement was the oval staircase hall which, as well as its cantilevered staircase with crinoline balusters by Paine's favourite ironworker called Wagge, has a bewildering array of architectural sleights of hand.

The Fosters made considerable changes at Stockeld, adding a large wing and raising the entrance so that the original ground floor was sunk into a basement. They remodelled interiors – but gave them suitably neo-classical appearances. The library, with its screen of grand scagliola columns, was originally the gallery for the Middletons' chapel and the double doors to the drawing-room, the broken pediments and plaster ceiling were all added by the Fosters. The drawing-room chimney-piece is Paine's original; the one in the library was added and came from 145 Piccadilly, the London home of the Queen Mother's family. When the fireplace was inserted, it was discovered that Paine's arrangement of flues was so complicated that rather than linking into it, a new one was built accounting for the curious single chimney stack on one side of the house.

The loss of the chapel in the house was rectified by the Fosters when they made another one adjacent to the stable block in what had been an old orangery. These alterations were designed by Detmar Blow and included a fine organ. These buildings and the splendid park containing a cricket ground give Stockeld a setting to complement its architectural distinction.

SCOTLAND

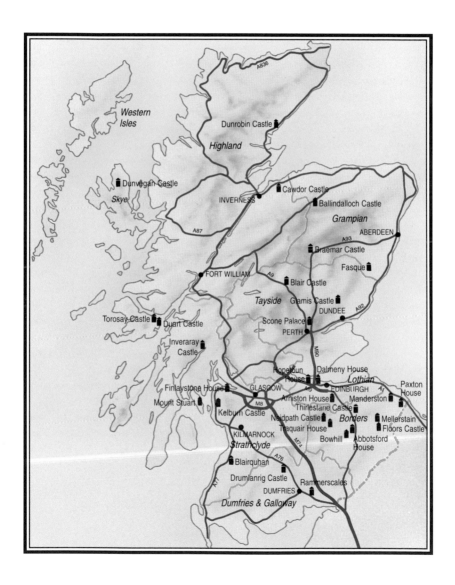

Western
Isles

Dunrobin Castle

Highland

Dunvegan Castle

Skye   Cawdor Castle

INVERNESS   Ballindalloch Castle

                        Grampian

            A87   ABERDEEN

                            A93

                        Braemar Castle

                                    Fasque

FORT WILLIAM   A9   Blair Castle

                Tayside   Glamis Castle

Torosay Castle   Scone Palace   DUNDEE

        Duart Castle   PERTH

Inveraray
Castle

                        Hopetoun   Dalmeny House
                        House   Lothian   Paxton
Finlaystone House   GLASGOW   EDINBURGH   House

Mount Stuart   Arniston House   Manderston

                Kelburn Castle   Thirlestane Castle   Mellerstain
                        Neidpath Castle   Borders   Floors Castle
                        Traquair House
                KILMARNOCK   Bowhill   Abbotsford
                                            House
        Strathclyde

        Blairquhan

        Drumlanrig Castle   Rammerscales

                DUMFRIES

        Dumfries & Galloway

ABBOTSFORD HOUSE, *Melrose*

Mrs P. Maxwell-Scott
Tel: 01896 752043

Off A72, 5 km (3 miles) west of Melrose
Open: late Mar to end Oct, daily 10–5 (Sun, 2–5)
£3, children £1.50
Tea room

Abbotsford is a shrine to the life and achievements of Sir Walter Scott. The affection that he poured into his home between 1811, when he purchased the original farm, and his death in 1832 remains evident and accounts for the strong personal presence that survives.

It was the success of his writing – in particular the Waverley Novels begun in 1814 – that provided the necessary funds for Abbotsford. Scott gave the place this name because it had been owned by the Abbot of Melrose whose monks had crossed the Tweed at a nearby ford. This and the house's appearance, irregularly battlemented, turreted, towered and gabled, celebrated the romantic Scottish history that Scott extolled in his writing. Together the place and his books were the major impetus for the advent of Scottish baronial architecture and the explosion of Victorian enthusiasm for Scotland.

Scott had originally purchased a farm of 44.5 ha (110 acres) and extended the existing house. But in 1822 this was pulled down and replaced with the more substantial present one, to which the west wing was added during the 1850s. Scott and his family first moved into their new home in 1824 and for the next few years he decorated the house and filled it with gifts from eminent friends and admirers: a lock of Bonnie Prince Charlie's hair; a glass that belonged to Burns; Rob Roy's purse; a desk from George IV (who made him a baronet in 1820); an urn from Byron.

The warm, rich character that Scott gave to Abbotsford radiates from his portrait by Raeburn in the drawing-room and ensured that from the first year after his death, visitors would be irresistibly drawn – as they have been ever since. Queen Victoria went in 1867 (although she thought it was 'rather gloomy') and in 1883 a total of fifteen hundred people visited the house. Unbroken family ownership, together with the richly carved wooden panelling, the important collection of armour, the library lined with leather-bound volumes, and the quantity of artefacts, combine to perpetuate the memory of one of Scotland's favourite sons.

BOWHILL, *Selkirk*

The Duke of Buccleuch and Queensberry
Tel / Fax: 01750 22204

On A708, 5 km (3 miles) west of Selkirk
Open: July, daily, 1–4.30
£4, concessions
Tea room

The long, rambling house of Bowhill is well suited to the gentle contours of the Scottish Borders. Despite boasting a continuous length of 133.19 m (437 ft) there is a softness about the building which inspired Sir Walter Scott – neighbour and frequent visitor during the period when the original eighteenth-century house was encased and expanded – to name it 'sweet Bowhill'.

Certainly it does not have the ducal grandeur of the other Buccleuch seats, Drumlanrig Castle or Boughton House, and as a result the visitor may not be prepared for the interior which contains one of the most superlative art collections in any house in Britain. Here the family portraits are masterpieces and the collections of Old Master paintings, French furniture and continental porcelain alone are testament to the combination of munificent patronage and collecting which has characterized successive generations of the family.

In 1812 the 4th Duke of Buccleuch commissioned William Atkinson to alter the house. The Duke died five years later but the work was continued by his son, the 5th Duke who was laird of Bowhill for the next sixty-five years. He employed two architects, William Burn and David Bryce. The arrangement of the house and much of its atmosphere originates from this halcyon period as home to the Duke and Duchess and their seven children.

Many of the contents were either commissioned or collected during the previous century, for it was the 3rd Duke of Buccleuch who brought about the union of the three families of Montagu, Douglas and Scott along with their estates, houses and possessions. In 1767 he married Elizabeth, daughter and heiress of George, Duke of Montagu, and just before the end of his life, in 1810, he succeeded to the dukedom of Queensberry with its accompanying titles and the Douglas estates.

As befitted one of England's greatest heiresses, Elizabeth Montagu was painted by Reynolds in a portrait at Bowhill that many experts consider his finest work. While she is almost regally elegant, Gainsborough's portrait of her husband in the dining-room reveals a supremely cultivated gentleman. Their eldest son is the 'Pink Boy' by Reynolds but for most visitors it is the artist's portrait of his sister, Lady Caroline Scott, as 'Winter' which is the most enchanting discovery in the whole house.

Bowhill reminds visitors that the original Buccleuch earldom became a dukedom when the family heiress, Anne, married James Duke of Monmouth, the son of Charles II and his most attractive mistress, Lucy Walter. The family (and their estates and titles) survived the upheaval of the Duke's rebellion against his uncle, James II, and his execution in 1685. A number of the works of art at Bowhill were gifts to Monmouth from his father and the Duke himself is remembered in the Monmouth room which appeals to varied taste: as well as grand full-length portraits of himself (by Lely) and his Duchess and two sons (by Kneller), there is his cradle, his wonderfully ornate saddle and the shirt he wore at his execution.

Such upheavals seem far removed from Bowhill today. Instead it is easier to envisage the assured connoisseurship which gathered together the Mortlake tapestries in the Gallery Hall and the full-length portraits below, the scenes by Canaletto, Guardi and Claude Lorrain and Jacob van Ruysdael, and the eighteenth-century Sèvres porcelain often either on or near contemporary French furniture. Other numerous pieces combine curiosity with quality, such as the longcase clock by the Scottish maker John Smith of Pittenweem, which plays eight different Scottish airs every twenty-four hours but is silent from midnight on Saturday until midnight on Sunday. Equally important, the tradition established by the 5th Duke during his long tenure, that Bowhill was the focus of a thriving estate, has been continued by his descendants, not least since the present Duke succeeded in 1973.

FLOORS CASTLE, *Kelso*

The Duke of Roxburghe
Tel: 01573 223333

Off A6089, 1.6 km (1 mile) north of Kelso

Open: Easter to end Sept, daily except Fri, 10.30–5; Oct, Wed and Sun, 10.30–4.30
£3.90, children £2.50, concessions
Restaurant

As originally built by William Adam for the 1st Duke of Roxburghe between 1721 and 1726, Floors was one of the Borders' most impressive houses and enjoyed an enviable position overlooking the River Tweed. This is confirmed in the painting of 1809 by William Wilson that hangs in the castle. The position remains unchanged but alterations for the 6th Duke, carried out by the Edinburgh architect, William Playfair, transformed

the house from impressive to palatial. Playfair joined the central block to its pavilions and extended the whole, so now the north – entrance – front seems endless in width, while from the river to the south the roofscape is a dazzling mêlée of pepper-pot turrets, chimneys and castellations.

In 1903 the 8th Duke followed the example of other leading aristocrats and married an American heiress, May Goelet of New York, and it is her contribution that makes the greatest impact in the rooms open to visitors. She inherited and expanded a superb art collection and also replaced Playfair's Scottish baronial style in some rooms with eighteenth-century re-creations. She remodelled the drawing-room to accommodate the set of seventeenth-century Brussels tapestries called the 'Triumph of the Gods' that came from her family home on Long Island, and similarly transformed Playfair's ballroom to accommodate two equally fine Gobelins tapestries from the series 'Les Portières des Dieux'.

Many rooms contain Duchess May's oriental porcelain and French furniture, notably the Louis XV and XVI cabinets and commodes in the drawing-room, the Louis XVI escritoire in the needle-room, the sets of gilt and tapestry chairs in both rooms and a number of fine French clocks. A more surprising discovery is her collection of paintings in the needle-room including works by Matisse, Bonnard and the Englishman, Sir Matthew Smith.

Duchess May's additions complement the grand scale of Floors but there is a pleasing element of contrast in the smaller rooms such as the sitting-room where the Wilson view of Floors hangs, the ante-room with a rare early-sixteenth-century Gothic tapestry woven in Brussels, and the hall, where Hendrick Danckerts's view of Charles II and his Court walking in the Horse Guards Parade is outstanding among a group of English topographical pictures. The series of likenesses of successive Earls and Dukes of Roxburghe was completed in 1988 with an arresting portrait of the present Duke by Howard Morgan.

MANDERSTON, *Duns*

The Lord and Lady Palmer
Tel: 01361 883450

On A6105, 3 km (2 miles) east of Duns

**Opens: mid-May to end Sept, Thur and Sun; also late-Spring and
Aug Bank Holiday Mon; 2–5.30**
Prices available on request
Tea room

Manderston can claim to be the most sumptuous Edwardian house in Britain, and if anyone wants to savour the blend of opulence, indolence and quality that form the popular conception of upper-class life during that era, there is no better place to experience it. However derivative its architecture and every detail of its interior decoration, the unfailing quality of the execution more than compensates.

It is the Edwardian story par excellence: a fortune made out of the most uninspiring of trades, hemp and herrings, is married to aristocratic grandeur, the daughter of Lord Scarsdale of Kedleston Hall, and Manderston and its policies are transformed like Cinderella. But for a cherry stone it might not have happened. The fortune was made by Sir William Miller, who himself first altered the original eighteenth-century house and gave it a French Renaissance look, but his eldest son, William, died a schoolboy at Eton after choking on a cherry stone and the inheritance passed to his younger brother, James. Little wonder he was always known as 'Lucky Jim'.

He inherited in 1887 and five years later married the Hon Eveline Curzon, one of the eleven children of the rector, Lord Scarsdale. She had been brought up at Robert Adam's masterpiece, Kedleston, and when her husband commissioned John Kinross – the best and most fashionable Scottish architect of the period – to begin work at Manderston, his wife's home was to be the model. Georgian elegance was to be blended with Edwardian comfort. The end result was impressive and expensive – fortunately Kinross had been told that there was no limit to the budget.

Externally, the house is faithful, immaculate neo-Georgian but even here there are the ingenious touches that all aided the easy flow of Edwardian life; at the base of the four Ionic pillars of the new entrance portico are metal lions' heads, two of which are bell-pulls in reach of a horseman's boot. It was, however, inside Manderston that Kinross worked to greatest effect and where the inspiration of Kedleston is constantly evident. From the oval entrance hall through vestibules and ante rooms to the main hall and a suite of reception rooms – a circular morning-room, tea-room, dining-room, library, drawing-room and ballroom (these two decorated as a pair in Sir James's racing colours of primrose and white) – the progression is a remarkable ensemble of Adam features: rich plaster ceilings and wall panels, urns on carved pedestals, inlaid marble

floors, columns of varying order and arched doorcases containing perfectly hung mahogany doors.

The overall richness is enhanced by silk and velvet wall hangings and curtains – all original – gilded and painted, covered in tapestry and French furniture, and the standard of work is almost unnervingly high. The climax – which some guests at Manderston's house parties may have secretly considered rather vulgar – is the cantilevered marble staircase with a swirling silver-plated balustrade and solid brass top rail.

Sir James ensured that not only his guests were afforded the utmost comfort. His passion for hunting and racing meant that his horses lived in what are widely acknowledged to be the grandest stables in Europe; one commentator wrote that their teak and tiled troughs were 'reminiscent of luxuriant hotel basins'. And it is the whole composition of Manderston: house, stables, Gothic marble dairy, terraced gardens, the boathouse built for his wife in the style of a Swiss chalet, cottages, kennels and home farm – all designed by Kinross – and the huge gates gilded to catch the setting sun, which together submerge the visitor in a vision of luxury. The only note of melancholy is the knowledge that Sir James only enjoyed it for a few months. He died childless aged forty-two from pneumonia brought on by a cold caught out hunting. Today Lord Palmer (the great-grandson of Sir James's sister), his wife and children cope with maintaining Manderston to a standard his great-great-uncle would have approved of, without the army of staff that kept the wheels silently turning.

MELLERSTAIN, *Gordon*

The Mellerstain Trust
Tel: 01573 410225

Off A6089, 11 km (7 miles) north-west of Kelso
Open: Easter; May to end Sept, 12.30–4.30
£4, children £1.50, concessions
Tea room

It is an indication of the grandeur of the Earls of Haddington that until the present Earl inherited the title, Mellerstain, one of the outstanding Adam houses in Scotland, was the family's secondary residence. They were among Scotland's foremost peers when, in 1717 the heir to the 6th Earl married Rachel Baillie, heiress to Mellerstain. As their eldest son inherited the Haddington title and estates Mellerstain passed to their second son, George, who built the house. Two generations later his grandson inherited the earldom from his cousin.

George Baillie and his future wife, Lady Grisell, were a romantic couple who suffered at the hands of the Stuart government and fled to Holland after his father had been executed. They subsequently saw their fortunes – and family estates – restored by the accession of William of Orange, after which they married in 1691. In 1725 George commissioned William Adam to build a new house at Mellerstain, but only two wings were completed. Forty years later, his grandson, also George (who had assumed the Baillie surname) commissioned William's son, Robert Adam, to complete the plan by building the required house between his father's two wings.

Mellerstain's north-facing entrance front, a harmonious balance of the father's wings and son's central block, presents an elegantly welcoming scene. The south-facing front with its undecorated pattern of windows and castellated roof-line is austere to a point of bleakness and certainly not the younger Adam's most inspired design. Thus his work inside the house comes as something of a surprise, for even his greatest commissions in England – Kedleston, Harewood and Syon – can hardly rival the delightful interiors which remain almost unchanged.

In the succession of rooms along the south front – sitting-room, library, music-room, drawing-room, small drawing-room and small library (originally two rooms) – Adam's skill at arranging a series of classical decorative compositions is triumphantly displayed. Each has a plaster ceiling, the one in the library in pink and green with painted panels of Minerva flanked by Teaching and Learning by Zucci, perhaps the finest. The books were collected by Adam's patron and above their shelves are four classical reliefs and, in niches, portrait busts, two of Lady Grisell Baillie and her daughter, Lady Murray, by Roubiliac. Adam's green and white marble fireplace sets the standard for those that follow in the other main rooms.

Adam's most coolly classical room is the apsed entrance hall and his hand continues in the double staircase and, indeed, to the top of the house beyond the main bedrooms, where visitors discover the great gallery with a long curving ceiling, Ionic columns and a classical plaster frieze. Throughout the house portraits illustrate members of the family through three hundred years, in many rooms hanging next to fine Dutch paintings and the furniture is of similar quality and varied interest.

In 1909 Sir Reginald Blomfield, the fashionable Edwardian architect and garden-designer, was commissioned to lay out the formal terraces below the south front. These make an imposing foreground to the magnificent view that stretches over a long sweep of lawn to the lake and the Cheviot Hills in the background.

NEIDPATH CASTLE, *Peebles*

The Lady Elizabeth Benson
Tel: 01721 720333

On A72, 1.6 km (1 mile) west of Peebles
Open: Easter to end Sept, Mon to Sat, 11–5, Sun, 1–5
£2, children £1, concessions

Perched on a bluff overlooking the River Tweed, Neidpath's defensive origins are clear and the castle seems to have made few concessions to modernity since it was built during the late-fourteenth century. Altered inside during the sixteenth and seventeenth centuries, it was not extended and thus remains essentially a medieval tower house: a compact L-shape, with immensely thick walls, the height and limited ground-area giving maximum assistance to defenders warding off attack. This came regularly. In 1307 before the castle was built the local laird, Sir Symon Fraser, fought – and defeated – English armies three times in one day. Neidpath passed with his daughter to the Hay family who owned it for three hundred and eighty years, becoming Earls and Marquesses of Tweeddale. In 1686 the 1st and last Marquess sold Neidpath to the Duke of Queensberry; in 1810 it was inherited from the 3rd Duke by the Earl of Wemyss.

Although partially ruined and unoccupied, Neidpath gives an absorbing illustration of grim medieval life and how the castle was subsequently altered to provide a home with a modicum of comfort. Originally consisting of three main levels, all vaulted, these were divided during the sixteenth- and seventeenth-century alterations, providing rooms with lower ceilings. Original medieval features such as arrow-slits, the corbels for defensive bretasches, and the guard room with a trap dropping into the grim pit-prison below, mix with later alterations including most of the windows and some panelling, but it is the picturesque scene as a whole which leaves visitors with the most abiding memories of Neidpath.

PAXTON HOUSE, *Berwick-upon-Tweed*

The Paxton Trust
Tel: 01289 386291

On B6461 (signed from A1), 8 km (5 miles) west of Berwick-upon-Tweed
Open: Easter to end Oct, 12–5
£3.75, children £1.75

John and James Adam did not achieve the illustrious reputation of their brother Robert (nor did the fourth brother in the architectural partnership, William, like their father). But in Paxton House they demonstrated an ability to design and build a Palladian house of the utmost elegance. The house was commissioned by Patrick Home, after he had

returned from an exciting time in Europe which included staying at the court of Frederick the Great and nearly marrying the emperor's daughter, Catherine. But the romance foundered and Patrick travelled on to Italy for a grand tour. Work on Paxton began in late 1757 and the impeccably proportioned seven-bay façade of the central block, with its imposing portico covering the central three, remains unaltered and faces across a courtyard flanked by two-storey side pavilions linked to the central block by neat balustraded galleries. Positioned overlooking the River Tweed, the house also enjoys superb views down the valley towards Berwick.

As correct for a Palladian house, the main rooms are on a *piano nobile*, over a basement floor lit by half-size windows matched by those of the upper, second floor. There are fine interiors by the Adam brothers, with painted plaster ceilings and marble chimney-pieces, and important furniture supplied by the firm established by Thomas Chippendale, Chippendale, Haig and Co, as well as later pieces by Thomas Chippendale, Jnr. This furniture was bought for the house by Ninian Home, who purchased Paxton from his cousin (the builder Patrick's nephew) in 1773, and the decoration of the interiors was also completed for him with the most famous Adam brother, Robert, having a hand.

In 1811 George Home commissioned the Edinburgh architect, Robert Reid, to build a corridor and library leading to a picture gallery that stands behind the east pavilion or stable block. The bookcases in the library and furniture in the domed picture gallery were made by William Trotter of Edinburgh. The gallery was originally built by George

255

Home to display the picture collection of his uncle Patrick, but the collection was sold earlier this century and the gallery now contains pictures on loan from the National Gallery of Scotland.

In 1988 John Home Robertson (of whom there is a fine portrait with his wife by Richard Gale) presented Paxton to the Paxton Trust who now administer this distinguished house and its collections.

THIRLESTANE CASTLE, *Lauder*

Thirlestane Castle Trust
Tel: 01578 722430

Off A68, 45 km (28 miles) south of Edinburgh
£4
Open: details available on request
Tea room

Thirlestane's massive T-shaped plan, with thrusting central towers and turrets extending into broad wings is the product of three phases of architectural activity: in 1590 when the original keep was completed for John, 1st Lord Maitland who was Lord Chancellor of Scotland; from 1672 to 1678 when Sir William Bruce extended the castle for the chancellor's grandson, the Duke of Lauderdale, who had married the Countess of Dysart, heiress of Ham House; and in 1840 when the Edinburgh partnership of David Bryce and William Burn added the matching wings and adapted many of the rooms for Victorian country-house life.

It was in 1972, however, that the most decisive point in the six centuries of Maitlands at Thirlestane was reached. Captain Maitland-Carew, the grandson of the 15th Earl of Lauderdale, inherited the castle from his grandmother with much of it in a dangerous state of disrepair. The resulting rescue operation was one of the most ambitious and successful carried out to date. Among the major problems, the central tower with which Bryce had topped the sixteenth-century keep in typically theatrical Victorian style, was in danger of collapsing and throughout the castle the fabric was in urgent need of attention. Grants from the Historic Buildings Council for Scotland enabled the repair work to be carried out. Subsequently Captain Maitland-Carew passed most of Thirlestane and its contents into a charitable trust which could be endowed by the National Heritage Memorial Fund, thereby helping to assure its future.

Bruce's contribution adds the greatest note of quality to Thirlestane. This is not surprising considering that his patron had been elevated to a dukedom by Charles II; Landerdale's name supplied the last letter in the King's five-member Cabal. Bruce's approach, a grand balustraded staircase leading to two new towers projecting from the old castle and a fine Baroque doorway demonstrated how Restoration architecture could be adapted to a Scottish castle. With access to the superlative craftsmen working either for himself at Holyroodhouse or for his patrons in their lavish remodelling of Ham, Bruce added some of the most vigorous interior features to be found in any Restoration house, notably the plaster ceilings which were mostly executed by the Englishman George Dunsterfield. The Baroque doorcases in the ante-room were almost certainly the work of Thomas Carter who was working at Ham.

Only portraits of Charles II himself evoke the Restoration period more forcefully than that of the red-haired Duke over the dining-room fireplace, but as the rest of the room which is part of Bryce and Burn's work illustrates, Thirlestane moved on from his period and influence and successive generations enjoyed it as a country home rather than an illustration of political power. Paintings span the seventeenth, eighteenth and nineteenth centuries, but the furniture in most rooms dates from the nineteenth century.

An important and unfailingly popular attraction – to both young and old – is the historic toy collection. The Maitland-Carew family live in the north wing and the south wing is given over to a museum of Border Country Life.

TRAQUAIR HOUSE, *Innerleithen*

Mrs Peter and Ms C. Maxwell Stuart of Traquair
Tel: 01896 830323

At junction of B709 and B7062, 1.6 km (1 mile) south of Innerleithen
Open: mid-April to end Sept, daily, 12.30–5.30 (July and Aug, 10.30–5.30);
Oct, Fri to Sun, 2–5; last admission 5
£3.80, children £1.80, concessions
1745 Cottage restaurant

The upper reaches of Tweeddale present some of the most beautiful Border country and the setting makes its own contribution to Traquair, perhaps the most eulogized of all Scottish houses. For more than three centuries from 1107, when Alexander I visited, Traquair was a royal demesne, where Scottish kings stayed and hunted. In 1491, having earlier been given by James III to one of his favourites, it came to James Stuart, 1st laird of Traquair, who established five centuries of unbroken family occupation. Generations later, in 1745, the story goes that Prince Charles Edward stayed and as he left, his host, the 5th Earl of Traquair, closed the gates and vowed they would never be opened until the Stuarts were restored to the English throne.

They have remained closed ever since and brought to Traquair a note of romance enhanced by the lack of change since that day. The family's period of greatest prosperity was during the sixteenth and seventeenth centuries, when the house was built in successive stages and they acquired an earldom (which died out in 1861). After 1745 their Jacobitism and Catholicism meant safety in anonymity, and successive generations were happy to enjoy Traquair and its historical connections. They did not display their Catholicism until emancipation came to Scotland during the nineteenth century, when the intimate chapel was made.

The view from the house, which grew in stages from a fourteenth-century Pele-tower, across the forecourt with its elegant late-seventeenth-century screen and gates to the broad avenue beyond and the closed bear gates or 'Steekit Yetts' at the far end, has not changed since 1745. Inside, the period of the family's close involvement with the Scottish kings is widely represented. Mary, Queen of Scots's rosary and crucifix and the cradle in which she rocked her son, James VI and I, recall her visit with her husband, Darnley. There is also fine engraved Jacobite glass.

The library, which dates from the eighteenth century remains intact and is full of treasures: the *Nuremberg Chronicle* (1493), a Koberger Bible (1479) and a fourteenth-century illuminated psalter. The room has a cove painted unusually in grisaille which is one of a number of decorative curiosities in the house, in particular the *trompe l'oeil* overmantel and overdoors. Most important, however, and the draw for visitors, is the atmosphere which pervades the whole place, enshrined in the stories and poetry that Traquair's history has inspired.

DRUMLANRIG CASTLE, *Thornhill*

The Duke of Buccleuch and Queensberry
Tel: 01848 330248

Off A76, 5 km (3 miles) north of Thornhill
Open: end Apr to end Aug, daily except Thur, 11–5 (Sun, 1–5)
Prices available on request

The first view of Drumlanrig is an experience never forgotten and something that every country-house enthusiast should enjoy. Among the gentle wooded hills of Nithsdale the castle seems to float on an elevated plateau and on a sunny afternoon it gives the impression of being spotlit as the sun picks up the pale pink hue of its sandstone. It presents an Arcadian harmony of architecture and landscape that few places can match.

The third castle on the site where Douglas's had lived for over three centuries, Drumlanrig was built between 1679 and 1691 by the 1st Duke of Queensberry, who became the most powerful man in Scotland after the restoration of Charles II. The existing site and old castle probably contributed to the plan of a rectangle around a central courtyard, but the new castle demonstrated the status of its builder and – to a startling degree on the entrance front – the Carolean Baroque style of the age. One does not expect the rich composition that Robin Fedden described, '…curving perron, arcaded loggia, giant pilasters, ranks of pedimented windows, balustrades, and a lavishly decorated porch with trophies and swirling coats of arms. This burst of exuberance is echoed by the forest of turrets breaking the skyline over the four corner towers.'

Drumlanrig and its gardens nearly bankrupted the Duke; the fortunes were restored by his son before coming under siege again later in the eighteenth century. The wife of the 3rd Duke was Kitty Hyde, whom one contemporary described as 'Kitty, beautiful and young, and wild as colt untamed'. When her husband died without a son, the titles and estates passed to his cousin William, a dissolute rake called 'Old Q' whose carryings-on in London took their toll on his Scottish estates. He had no sons and left his money to an illegitimate daughter who used it to launch the Wallace Collection. The Queensberry titles and estates passed to the Duke of Buccleuch.

From this moment serenity and a steady influx of artistic riches were the happy lot of the Douglas stronghold and Drumlanrig is a similar treasure-trove to the other Buccleuch homes, Bowhill and Boughton. Rembrandt's 'Old Woman Reading', Leonardo da Vinci's 'Madonna with the Yardwinder' and Holbein's portrait of Sir Nicholas Carew – the three masterpieces among serried ranks of outstanding pictures – all came from the Montagu family.

Much of the outstanding French furniture was similarly imported. Nonetheless Douglas and Queensberry family members are well represented; Kitty Queensberry is painted by Jean-Baptiste Van Loo and there is a conversation piece of her with her husband and two sons by George Knapton, while wood carving by Grinling Gibbons testifies to the quality of the 1st Duke of Queensberry's original decoration of the interiors.

The family's position and patronage at the time combine to make Drumlanrig an all-round illustration of seventeenth- and eighteenth-century art of the highest quality; the enlightened custodianship of subsequent generations has ensured that their connoisseurship is preserved for visitors to enjoy.

RAMMERSCALES, *Lockerbie*

M.A. Macdonald
Tel: 0138 781 0229

On B7020, 4 km (2½ miles) south of Lochmaben

Open: last week of July and first 3 weeks of Aug, daily except Sat, 2–5
£5, children £2.50

Rammerscales was built on an eminence to take advantage of the majestic views over Annandale that the house still enjoys. The house was built by James Mouncey, who made a fortune as a doctor to the Imperial court and military in Russia. He built Rammerscales after his return to Scotland in 1762 and his neat, sober Georgian box remains little altered outside. Its ashlar façades are undecorated save for the cornice and balustrade, and the loggia with Tuscan pillars with a pedimented window above, on the entrance front.

Interior work was completed after Mouncey died in 1773, including the well-crafted rail and baluster for the spiral staircase and, possibly, the long gallery with bowed ends, that is hidden away on the second floor. This was made into a library, largely to house the outstanding library collected by William Bell Macdonald, who inherited in 1837. More recent additions to the house are the modern paintings and works of art including work by Rodin, Barbara Hepworth, Segonzac, Lowry and Wyndham Lewis.

BALLINDALLOCH CASTLE, *Grantown-on-Spey*

Mr and Mrs Oliver Russell
Tel: 01807 500205

On A95, 23 km (14 miles) north-east of Grantown-on-Spey

Open: Easter to end Sept, daily, 10–5
£3.95, children £2 (5 and under free), concessions
Tea room

Transformation from defensive tower house to Victorian country house is the story of many Scottish castles, nowhere more so than at Ballindalloch, set in the superb countryside of Speyside. Mrs Russell is the only daughter of Sir Ewan Macpherson-Grant, 6th Bt, and the family have lived here since 1546. The Macpherson and Grant families, long the two main clans of Strathspey, were united when the eighteenth-century General Grant was succeeded at Ballindalloch by his great-nephew, George Macpherson of Invereshie. Awarded a baronetcy in 1838, he became Sir George Macpherson-Grant. The rebuilding of Ballindalloch into the imposing building of today,

complete with crow-stepped gables and conical turrets, was carried out for his son, Sir John, by Thomas MacKenzie in 1850. Sir John's son added a further wing in 1878, but this was removed during the 1960s as part of extensive renovation of the castle by Sir Ewan and Lady Macpherson-Grant.

MacKenzie's remodelling is evident throughout the house, not least in the hall with its unusual umbrella design and fan vaulting, and in the panelled dining-room and library which houses a distinguished collection of books. General Grant's eighteenth-century parts of the castle remain evident in the elegant drawing-room, where the 18th-century furniture is some of the finest in the castle. Sir John Macpherson-Grant, for whom the 1850 work was carried out, served as a Secretary in the British legation in Lisbon and brought to Ballindalloch the collection of seventeenth-century Spanish paintings that are among the castle's most important treasures.

BRAEMAR CASTLE, *Braemar*

Captain A.A.C. Farquharson of Invercauld Trusts
Tel: 013397 41219

On A93, 1.6 km (1 mile) north-east of Braemar
Open: May to mid-Oct, daily except Fri, 10–6
£2, children £1, concessions

It is ironic that Braemar is home to the Farquharsons, for it was built in the early seventeenth century by the Earls of Mar to fend off their threatening Farquharson neighbours. The vicissitudes of the two families dominated the castle's development for nearly two centuries, during which time it was a ruined shell for sixty years after being burnt out in 1689 by the legendary 'Black Colonel', John Farquharson.

In 1732 the castle was purchased by the colonel's descendant, John Farquharson of Invercauld, but its ruined state rendered it uninhabitable and in 1748 he leased it to the Hanoverian government for £14 per annum, to house one of the garrisons established to control the Highlands after the Jacobite risings. At the time John Adam, brother of Robert, held the position of Master Mason to the Board of Ordnance, and as a result he designed the restoration necessary before the castle could house its garrison. Adam's work, grafted on to the original seventeenth-century fortress, is responsible for Braemar's appearance today.

No doubt because Adam was planning for defence, the castle was not expanded and it retains the appearance of a miniature fortress, its five-storey battlemented walls towering over the courtyard which he protected with the curtain wall. When the Farquharson family took up occupation in 1807, peace had been restored to Deeside and the small rooms of the garrison stronghold became a family home of surprising intimacy compared to the castle's imposing exterior. Nonetheless, despite the cosiness, there are plenty of reminders of Braemar's violent past, in particular the iron grille in a stone passage which covers the 'Laird's Pit', an uninviting stone cell into which unfortunate prisoners were dropped.

FASQUE HOUSE, *Fettercairn*

The Gladstone family
Tel: 01561 340569/202

On B974, 1.6 km (1 mile) north of Fettercairn
Open: May to end Sept, daily, 11–5.30 (last admission 5)
£3, children £1, concessions

Aberdeenshire is an area of Scotland richly endowed with substantial houses as opposed to castles, but few rival Fasque for scale and symmetry. Its broad stone front, with castellated turrets in descending size from the centre, and simple Georgian windows looking out over the deer park, is an impressive sight. It is no surprise to hear that the project ruined its builder, Sir Alexander Ramsay. His architect was Paterson of Edinburgh, who controlled the Scottish projects of the Adam brothers once they were based in London, and Fasque has all the assertive confidence of this family partnership. The house's interiors continue the tone of grand austerity, with the one architectural flourish of the double curving, cantilevered staircase.

Ramsay's plight forced him to sell in 1830, and Fasque was bought by John Gladstone. A Leith boy who made a fortune in Liverpool, he returned home to Scotland to establish himself with a country seat. And it is for the Gladstone connection which most people visit Fasque, as John Gladstone's youngest son was William Ewart Gladstone, the Liberal Prime Minister. Fasque was his home from 1830 until his father's death in 1851 and it is easy to imagine him immersing himself in the leather-bound volumes in the library.

The Prime Minister's eldest brother, Thomas succeeded to Fasque and to the baronetcy their father had been given. Thomas was succeeded by his only son John, who lived in the house until 1926. Thereafter the family based themselves at Hawarden Castle in Wales and only occupied Fasque on an occasional basis. The lack of change since the 1920s – fine Georgian and Regency furniture and paintings in the main rooms have not been moved – means that visitors are able to enjoy an intriguingly unchanged period atmosphere.

CAWDOR CASTLE, *Inverness*

The Dowager Countess Cawdor
Tel: 01667 404615

On B9090, 8 km (5 miles) south-west of Nairn
Open: May to Oct, daily, 10–5.30 (last admission 5)
£4.70, children £2.50, concessions
Restaurant

The Cawdor motto is 'be mindful' and for centuries successive generations of the family were well advised to remember it. Their title of Thane (once held by many Scottish barons) emphasizes a sense of antiquity, deriving from the Saxons who took the word from the Norse thegn 'trusted servant of the king.' Even without the shroud of legend that Shakespeare threw around the place in *Macbeth*, there is plenty of evidence of violent goings-on which terminated at Culloden field only a few miles away.

Certainly the family appear to have remembered the motto when building their castle. Even today with its surroundings of peaceful park and woods, and delightful gardens, Cawdor has an air of impregnability. The feeling that it was built with security firmly in mind is confirmed as one approaches across a small drawbridge. Like many Scottish castles it has expanded from an original tower-house, built around 1370 and crenellated by royal licence in the middle of the next century.

The other buildings which now enclose small courtyards to the east and north of the tower date mainly from the seventeenth century, with additions during the nineteenth century which marked the beginning of unbroken – and peaceful – occupation by the family. Part of the reason for the buildings' surviving austerity is the absence of the family from Cawdor throughout most of the eighteenth century when it was looked after by successive factors. The family's absence from Cawdor was partly due to its remoteness and because they had homes elsewhere, in London and in Wales where they

had further large estates. In the survey of 1883 Earl Cawdor was one of the twenty-eight men to possess more than 40,470 ha (100,000 acres) in Britain. A fire in 1819 burnt part of the tower, and repairs by the 1st Earl Cawdor signalled the family's return.

Today Cawdor is very much the family base. Paintings and works of art have been brought to the castle from other houses to make the various rooms surprisingly rich compared to the forbidding exterior. Many early pictures were destroyed in the fire but full-length portraits of the the 1st Baron Cawdor by Reynolds, his wife Caroline (daughter of the Earl of Carlisle) by Beechey and their son, the 1st Earl, confirm the status the family had achieved by the late-eighteenth century.

Sets of tapestries are traditional decoration for castle walls. At Cawdor there is a fine collection: seventeenth-century Arras, Brussels and Franco-Flemish, depicting the story of Noah, the Arts and Sciences and the story of Don Quixote. Less expected are the examples of modern and contemporary art, including a bronze girl by the Japanese sculptor, Churyo Sato; 'St Ives' by Stanley Spencer; and a plate by James Campbell.

James Campbell is the brother of Hugh, 6th Earl Cawdor, who died in 1993 aged sixty-one and who did so much to make Cawdor enjoyable for visitors. With his blend of irreverence, wit and connoisseurship, well displayed in the guide that he wrote, he made Cawdor history that was fun and brought the place and its contents to life to a degree reflected by its enduring popularity.

DUNROBIN CASTLE, *Golspie*

The Countess of Sutherland
Tel: 01408 633177/633268

On A9, 1.6 km (1 mile) north-east of Golspie
Open: Easter weekend to mid-Oct, daily, 10.30–5.30
(April, May and Oct, 10.30–4.30; Sun, times vary)
£4.40, children £2.80, concessions
Tea room

Dunrobin is a place of fantasy more suited to Ludwig II's Bavaria than the far north-eastern Scottish coast where it stands perched dizzily above its terraced gardens, indisputably what it was built to be, the grandest and most impressive building in the northern Highlands. More modest predecessors were homes to the Earls of Sutherland whose ancient title dates from the thirteenth century and whose vast estates stretched the length and breadth of the Highlands encompassing in excess of 404,700 ha (1 million acres).

The earldom may be held by a female. In 1785 land and lineage became merged with huge wealth when Elizabeth, Countess of Sutherland married George, Marquess of Stafford. He inherited not only his own family's wealth and estates, but those of his uncle, the 3rd and last Duke of Bridgwater. Months before Lord Stafford's death in 1833, he was created 1st Duke of Sutherland and his wife was thereafter known as the Duchess-Countess.

Dunrobin celebrates the union of the Stafford and Sutherland largesse and the

Victorian period when it was most lavishly displayed. A committed reformer and philanthropist, the 1st Duke initiated the misguided Clearances that caused such unhappiness and ill-feeling, but his son had different ideas. He commissioned the fashionable architect Charles Barry to remodel his three seats: Dunrobin, Trentham in Staffordshire and Cliveden on the Thames. Between 1835 and 1850 Barry transformed Dunrobin into the French-style château one sees today.

The 2nd Duke, his son and grandson all entertained lavishly at Dunrobin. Queen Victoria made the long journey from Balmoral in 1872 and her son, Edward VII, to whom the comfort greatly appealed, was a more regular guest. In 1915 when the castle was being used as a hospital, fire gutted most of Barry's interiors and the 5th Duke commissioned Sir Robert Lorimer to carry out extensive restoration.

Despite this the castle retains an atmosphere of grand Victorian Scottish living in its warmly panelled rooms. In recognition of her contribution to the family fortunes, there are portraits of the Duchess-Countess by Hoppner, Reynolds and Lawrence. Dunrobin's zenith is evoked by two portraits of the 2nd Duke's wife, Harriet, one with her daughter, Elizabeth by Lawrence, the other by Winterhalter, and the later portrait of Eileen, 5th Duchess, by de Lazlo. Foremost in the collection, however, are the pair of Canalettos of the Doge's Palace in the spacious drawing-room that Lorimer made out of two smaller rooms.

ARNISTON HOUSE, *Gorebridge*

Mrs A. Dundas-Bekker
Tel: 01875 830239

On B6372, 1.6 km (1 mile) south-west of Gorebridge
Open: July to mid-Sept, Tues, Thur and Sun, 2–5
£3
Home-made teas

A canny wife was responsible for the purchase of the Arniston estate in 1571 by the Dundas family, who had been established at Dundas Castle in South Queensferry since 1180. Katherin Oliphant was the second wife of George Dundas and when she discovered that the family castle would be inherited by his son by his first marriage, and not by the son born to her in 1570, she insisted on the purchase of the Arniston estate, which her son James duly inherited. James Dundas founded a dynasty of distinguished Presbyterian lawyers. His grandson, Robert, became a judge of the Court of Session and was followed by his own son, also Robert, who became Lord President of the Scottish Supreme Court, as did his son – another Robert.

Robert the elder had plans to rebuild the old house at Arniston but never got further than redesigning a small part of the garden. In 1725, however, his son commissioned William Adam, senior member of Scotland's foremost architectural family, and in 1726 work began on the new house. The result was the imposing, Scottish Palladian mansion that stands today, looking out over parkland (which formerly boasted a formal garden), also designed by Adam, to the Moorfoot Hills beyond.

With its central block joined to matching side pavilions around an open courtyard, Arniston is imposingly elegant outside. Inside, the house greets the visitor with a superb Baroque flourish in the hall, where Adam employed the Dutch craftsman, Joseph Enzer, to execute the decorative stuccowork, which took seven years to complete. Enzer's stucco work is also evident right at the top of the house, in the Porcelain Room, which was the library until Victorian Dundas's found it too inconvenient to climb two storeys every time they wanted a book.

Generations of Dundas's comprise a distinguished collection of family portraits, in particular the paintings by Ramsay and Raeburn, many of which hang in two of Arniston's most welcoming rooms, the old school-room and the oak-room. They hint at the varying characters, whether the brilliant, scholarly lawyers, or the more rumbustious Henry Dundas (younger son of Robert II) who was made 1st Viscount Melville by William Pitt the Younger and described on one occasion in London as being 'very hearty, in great spirits, and drinks wine liberally; speaks such broad Scotch that he can hardly be understood'.

William Adam's work at Arniston was completed by his son, John (brother of the more famous Robert). In recent years the John Adam parts of the house have seen ambitious restoration by Mrs Dundas-Bekker (whose father was Sir Philip Dundas, 4th Bt), to cope with a disastrous outbreak of dry rot. It has been a brave project and has enabled visitors to continue enjoying one of Scotland's lesser-known, but most distinguished houses.

DALMENY HOUSE, *South Queensferry*

The Earl of Rosebery
Tel: 0131 331 1888

Off A90, 5 km (3 miles) east of South Queensferry
Open: July and Aug, Mon and Tues, 12–5.30, Sun, 1–5.30
£3.50, concessions
Home-made teas

Dalmeny, full of history and treasures, is a house to return to; one visit gives a taste of the diverse art collection but will also leave the visitor wishing to see more. Fortunately it is the most accessible country house from Edinburgh. The family home of the Earls of

Rosebery, it was built in 1815 by the 4th Earl's friend, Wilkins, designer of King's College, Cambridge, and the National Gallery. He created a fine Tudor-Gothic mansion with wonderful views up and down the Firth of Forth. The style continues inside with the great hall and state corridor, off which run a sequence of formal Regency rooms. On the garden side are the more intimate rooms of the original family wing.

The family's great art collection, including that of the present Earl's grandmother, Hannah Rothschild, is clearly and carefully arranged. The hall boasts family portraits, original Wilkins furniture and the delightful Goya tapestries of 'Children at Play'. The adjacent library contains furniture owned by Warren Hastings. This room is now used as a family drawing-room – not surprisingly when you enter the state drawing-room. Here is a remarkable display of French eighteenth-century furniture of the highest quality, set on a Louis XIV Savonierie carpet and surrounded by Beauvais tapestries designed by Boucher. The paintings are by Greuze and his contemporaries and the small porcelain dog on a cushion from the Sèvres factory is naturally modelled on Marie Antoinette's pet.

The Napoleon room comes as a wonderful contrast. The richness of the eighteenth century is replaced by masculine severity. Here are objects not normally seen outside France: the Appiani portraits of the Emperor; and the Lefevres and Gerard portraits of his family; the Consular throne; his shaving stand with his own profile portrait life-size in ormolu; furniture and personal possessions from St Helena. In the dining-room hang not just the family portraits but the eighteenth-century political portraits by Gainsborough, Reynolds, Lawrence and Raeburn, collected by the 5th Earl who married Hannah Rothschild. He became Prime Minister during the 1890s, but once remarked that he would prefer to own the winner of the Derby – which he did in consecutive years.

In the family wing are rooms devoted to the passion for racing which generations of Roseberys have enjoyed under their famous Rose and Primrose colours, as well as French porcelain, furniture and paintings, and a room devoted to the Rothschild family. They complete a house of intriguing historical and artistic interest.

HOPETOUN HOUSE, *Nr South Queensferry*

The Hopetoun House Preservation Trust
Tel: 0131 331 2451

Off A904, 3 km (2 miles) from Forth Road Bridge
Open: April to end Sept, daily, 10–5.30 (last admission 4.30)
£4.20, children £2.10, concessions
Restaurant and tea room

Hopetoun is Scotland's largest house, and could be considered architecturally the most important in that it was built by the country's two most distinguished classical architects, or architectural families, William Bruce and the Adams. Bruce's house built between 1699 and 1703 is preserved in the west-facing garden front and reveals distinct similarity to his own home, Balcaskie, in its French-influenced classicism. William

Adam's entrance front begun in 1721 is altogether more monumental, the curving colonnades and pavilions with their cupola-topped towers balancing the massive proportions of the central block.

Inside the contrasting scales of classicism continue, with the important influence of the Hope family's elevation from the Earldom of Hopetoun dating from 1703, to the Marquessate of Linlithgow in 1902. The 1st Marquess was the first Governor-General of Australia, his son was the longest serving Viceroy of India, from 1936 to 1943. Their full-length portraits, both as Knights of the Thistle (Scotland's equivalent of the Garter), greet the visitor in the entrance hall which was completed by William Adam's son, John.

The main staircase is Bruce's work, with rich wood carving by Alexander Eizat who worked for him at Holyroodhouse, as are the parlour and bedchamber in the centre of the west front, the last containing the splendid state bed made by Mathias Lock and supplied by James Cullen, who was responsible for most of the furniture for the Adam apartments. Also in the bedroom is an unusual pattern chair which Cullen made for the 2nd Earl to enable him to choose from a variety of carving styles for the new apartments. Here, and continuing in rooms above, are a series of allegorical paintings commissoned by the 1st Earl from Philip Tideman.

The large library, as it is now, was a conversion from a bedchamber and small drawing-room, in the early part of the 19th century by Sir James Gillespie Graham, employed by the 4th Earl. Three grand rooms make up the major Adam contribution to the interiors: the yellow drawing-room, red drawing-room and dining-room (which it became after considerable alteration during the early nineteenth century). The two drawing-rooms survive as remarkably complete examples of Adam decoration, with rich coved plaster ceilings and suites of splendid furniture, all as supplied for the original scheme by Cullen.

The work at Hopetoun also reflects the classical education of Robert Adam. In 1754 he visited Italy with Charles Hope Vere (or Weir), the second son of the 1st Earl, a journey that profoundly influenced his architectural style. The most impressive example is the marble chimney-piece in the red drawing-room, for which Adam sent the design from Rome, to be carved by Michael Rysbrack. Charles Hope Vere (who died aged only twenty-six) is shown as a boy with his brother, James, and their tutor in Nathaniel Dance's portrait.

All three rooms contain fine paintings and among the portraits the most significant is the 2nd Earl Annandale by Andrea Procaccini. The Earl was a noted connoisseur and collector, whose sister married the 1st Earl of Hopetoun. When Lord Annandale died, his sister inherited his art collection. Most of it was dispersed during the nineteenth century when it was replaced with the present collection of Italian, Dutch and Flemish Old Masters.

George IV came to Hopetoun on his visit to Scotland in 1822 and knighted the artist, Henry Raeburn, and Captain Adam Ferguson, Keeper of the Scottish regalia, in the yellow drawing-room. The King would certainly have appreciated the house's splendours, but he is unlikely to have made the journey to the roof as visitors can do today, to enjoy the spectacular views across Hopetoun's park to the Firth of Forth and its twin road and rail bridges.

BLAIRQUHAN, *Maybole*

James Hunter Blair
Tel: 0165 57 239

Off A77, 23 km (14 miles) south of Ayr

**Open: mid-July to mid-Aug, daily except Mon, afternoon
£3, children £2, concessions**

The approach to Blairquhan, along a 5-km (3-mile) drive which capitalizes on the picturesque setting of the River Girvan, is the ideal preparation for the house that lies ahead, on first impressions a pure Gothic castellated mansion which J.P. Neale described in his *Views of Seats* as 'a correct specimen of the architecture of Henry VII's time'.

But the house's architect, William Burn, shared an enthusiasm for Greek revival architecture with Robert Smirke in whose offices he studied. Blairquhan, built in the

1820s during the height of the Greek revival movement, clearly reveals this inspiration in the clean crisp lines of the ashlar stone with which it is built and makes the house, both outside and in, an intriguing blend of styles.

The main rooms, all arranged round an impressive two-storey saloon with a double staircase beyond, form an easy progression enhanced by their elegant, unfussy proportions. Certainly Burn's work is an intriguing contrast to the fantasy-like appearance of some of his other projects, such as the extraordinary staircase at Harlaxton Hall in Lincolnshire. But perhaps the most enjoyable feature of Blairquhan's interiors is the survival of the furnishings and other works of art that Burn's patron, Sir David Hunter Blair, originally commissioned for the house. Redecoration and modernization by the present owner, James Hunter Blair, has done nothing to disturb this happy situation.

Without doubt the most important addition since Sir David's time is the collection of pictures by Scottish Colourist artists, put together by the present owner's father, Sir James. Notable among these are the works by F.C.B. Cadell which predominate in the picture gallery. And as one leaves, the house's setting confirms the great contribution made by Sir David's extensive tree planting which, with the natural landscape, does so much to display the house to its best effect.

DUART CASTLE, *Isle of Mull*

Sir Lachlan Maclean, Bt
Tel: 01680 812309

Off A849, 3 km (2 miles) south-east of Craignure
Open: May to mid–Oct, 10.30–6
£3.30, children £1.65, concessions
Tea room

Even among Scottish castles, Duart seems to encapsulate the strange combination of romance, violence and hardship integral to the history of the Highlands and their clans. Its remoteness is immediately evident as it is glimpsed, perched on a rocky promontory called Black Point that sticks out into the Sound of Mull, facing Lismore Island and the mainland beyond.

The oldest part of the castle dates from the thirteenth century, from which time until the end of the seventeenth century the Macleans appear to have been constantly fighting – among themselves, with the Macdonalds, but principally against the hated Argyll Campbells who, with support from the English government, eventually defeated them in 1691. Duart was then razed in 1756 when the English garrison departed.

It remained a ruin for about a hundred and fifty years until 1911 when the surviving building and peninsula on which it stood were purchased by Sir Fitzroy Maclean, 26th Chief of the Clan and a man in the mould of his ancestors, who fought as an Hussar in the Crimea and lived to be a hundred. He engaged the architect, Sir John Burnet, to rebuild the small castle and make it the habitable home visitors enjoy today. The major addition was the sea room whose huge windows give spectacular views across the Sound of Mull and Loch Linnhe.

The castle contains regular reminders of stirring deeds by Macleans: dirks and uniforms and a portrait of Sir John Maclean who fought at Killiecrankie shortly before the clan's rout by the Campbells, as well as portraits of the castle's saviour, Sir Fitzroy, and his grandson, Lord Maclean, who was Chief Scout and Comptroller of Elizabeth II's Household. Duart's romantic history and position make it a place of irresistible pilgrimage for Macleans from the world over.

FINLAYSTONE HOUSE, *Langbank*

Mr and Mrs G. MacMillan
Tel: 01475 540285/505

On A8, between Langbank and Port Glasgow
Open: Apr to Aug, Sun, 2.30–4.30
£2, children £1.20, Senior Citizens £1.50
Tea room
Doll and Toy museum in the Visitor Centre

Overlooking the Clyde estuary a few miles west of Glasgow airport, Finlaystone was for some four centuries a seat of the Earls of Glencairn, whose number included an ardent supporter of John Knox, a Chancellor of Scotland, and a leading patron of Burns. Their house dated from the fourteenth century but was rebuilt around 1760. They did not have long to enjoy their improvements; in 1796 the last Earl died and that family's occupation of Finlaystone ended.

By the end of the nineteenth century the Clyde was among the most important shipping centres in the world and Finlaystone was bought by George Jardine Kidston, chairman of the Clyde Shipping Company. The house was in need of considerable repair and he commissioned Sir John James Burnett to carry out the work, completed around 1900. The house retained an eighteenth-century façade. The top storey (which Kidston added to accommodate his nine children) added an attractive hipped roof and dormers. On one side symmetry is interrupted by the square tower which rises above the roofline. In true plutocratic style Kidston lavished huge sums on the house. Marble pillars were inserted to support the old north wall and heavy marble chimney-pieces were put in the main rooms which were also given decorated plaster ceilings.

General Sir Gordon MacMillan married Kidston's granddaughter and their family have lived at Finlaystone since the Second World War. The Edwardian atmosphere survives in the house where new interests include an important collection of dolls in the billiard-room. In recent years the MacMillans have made major new introductions in the garden, redesigning the walled garden and extending the traditional garden of yew hedges, herbaceous borders, and sweeping lawns by incorporating more informal areas in the surrounding woodland and unusual features such as the Celtic pattern of paving.

INVERARAY CASTLE, *Inveraray*

The Trustees of the 10th Duke of Argyll
Tel: 01499 302203

On A819, north of Inveraray on Loch Fyne

Open: 1st Sat in Apr to 2nd Sun in Oct, daily except Fri, 10–1, 2–5; July and Aug, daily 10–5.45 (Sun 1–5.45)
£4, children £2, Senior Citizens £3
Tea room

Inveraray Castle is the most brilliant example of how Highlanders progressed from centuries of warring with their enemies to the height of eighteenth-century sophistication. Architecturally, and in its decoration and contents, Inveraray reveals a depth of quality that two disastrous fires in 1877 and 1975 have mercifully not impaired.

The ancient seat of the Clan Campbell, of whom the Dukes of Argyll are head, was ruined Innis Chonnell Castle on Loch Awe. When the 3rd Duke inherited in 1743 he commissioned the Englishman, Roger Morris, to design the new castle outside its eponymous town. The family's pro-English connections, so hated by their enemies the Macleods and Macdonalds, dated from the 10th Earl of Argyll who was made a Duke by William of Orange for his support in opposition to the Stuarts, who had beheaded both his grandfather and father for treason.

Morris's castle, whose construction was supervised by William Adam and his two sons, John and Robert, was a vigorous early example of the

Gothic revival, its four-square proportions undiminished by any wings or extensions. The Gothic character was best displayed in Morris's central tower, 21 m (70 ft) tall, although its impact was reduced by alterations by Anthony Salvin after the 1877 fire, when the original roof battlements were replaced by the present dormer windows. Salvin also added the conical turrets to the corner towers, making the castle's appearance more Scottish than the original, and redesigned the inside of the tower (which had been gutted) with the present armoury hall.

Internally Inveraray's main delight is the series of painted rooms designed by Robert Mylne for the 5th Duke during the 1780s, which are without equal. The 5th Duke and his beautiful Irish wife were Francophiles and most of the painters employed at Inveraray were French; the wonderful patterns have a lightness of touch compared, for instance, to similar painted rooms executed by Robert Adam. The decoration is complemented by an abundance of gilded chairs covered in French tapestry, and by the set of Beauvais tapestries that hang in the drawing-room with Hoppner's portrait of the 5th Duke's daughter, Lady Charlotte, as Aurora.

The 5th Duke's four sons were all painted in a notable series by Opie which hang in the saloon – originally the entrance hall – along with other distinguished family portraits. Elsewhere in the house are reminders of the marriage in 1871 of the Marquess of Lorne to Queen Victoria's daughter, Princess Louise. This was six years before the first of Inveraray's fires and the visitor should marvel that the family's determined efforts on two occasions have been so successful while sympathizing with the strain the restorations have placed on the estate.

KELBURN CASTLE, *Largs*

The Earl of Glasgow
Tel: 01475 568685

On A78, between Largs and Fairlie

Open: July and Aug, p.m
£1.50 (castle only), concessions

Kelburn, home of the Boyle family, Earls of Glasgow, is among the select group of Scottish castles vying for the unprovable distinction of being the country's oldest inhabited home. Continuous occupation since 1140 by the de Boyvilles (who came to Britain with William the Conqueror), then by Boyles, combines with the existence of the castle itself by the reign of Alexander III (1249–86) as impressive evidence. Certainly they chose their position well, with the picturesque Kelburn glen tumbling down on one side and views across the Firth of Clyde to Arran and the closer island of Great Cumbrae – most of which they owned.

The earldom came to David Boyle in 1703 in thanks for his active support of the Act of Union. To demonstrate his new-found importance, he transformed Kelburn from a modest defensive tower house into a seat of substance by adding the wing which today forms the largest body of the castle. The family prospered for nearly two centuries, until the 6th Earl threatened total ruin through – even by Victorian standards – one of the more unusual forms of profligacy, a mania for building churches. He funded their construction all over Scotland. The most ambitious were the Cathedral of the Isles on his own Cumbrae and the Episcopalian cathedral in Perth. Cumbrae and his other possessions did not remain his for long. By the 1880s he was bankrupt, the family's considerable estates and most of the contents of Kelburn were sold and the castle itself was only saved when his cousin – who eventually inherited the title – bought it in 1886.

The 7th Earl was a sailor who served in the Crimea and China and became Governor of New Zealand. Kelburn today has many reminders of his career – some quite ordinary such as the quantity of marine pictures, other extraordinary such as the ghariol (a relative of the crocodile) which climbs the banisters of the 1st Earl's impressive staircase. And although most of Kelburn's original contents were dispersed in the sale, its vigorous early-eighteenth-century interiors executed for the 1st Earl both in his new wing and the main rooms of the old tower house, notably the grandiose drawing-room with Corinthian pilasters and a frieze incorporating the rose and thistle in honour of the Union, survived and remain great attractions.

Since opening Kelburn to the public the present Earl and Countess have emphasized the qualities of the castle's surroundings and made the old eighteenth-century home farm into the Kelburn Centre. It is along the path that follows the burn up its glen that one discovers the marvellous classical monument to the 3rd Earl, erected by his widow after his death in 1775, the design commissioned from no less a figure than Robert Adam, by that time at the zenith of his career. The elegant monument's position here is entirely apt, for the 3rd Earl's main contribution at Kelburn was landscaping the picturesque glen and improving the gardens which today are integral to Kelburn's attraction. It is especially fortunate that the charming painting of his four children playing in the garden survives in the castle.

MOUNT STUART, *Isle of Bute*

The Mount Stuart Trust
Tel: 01700 503877

9 km (5½ miles) south of Rothesay pier via ferry from Wemyss Bay
Open: May to end Sept, daily except Tues and Thur, 11–5
(last admission 4.30)
£5.50, children £2.50, concessions
Tea room

Mount Stuart is the most fascinating house to have opened its doors to the public since the first edition of this book was published in 1994. Indeed it is one of the most remarkable houses in Britain, home of the Crichton-Stuart family, Marquesses of Bute, generations of whom have combined enormous wealth founded on their estates in South Wales, with great scholarship and patronage of the arts.

The family history stretches back to the reign of David I and the island of Bute was always their most established stronghold. The earldom of Bute was awarded in 1702 and the 3rd Earl, confidant and adviser to George III, was Prime Minister. Collector and patron, his principal home was Luton Park (replaced by the present house, Luton Hoo), and many of the paintings and furnishings from that seat are now at Mount Stuart. His son was made Marquess of Bute and secured the family's fortunes by marrying the daughter of the Earl of Windsor, who inherited the South Wales estates. (He proceeded to further enhance the Bute wealth by marrying the daughter of Thomas Coutts, the banker, as his second wife.)

The 2nd Marquess developed the city and docks of Cardiff that were to make his son the richest man in Britain. With William Burges as his architect, the 3rd Marquess restored Cardiff Castle, and then turned his attention to Mount Stuart, when a fire in 1877 gutted the central block of the old eighteenth-century house. He decided to retain the surviving wings, but rebuild the central block from scratch, using the Scottish architect, Sir Robert Rowand Anderson. It is important to understand the degree to which Bute's personality and interests influenced the appearance of his new house. As a young man he had converted to Roman Catholicism and his new religion combined with scholarly aestheticism to closely affect the architectural details of the new house.

Built in deep red Corsehill sandstone, the house has been described by Gavin Stamp as 'one of the most astonishing monuments to the Victorian age'. Work began in 1880, but by the time of the 3rd Marquess's premature death in 1900 many details were unfinished. These were carried out under the supervision of his widow. Bute appears to have been dissatisfied with Anderson at one stage and replaced him with William Frame around 1886, but Anderson was called back in 1890.

The house's powerful Gothic exterior combines the sheer size of the central block rising through four storeys, with the detail of windows and stonework and the pinnacled lantern tower over the chapel, to make a memorable picture. The greatest drama lies inside, however, in the square central hall rising to 18 m (60 ft). Tiers of marble columns support Gothic arches and light pours in from above, through the stained glass of the third-floor windows. Even without decoration or furnishings it is one of the most dramatic interiors of any house in Britain. With two staircases, one on either side of the hall, the main rooms are laid out on the *piano nobile* above a ground-floor basement, with principal bedrooms on the second floor and two further floors above. Perhaps not surprisingly, the house was built with a number of innovations. It was the first to contain a heated pool (Gothic in design) in any house, and the first in Scotland to be lit by electricity. Throughout the main rooms the rich variety of carved decoration, vaulted ceilings, stained glass, and heraldic patterns, make it easy to understand how the work took so long.

From the entrance hall to the great marble hall the visitor is simply overwhelmed. But progression to some of the main apartments, in particular the dining-room and drawing-room, the quality of Mount Stuart's collections becomes evident. The dining-room and its ante-room contain one of Britain's foremost groups of eighteenth-century portraits (nearly all full-length): works by Romney, Raeburn, Reynolds, Gainsborough and Batoni, and, in particular, Allan Ramsay who owed his position as Principal Painter in Ordinary to George III (rather than Reynolds) to active support from the 3rd Earl of Bute. The drawing-room contains the Old Masters collected by the 3rd Earl and his son, as well as a superb group of clocks and eighteenth-century French and English furniture. The most dazzling interior is the chapel, lined in white Carrara marble, and lit through red glass in the octagonal lantern modelled on the La Seo Cathedral in Zaragoza, Spain.

Such a description can only give a brief impression of the scale and riches at Mount Stuart, which are added to by the gardens – with work by the Edwardian designer, Thomas Mawson, and more recent work by Rosemary Verey, and wonderful views out from the larger policies laid out for the 3rd Earl. But few visitors will leave without heartily agreeing with Gavin Stamp's description quoted earlier.

TOROSAY CASTLE, *Isle of Mull*

Mr Christopher James
Tel: 01680 812421

On A849, 1.6 km (1 mile) south-east of Craignure
Open: Easter to mid-Oct, 10.30–5.30
£3.50, children £1.50, concessions
Tea room

For most visitors Torosay epitomizes Victorian Scottish baronial and it is no surprise that its architect was a leading light of the movement, David Bryce. Compared to its more rugged and exposed neighbour, Duart (a ruined shell when Torosay was being built during the 1850s), Torosay, set in neat protective parkland, well illustrates the gentrification of Scotland by the Victorians. Its ambitious scale, however, proved too

much for Bryce's patron, John Campbell. He was forced to sell in 1865, only seven years after completion, and it was bought by Arbuthnot Charles Guthrie, ancestor of the present owner.

Inside and out, Torosay provides an absorbing picture of Victorian and Edwardian life. Probably the most important additions were the three Italianate garden terraces below the south front and the statue walk lined with a series of eighteenth-century Venetian stone figures, all designed by Sir Robert Lorimer. They were commissioned by Walter Murray Guthrie whose first reaction on hearing he had inherited Torosay — which he had never seen — was to put it on the market. Fortunately his first visit changed his mind and he fell in love with the place. His wife was the daughter of Sir John Leslie, something of a polymath and accomplished artist. Some of his best pictures, including a full-length portrait of his wife and a more modest likeness of his four-year-old daughter, hang in the castle.

BLAIR CASTLE, *Blair Atholl*

The Duke of Atholl
Tel: 01796 481207

Off A9, 11 km (7 miles) north of Pitlochry
Open: Apr to end Oct, daily, 10–6 (last admission 5)
£6, children £4, concessions

Blair Castle presents a surprising contrast. From the outside the sprawling white-harled building composed of tall vertical blocks with proportionally small windows, crow-stepped gables and conical turrets is exactly what one would expect of a ducal Scottish seat. The feeling is encouraged by the knowledge that the ancient family has been established for over seven centuries on the site of enormous strategic importance on the main route through Scotland. The family history is closely linked to the fortunes of Scottish royal history, reaching a peak during the Jacobite uprisings. The 1st Duke and his heir supported the English government, but his other three sons took active part for the Stuarts. One, Lord George, actually laid siege to his old home in 1746, giving Blair the distinction of being the last castle in Britain to be besieged.

But there is an air of spaciousness in Blair's setting that suggests something more elegant than a castle in the Highlands. Indeed there is, for the 2nd Duke – possibly to atone for the anti-English activities of his brothers – created one of the most notable series of eighteenth-century interiors to be found in any Scottish house. The work was done in the English Georgian tradition, with a roll-call of distinguished craftsmen all making their contributions; among Scottish houses only the Duke of Argyll's Inveraray Castle rivals Blair in this manner.

Many of the craftsmen were English. Thomas Clayton executed the superb plasterwork, at its most florid Baroque in the ceiling, wall panels and overmantel in the dining-room, and finely elegant in the frieze of the tea-room. Thomas Carter carved the marble chimney-pieces and furniture was supplied by a series of leading makers – John Hodson, George Cole and John Gordon. Throughout all the rooms open to the public the wide range of furniture is of unfailing quality. For the bed enthusiast there is a feast of five grand four-posters, the most impressive being the William and Mary one hung with damask in the tapestry room.

Here is another of Blair's treasures, a set of Brussels tapestries made for Charles I and bought by the 1st Duke of Atholl when sold by Cromwell. Among the pictures which chronicle successive generations of Atholls and Murrays the most enjoyable are conversation pieces of the 3rd and 4th Dukes with their families by Johann Zoffany and David Allen. The most magnificent is the full-length portrait of the 1st Marquess of Atholl by Jacob de Wit on the picture staircase. One commentator described the portrait as looking like 'one of Louis XIV's marshals'.

To help understanding of the castle's evolution it is suitable that the first and last major rooms among the thirty-plus seen – the entrance hall and the ballroom – both date from the Scottish baronial additions for the 7th Duke during the 1870s. This work incorporated the surviving medieval parts of the castle and some Georgian alterations and accounts for the present exterior appearance.

Today Blair's strategic position is more important in attracting visitors than for defensive reasons, and it is the most visited historic house in Scotland. No doubt its popularity is partly due to the variety on offer; if the interior decorations and works of art are not to one's taste, you can always have a cannon fired for you by a detachment of the Duke's private army (the only one in Britain) or be greeted by your own piper.

GLAMIS CASTLE, *Glamis*

The Earl of Strathmore and Kinghorne
Tel: 01307 840 393/242

In Glamis off A928

Open: Apr to late Oct, daily, 10.30–5.30 (last admission 4.45)
£4.70, children £2.50, concessions
Restaurant

The first view of Glamis, the unusually tall central block framed at the bottom of a long double avenue, confirms expectations of romantic history, from the distant past as celebrated by Shakespeare in *Macbeth*, and more recently as the childhood home of Queen Elizabeth the Queen Mother who was born Lady Elizabeth Bowes Lyon. Like many Scottish castles, Glamis is impressive rather than beautiful and one agrees with the poet, Thomas Gray, who visited in 1765 and wrote, 'Very singular and striking in appearance, like nothing I ever saw.'

A medieval royal hunting lodge, Glamis was the scene of the death of King Malcolm in 1034. In 1372 it was granted to Sir John Lyon by Robert II and thus began the family's occupation which has continued unbroken ever since. Lyon became Lord Glamis in 1445 and during the seventeenth century the family became Earls of Kinghorne and Strathmore. More important for the family fortunes was the eighteenth-century marriage of the 9th Earl to the heiress Mary Bowes of Durham, from which point the family name became Bowes Lyon.

From a fifteenth-century core, parts of which are preserved in the east and central blocks, Glamis expanded, mainly during the seventeenth century. At this time the west wing was added to balance the existing east wing of the old tower, which produced the unusual arrangement of the main entrance facing out from its tower on the angle of the two wings. The further eastern extension was made principally during the nineteenth century. It is this period which greets the visitor in the dining-room where the combination of features, notably the ceiling, remain a vigorous Jacobean re-creation. As was popular among Victorians, the family history is told in heraldry by the succession of shields arranged in chronological order.

The atmosphere of Glamis's distant, violent past is prevalent in the crypt and in Duncan's Hall (the legendary scene of Duncan's murder by Macbeth although the deed actually took place near Elgin). One can sympathize with Sir Walter Scott who wrote after staying in the castle: 'When I heard door after door shut, after my conductor had retired, I began to consider myself as too far from the living, and somewhat too near the dead.'

It is a relief to escape to warmer, more welcoming parts of the castle and the drawing-room, billiard-room and royal apartments in particular are full of delights. In the drawing-room the 1621 arched ceiling, decorated with plasterwork, is the outstanding feature of the work by the 2nd Earl, and the overmantel with the royal arms is almost certainly contemporary. More plasterwork from the same period can be found in King Malcolm's bedroom which has a delicate ceiling pattern of the 2nd Earl's cypher and coronet and his arms in the overmantel.

The billiard-room is notable for the set of seventeenth-century English tapestries depicting the life of Nebuchadnezzar and 'The Fruit Market', a painting attributed to Frans Snyders. The drawing-room contains the best selection of the castle's portraits, including a fine group of the 3rd Earl and his sons and a more melancholy likeness of the 9th Lord Glamis aged eight, whose great-grandmother was burnt as a witch by James V in 1540 for no better reason than hatred of her family.

Such disturbing memories disappear completely in the elegant but friendly royal apartments, arranged during the 1920s for the Duke and Duchess of York, who became George VI and Queen Elizabeth. One delightful touch by the young Duchess's mother was to incorporate into the hangings the initials C and C (for herself and her husband) and the names and dates of birth of all their ten children. She also passed on to her daughter a love of gardening, evident in the enclosed Italian garden that Lady Strathmore created, which makes a delightful contrast to the more expansive parkland surrounding the castle's approaches.

SCONE PALACE, *Perth*

The Earl of Mansfield
Tel: 01738 552300

On A93, 3 km (2 miles) north-east of Perth
Open: Good Fri to mid-Oct, daily, 9.30–5
£4.70, children £2.60, concessions
Restaurant, home-made teas

Scone was steeped in Scottish history for centuries before Edward I removed its stone to Westminster to confirm English royal authority over Scotland, and it continued to be thereafter until James VI conferred the property to Sir David Murray who initiated four centuries of family occupation.

After opposition to the Act of Union and active support for the Jacobite risings, the family's fortunes might have been doomed but for William Murray, younger brother of the 6th Viscount Stormont, who became the outstanding lawyer of his generation. 'Silver-tongued Murray' twice became Lord Chief Justice and Chancellor and was made 1st Earl of Mansfield. By judging in favour of a runaway slave, he helped to launch the anti-slavery movement.

He lived mostly in London – in splendour at Kenwood House – and therefore Scone remained unchanged through his lifetime, as it did when his nephew, David, inherited the earldom in 1793 but only lived for another three years. David's son of the same name commissioned William Atkinson, who had been introduced to the Gothic style by his tutor James Wyatt, to transform the old gabled house into Gothic: castle outside, palace within.

The Chancellor Earl's portrait by Martin shows him with the Bernini bust of Homer that he proudly acquired. Today the portrait is flanked by the bust on one side and Rysbrack's bust of the Earl on the other. They are in the library where the bookshelves are mainly filled with Scone's magnificent porcelain: the 1st Earl's oriental armorial set, eighteenth-century Meissen, Ludwigsberg and Sèvres, early Chelsea, Worcester and Derby.

In the drawing-room the set of Louis XV armchairs and the writing table made for Marie Antoinette by Riesener are part of the extensive collection of French furniture brought to Scone by the 2nd Earl, the family's most significant collector and ambassador in Paris from 1772 to 1778. He also collected the Vernis Martin pieces which are unique, but their numbers were tragically diminished by a serious burglary at Scone in 1994. They are displayed in the gallery, where, in 1842, Queen Victoria and Prince Albert were introduced to the mysteries of curling on the old bog-oak floor.

The dining-room contains continental ivories and is hung with portraits and Old Masters that are representative of the collection at Scone. The most delightful – Zoffany's portrait of the Chancellor's daughter, Lady Elizabeth Murray, with Dido, the daughter of the 1st Earl's housekeeper, whom the great lawyer freed from slavery – was commissioned by the connoisseur 2nd Earl.

DUNVEGAN CASTLE, *Isle of Skye*

John MacLeod of Macleod
Tel: 0147 022206

On A850, 2.5 km (1½ miles) north-west of Dunvegan
Open: end-Mar to end-Oct, daily, 10–5; also winter by appointment
£4.50, children £2.50, concessions
Restaurant

Inhabited by the Chiefs of the Clan Macleod for over seven hundred and fifty years, Dunvegan has a history stretching back to Norsemen and Celts. The family descend from Leod who, around 1270, first fortified the rocky site of Dunvegan. Until 1748 the only entrance to the castle was through the sea gate, reached via steps up from the sea and defended by barbican and portcullis. When Dr Johnson visited in 1773, the faithful Boswell recorded that the landward entrance dated from 1748. Evidence of various stages of the castle's development from Leod's time can be found, but, internally and externally, Dunvegan dates from two substantial periods of work, during the 1790s when the 23rd Chief of the Macleod clan determined to make it as much a habitable home as a castle, and during the 1840s when the exterior gained its uniform castellated appearance.

No change could detract from Dunvegan's magical position and visitors find themselves steeped in history, admiring strange and romantic relics. The Fairy Flag is the most prized, followed by the Dunvegan Cup, a wooden vessel encased in silver filigree, which was given to Sir Rory Mor (the 16th Chief) by the O'Neills of Ulster, in thanks for his help in their fight against the English in 1596. The silver is inscribed and dated 1493 but the vessel is much older. Flora Macdonald, Bonnie Prince Charlie's saviour, lived here for a time as her daughter married the tutor to the young Chief. Many of her personal souvenirs of the Jacobite uprising are on view at the castle. The outstanding paintings are by Allan Ramsay, full-length portraits of the 22nd Chief and his second wife, he in full Macleod dress, every inch a Highlander.

Map of HHA Regions

Sotheby's Regional Offices

SOUTHERN ENGLAND
Hensleigh Cottage, Nr Tiverton, Devon EX16 5NH.
Tel: 01884 243663. Fax: 01884 258692.

Cheviot House, 69–73 Castle Street, Salisbury, Wiltshire SP1 3TN.
Tel: 01722 330793. Fax: 01722 330982.

EAST ANGLIA AND THE SOUTH EAST
Cleveland House, 39 Old Station Road, Newmarket, Cambridgeshire CB8 8DT. Tel: 01638
561426. Fax: 01638 5600094.

Summers Place, Billingshurst, Sussex RH14 9AD (Salesroom).
Tel: 01403 783933. Fax: 785153.

MIDLANDS AND WALES
18 Imperial Square, Cheltenham GL50 1QZ.
Tel: 01242 510500. Fax: 01242 250252.

The George Hotel Mews, Stamford, Lincolnshire PE9 2LB.
Tel: 01780 51666. Fax: 01780 62086.

NORTHERN ENGLAND
Lightfoot Street, Hoole, Chester CH2 3AD.
Tel: 01244 315531. Fax: 01244 346984.

8–12 Montpellier Parade, Harrogate HG1 2TJ.
Tel: 01423 501466. Fax: 01423 520501.

11 Osborne Terrace, Jesmond, Newcastle-upon-Tyne NE2 1NE.
Tel: 0191 281 8867. Fax: 0191 212 0141.

SCOTLAND
112 George Street, Edinburgh EH2 4LH.
Tel: 0131 226 7201. Fax: 0131 226 6866.

130 Douglas Street, Glasgow G2 4HF.
Tel: 0141 221 4817. Fax: 0141 204 2502.

HEAD OFFICE
34–35 New Bond Street, London W1A 2AA
Tel: 0171 493 8080. Fax: 0171 409 3100.

INDEX

ACKNOWLEDGEMENTS

The author and publisher are grateful to all those owners who supplied photographs of properties.

Other photographs by: **Richard Bryant / Arcaid** pp 29, 83, 101, 133; **Michael Busselle** 198; **Mark Fiennes / Arcaid** 201, 225; **David Fowler / Arcaid** 273; **Clive Nichols** 2, 23, 60; **Clay Perry / Arcaid** 78, 93, 176, 220; **Tourist Board** 182; **Jeremy Whitaker** 12, 16, 18, 37, 92, 98, 104, 118, 121, 148, 159 165, 172, 177, 242.